# House of Hilton

House of

of

# HILTON

FROM CONRAD
TO PARIS:

A DRAMA OF WEALTH, POWER, AND PRIVILEGE

## JERRY OPPENHEIMER

 *CROWN PUBLISHERS   NEW YORK*

Published in the United States by Crown Publishers,
an imprint of the Crown Publishing Group,
a division of Random House, Inc., New York.
www.crownpublishing.com

Crown is a trademark and the Crown colophon is a
registered trademark of Random House, Inc.

Library of Congress Cataloging-in-Publication Data
Oppenheimer, Jerry.
    House of Hilton : from Conrad to Paris: a drama of
  wealth, power, and privilege / Jerry Oppenheimer.
      1. Hilton, Conrad N. (Conrad Nicholson), 1887–1979.
  2. Hotelkeepers—United States—Biography.    I. Title.
  TX910.5.H5O67    2006
  647.94092—dc22                              2006020926

ISBN-13:  978-0-307-33722-1
ISBN-10:  0-307-33722-7

Printed in the United States of America

*Design by Barbara Sturman*

10  9  8  7  6  5  4  3  2  1

First Edition

*For Caroline, Cukes, Trix, Louise, Max, Toby, and Jesse*

# PRIMARY *HILTON* FAMILY TREE

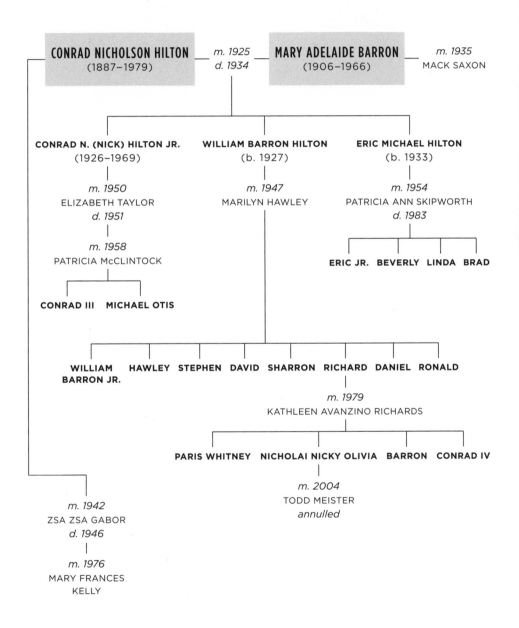

**CONRAD NICHOLSON HILTON**
(1887–1979)

*m. 1925*
*d. 1934*

**MARY ADELAIDE BARRON**
(1906–1966)

*m. 1935*
MACK SAXON

**CONRAD N. (NICK) HILTON JR.**
(1926–1969)

*m. 1950*
ELIZABETH TAYLOR
*d. 1951*

*m. 1958*
PATRICIA McCLINTOCK

**CONRAD III    MICHAEL OTIS**

**WILLIAM BARRON HILTON**
(b. 1927)

*m. 1947*
MARILYN HAWLEY

**ERIC MICHAEL HILTON**
(b. 1933)

*m. 1954*
PATRICIA ANN SKIPWORTH
*d. 1983*

**ERIC JR.    BEVERLY    LINDA    BRAD**

**WILLIAM
BARRON JR.**   **HAWLEY**   **STEPHEN**   **DAVID**   **SHARRON**   **RICHARD**   **DANIEL**   **RONALD**

*m. 1979*
KATHLEEN AVANZINO RICHARDS

**PARIS WHITNEY    NICHOLAI NICKY    OLIVIA    BARRON    CONRAD IV**

*m. 2004*
TODD MEISTER
*annulled*

*m. 1942*
ZSA ZSA GABOR
*d. 1946*

*m. 1976*
MARY FRANCES
KELLY

# House
## of Hilton

*T*here she is, standing tall beside the man.

From her four-inch stilettos, to her black thigh-high stockings, to the black garter belt and the itsy-bitsy, teenie-weenie Frederick's of Hollywood–style leopard-skin-print bikini barely covering her ass, to the matching leopard-skin-print push-up bra, to the sheer fingerless gloves, with the red, red nails of her right hand perfectly perched on her well-trained arched hip, and with her belly button tantalizingly beaming front and center, here is Paris Hilton, posing for the gazillionth time in all of her exhibitionistic glory.

As usual, the supervixen great-granddaughter of the late hotel magnate Conrad Hilton is pouting, preening, and letting it all hang out—not for a video camera recording a sex romp with a boy toy but rather for a swarm of photographers, including a female shooter for the usually staid *New York Times,* whose caption in the Sunday Styles section a week later declared, "Double Exposure." In just a finger snap, interest in Paris had veered from the "Enquiring Minds Want to Know" supermarket tabloid rabble to the "All the News That's Fit to Print" Upper East Side set.

And the man with whom Paris is cuddling? Hef.

There she is at the Playboy Mansion, the same place her maternal grandmother once partied, and where Paris's mother, Kathy Hilton, was a regular in the late '70s, and where Paris's Hollywood playboy paternal great-uncle, Nick Hilton, went in the late '50s to get some Bunny tail early in his second marriage (after Elizabeth Taylor). Following in her forebears' party-hearty footsteps, Paris, too, is a frequent frolicker at the Mansion, and in April 2006, she is a *very special guest.* For Hugh Hefner is celebrating his eightieth birthday, and Paris is there to sing "Happy Birthday" to him, on the eve of the launch of her latest incarnation—as a recording *artiste.* Through the latter part of 2005, Paris had been laying down tracks for her first CD, which she was supremely confident would go platinum overnight. As her producer (and occasional date who re-portedly gifted her with a Bentley), Scott Storch, a thirty-two-year-old music veteran with a slew of rapper hits, predicted in early 2006, "Paris's album is going to take everyone by surprise." But he fudged on whether Paris could actually sing. "If people are given the right circumstances, and the right track, and the right melody, it's about the conviction. It's not necessarily about being a God-given virtuoso." (By mid-year, though, he seemed to have soured on Paris's managers, claiming that they "smacked me in the face and disrespected me" because one of his tunes reportedly wasn't chosen as the first single from her CD.) Paris, meanwhile, gave her music two thumbs up. "I, like, cry when I listen to it, it's so good."

Even if she couldn't sing a note, her infamy catapulted her onto the charts. It had with every other of her many endeavors. The girl was an earner, no question.

When Paris sees the cameras aimed at Hef, she hustles over to have her picture taken with him—she can never get enough of getting her picture taken. And he naturally pulls her close against him—twenty-something girls (and younger) were always Hef's thing. Seeing the media closing in, Paris exclaims for all to hear, "Wow, Hef, this party is hot!" Hef glances at Paris like he has glanced at thousands of bimbos over the years and, in his courtly manner, responds with the lame playboy line, "Now it is. *You're* here."

At the stroke of midnight, when Hef officially turns eighty, Paris grabs a mike, and with still and video cameras trained on her she makes a feeble attempt to sing the birthday song, performing a gawky imitation of Marilyn Monroe's famous sultry rendition purred to President Kennedy in Madison Square Garden in 1962. Concluding her weird performance (in which it appears she has forgotten the birthday boy's name for a moment), Paris exclaims: "I love you, Hef. You're *amazzzzing*. You're eighty, but you act like you're twenty, you look like you're forty. You're hot. Love you. Happy birthday."

**SHAPELY SIXTEEN-YEAR-OLD** Lana Turner was licking an ice cream cone in a soda fountain across from Hollywood High when she was discovered by the publisher of the *Hollywood Reporter*. Ava Gardner was spotted at eighteen by an MGM errand clerk who was knocked out by her picture in the window of her brother-in-law's New York City photography studio. Twenty-one-year-old Paris's chance came after she and Rick Salomon, a well-endowed boyfriend a dozen years her senior (and the estranged husband of wildcat *Beverly Hills 90210* actress Shannen Doherty), performed sex acts in May 2001 in front of a video camera.

By the summer of 2002, the sleazy twenty-seven-minute homemade porno had been procured by an adult films distributor, and four minutes of the grainy movie landed on the Internet and was seen, downloaded, and either joked about or masturbated to around the world. With a click of a mouse, Paris had become internationally famous and infamous. Practically overnight, *1 Night in Paris* had outsold the video of *Gone With the Wind*.

Paris's parents went ballistic, or so it appeared.

"The Hilton family is greatly saddened at how low human beings will stoop to exploit their daughter Paris, who is sweet-natured, for their own self-promotion as well as profit motives," according to a prepared statement released to the world press. "Paris is working very hard on her career. The release of a private tape between a younger girl and an older boyfriend is more than upsetting. Anyone in any way involved in this video is guilty of criminal activity, and will be vigorously prosecuted." (There were lawsuits and counter-lawsuits, and in the end, Paris reportedly got a mid-six-figure piece of the video's financial action. Paris, however, denied ever receiving one red cent.) In July 2006, Paris actually contradicted the supposed anger her parents had about the video. She told Britain's upscale *Guardian* newspaper that she wasn't afraid of

Kathy and Rick Hilton's response to her X-rated starring role, acknowledged that "my mom heard about it [being released] before I did," and suggested they were supportive of her. "Well, they know I didn't do anything wrong. It's something everybody does, but it doesn't happen to everyone that a person actually shows it to other people." And she hadn't softened about her costar, calling him "a pig. He's disgusting. . . . I really loved him and I was a stupid little girl. So I've learned a lot from my mistakes." One of those lessons, she noted, was, "Don't ever trust anyone again like that, move on, and just forget about it.")

The publicity growing out of the titillating video was a monetary boon for Paris. Suddenly, she possessed an aggressive management team that included numbers crunchers, marketing experts, branding geniuses, shrewd New York literary agents, cutthroat Hollywood film and TV talent agents, and high-priced lawyers negotiating a portfolio of lucrative deals for her. Her savvy suits got her major product endorsements, including a 2005 too-pornographic-and-too-hot-for-TV spot showing her in a skintight swimsuit soaping up a Bentley and crawling all over it before taking a big bite out of a juicy chunk of Carl's Jr.'s new Spicy Burger. The commercial was called "soft-core porn" by the conservative Parents Television Council. However, before the spot was pulled, Spicy Burger demand soared.

Her marketing geniuses and agents provocateurs secured for her a hugely successful jewelry line on Amazon, as well as bankable fragrance and makeup products. Then there was the nightclub chain—the first Club Paris opened in beautiful downtown Orlando, Florida, the home of Disney World. The nightspot seemed to appeal to the town's tourist trade and the simple-life blue-collar locals, although it featured "a decadent VIP section" that included "a cozy boudoir area perfect for intimate encounters." But there also were the well-advertised specials—the three-dollar Corona beers, the five-dollar Jagerbombs, and sometimes "special Virgin drinks" for the thirteen- to seventeen-year-old set. In April of 2006, Paris's club promoted a three-day "School's OUT!" party. "Princess Paris knows how hard you've been studying and thinks you're definitely worth an A+" went the promotional material. "Since you're on Paris's honor roll you will be rewarded for being such a good student."

Paris, however, never made an honor roll, bounced from school to school, and, as one Hilton family insider notes, was lucky to get out of high school.

Nevertheless, Paris hit the *New York Times* bestseller list with her *Confessions of an Heiress,* and even her dog, Tinkerbell, got a book deal, *The Tinkerbell Hilton Diaries.* A third book with Paris's name on it, *The Heiress Diary: Confess It All to Me*—for young Britneys, Jennifers, and Megans to write in their innermost thoughts—was a rare dud.

*Confessions,* according to a member of Paris's team, was conceived to counter the negativity from parents regarding Paris's sex tape, plus the bet was her book, written by an actual writer, would register big sales for doing nothing but allowing her name and face to appear on the jacket. "With the book, we wanted the world to think of her as a role model for young girls," says one of her marketers.

Paris also became the costar of a much-criticized but hit Fox TV (and later E! Entertainment Television) reality series, *The Simple Life* (which, coincidentally, was based on a sitcom from the '70s called *Green Acres* that starred Eva Gabor, sister of Paris's great-grandfather's second wife, Zsa Zsa Gabor). A tabloid-fueled feud between Paris and her costar and childhood friend, Nicole Richie, helped the ratings, and secured Richie, an admitted former drug user, a book deal and appearances on the TV talk show circuit.

Meanwhile, Paris's mother, Kathy, parlayed her daughter's TV success into a reality show of her own, NBC's *I Want to Be a Hilton,* which received poor reviews. The *Hollywood Reporter*'s online critic observed, "When I was a kid, people wanted to be an Oscar Mayer Weiner. Now they want to be a Hilton. Or so we're told. Not that the two are so very different, actually. You don't want to know what's really inside either one—and both tend to hide behind their buns. . . . *I Want to Be a Hilton* supplies further evidence of the decline and fall of Western civilization . . ." The *National Review* took note of "the raw avarice displayed. . . . You'd need a strong stomach for vulgarity to be able to stand all this for more than a few minutes." *Variety* called Kathy Hilton's show "smirky."

Nevertheless, Kathy was the chutzpah behind much of Paris's success, pushing her relentlessly into the celebrity spotlight. Along with her,

Paris consulted with her father, Rick, on all her business deals. As a family insider asserts, "They are proud of everything she has done—even the video." Paris's grandfather, Barron Hilton, Rick's father, had taken to telling colleagues, "Good for her! She's the only one in that family making so much money."

With TV on her exploding résumé, Paris began making films—severely panned films, but films nonetheless—aimed at her prime demographic, pubescent teens; a director with a sense of irony in India even considered casting her in the role of Mother Teresa in a biopic of the beloved saint. For Paris's part in the 2005 feature *House of Wax,* she even won an award—a Razzie for "Worst Supporting Actress." Critics gloatingly took after her. Joanne Kauffman, writing in the *Wall Street Journal,* noted, "For the record, [Hilton] looks great in her red bra and matching thong. For the record, that's the most significant of her contributions." Nevertheless, Paris began to consider herself a movie star and showed up at the twenty-fifth annual Sundance Film Festival, infuriating its founder, Robert Redford, who suggested that celebrities like Paris were giving the event a bad name. "To the outside world, it's a big fat market where you have people like Paris Hilton going to parties," he said. "Now, she doesn't have anything to do with anything. I think the festival is close to being out of control."

With all of it, the cash started rolling in. In 2005 alone, Paris had banked as much as $20 million through her corporate entity, Paris Hilton Entertainment—all for just being famous for being famous.

Like her hotel magnate great-grandfather, a visionary who turned a fleabag hotel in a dirtbag Texas town into an international empire, Paris had the Midas touch, putting her mark on every conceivable kind of merchandise. In July 2004, the U.S. Commissioner of Trademarks received from Paris's Hollywood lawyers a drawing of a tiara with a fancy letter "P" on the crown, which she wanted as her trademark. Her business people imagined the tiara appearing on every form of goods and services from gymnastic and sporting articles to footwear, headwear, rubber stamps, decals, imitation leather goods, hair preparations, soaps, even kitchen utensils. Paris also hoped to trademark her most uttered two words—"That's hot!"—as exclusively her own. (By spring 2006, though, she announced on a TV talk show that she had dropped "That's hot" in favor of "That's sexy.")

Paris Hilton was no longer being viewed as just a party girl who had no interest in the family's hotel business. It was clear that this Hilton was a party girl with blond ambition, and naked greed. She had become big-time, generating as much as $200,000 to appear at a party or charity event for just a few minutes; and if she had a yen to fly to Japan to attend a bash, she'd get even more. In Vienna, she is said to have received $1 million to make a showing. "All I had to do," boasted Paris, "was wave like this." (She did an imitation of Queen Elizabeth II greeting the populace.)

She had become—*Paris Inc.*

Her amazing success even helped the bottom line of the Hilton Hotel Corporation. When her name became a household word, the hotels saw a more than 30 percent spike, which made Barron Hilton quite happy. Says a close associate: "Barron's horrified by all of Paris's vice and her shenanigans, but says, 'It's good publicity for the company; she's getting the Hilton name out there.'"

Her fame and infamy knew no bounds. She was named one of the "10 Most Fascinating People of 2004" in a Barbara Walters TV special that drew an audience of sixteen million. She was honored as one of *Rolling Stone's* ten top celebrities that same year. The magazine observed, "We have no idea where this girl is going, but we have the strangest feeling we are going there with her."

At the same time, Paris became the target of ongoing intense criticism as her fame skyrocketed. Andy Warhol's colleague, the writer Bob Colacello, ventured, "If she is the ultimate idol of a civilization that worships celebrity in and of itself, no matter how attained, then bring on the barbarians." Across the pond, where she had become a boldface name, the British actor Stephen Fry denounced Paris for having "a huge amount of greed and desire." One gossip writer, Lloyd Grove, filled an entire page of the *New York Daily News* with an angry denouncement, declaring that Paris had waged a "terrifying campaign for world domination." Grove resolved never to mention the name "Paris Hilton" in print again. *Ever.*

Meanwhile, Paris seemed on the brink of reinvention. She claimed that her porn video and party-girl shenanigans aside, she wasn't really a slut as the media portrayed her. "I'm not a sexual person," she maintained. "I really don't care about sex." She declared she was seeking responsibility and credibility by becoming a mother and having "three kids." Asked by Barbara Walters if she had a husband in mind to father them, Paris glibly responded, "I'll find one."

Subsequently, Paris announced she wanted to model her life on another publicity-mad, egomaniacal empire builder and TV reality show star, Donald Trump (whose modeling agency gave her one of her first catwalk gigs). Paris was called "the Donald Trump of the younger generation," and Trump, a friend of Paris's parents, respects her chutzpah and moneymaking abilities.

"Paris, in many ways, has done very well," he observes. "People like to knock her and criticize her for some of the things [she's done], but in many respects, Paris has done very well."

**WHILE PARIS HOLDS TITLE** to the Hilton name, she is not the hotel empire "heiress" who will inherit tens, if not hundreds, of millions of dollars, as has so often been reported. "One of the reasons she's working her tush off," asserts a Hilton family insider, "is because there's not going to be a big inheritance. She'll never be on the welfare line, but she's not a trust fund baby, either."

When Paris's paternal grandmother, Marilyn Hawley Hilton, died in 1999, she is said to have left some $60 million to be divided up among her eight children, one of whom is Paris's father, a Beverly Hills realtor and one of the executive producers of *I Want to Be a Hilton*. But that's about all the money that is forthcoming.

"Her grandfather, Barron, has a certain amount of independent wealth, but the huge dollar amounts are already owned by the Hilton Foundation," says an attorney with first-hand knowledge of the Hilton fortune. "There's no more for Paris." Paris, however, claims she "avoided" the family business "because I wouldn't just want to be given something."

So it did not come as a surprise to anyone in the Hilton inner circle that Paris was out and about trying to make her own bundle, to become her own corporate entity, and to corral a rich husband—two well-publicized contenders were young Greek shipping heirs Paris Latsis and Stavros Niarchos III.

Paris's parents were said to have been praying for one of those mergers to happen so there could be really big money in their immediate family. But the Latsises reportedly snubbed Rick and Kathy Hilton when they arrived in Greece to bond, and the engagement, announced by Kathy Hilton, was called off. As one cynical observer noted, Rick and Kathy "flew halfway around the world to be humiliated." The Latsis family felt that Paris was nothing more than "a promiscuous innkeeper's daughter." The word was that Paris Latsis vetoed a marriage to Paris Hilton on direct orders from his parents, and that Paris was livid.

Later, Kathy Hilton was overheard in a tony Hamptons restaurant rationalizing that the Latsis kid was just lazy and spoiled—a young man who didn't have the kind of motivation Paris possessed to make a name for himself. Paris's much-ballyhooed relationship with Stavros also hit a brick wall and ended.

Paris told the *New York Times,* which devoted a third of the Arts page to her in May 2005, "I'm glad I got the partying out of my system when I was young, because now I'm so over it and I can focus on my career. Now I'm trying to build an empire."

Speaking in the same vein to *TV Guide* around the same time about her success, she said, "This doesn't just happen. I mean I work. I'm a good person. I have good ideas and I'm smart and I'm a good businesswoman."

Her perception of herself, however, differs from how members of her management team view her, especially about the work part. As one close observer succinctly put it, "Work is not Paris's forte, but she's really kind of serious about all of it, and has amazing acumen. She's bright about three things—money, men, and how to get attention—and those are the only things she really *cares* about; she's basically classically self-involved and narcissistic. She doesn't speak in long sentences and words are not her game, but she can be clever and funny, and oddly makes fun of herself.

"I've spent an enormous amount of time with her, and after she leaves a meeting I always find myself wondering, where did this creature come from? What are the genetics happening here? Who's responsible for turning out a persona like Paris? Where'd she get her values and ethics and morals? What's her story?"

HILTON

BOOK I:
MATERNAL ROOTS

# CHAPTER 1

Like many children of the rich and famous, Paris Hilton didn't always get to spend quality time with her parents, especially her mother. A socially ambitious young woman, Kathleen Elizabeth Avanzino Richards Hilton, who had married into the celebrated Hilton Hotel family, was often out and about. With little time on her hands for mothering, she was cavalier about leaving her firstborn with the hired help or with relatives.

This was made abundantly clear to Patricia Skipworth Hilton, the first wife of Conrad Hilton's third son, Eric. A Texas beauty who had married into the Hilton family in her late teens, Pat, a mother of four, had become quite close over the years to her sister-in-law and brother-in-law, Marilyn and Barron Hilton, parents of Kathy's husband, Rick. The second of Conrad's three sons, Barron had succeeded the Hilton patriarch as head of the international hotel empire. Pat adored Marilyn, a former cheerleader who herself was a gorgeous teenage bride when she became part of the Hilton family. (The Hilton men, from Conrad on down, were known for taking young'uns for their brides.)

Whenever Pat visited Los Angeles from her home in Houston, Marilyn insisted that she stay at their spectacular estate. It was during one of those occasions, when Pat was "in the throes" of one of her many divorce actions in what was a hellish marriage to Eric Hilton—hellish marriages not being an oddity in the Hilton dynasty—that she observed new mother Kathy Hilton in action.

"I was there talking with Marilyn when here comes Kathy with Paris, who was nine months old and a great big, fat, pretty baby," Pat Hilton says in her Lone Star State drawl. "Kathy said, 'Meet Star'—she called Paris 'Star' from day one. 'Would you like to hold her for a minute?' That was the last I saw Kathy that day. She took off until that evening. I wanted to kill her! She didn't leave any instructions on what time Paris had to be fed. There weren't any diapers. She just left me in the lurch."

Furious, Pat vented to Marilyn, who listened sympathetically and knowingly, and rolled her eyes. "Marilyn said, laughing, 'Well, I guess you're *it* for the day. Kathy does this *all* the time. She just wants to go out. And she knew you'd take care of the kid.'"

When Kathy finally reappeared at day's end, Pat confronted her. "How dare you do this to me?" According to Pat, "Kathy's only reply was, 'Oh, I had to be somewhere. I didn't think you'd mind.' I warned her, *'Never, ever do this to me again!'* But it didn't bother her at all. Kathy Hilton's *very* selfish and *very* spoiled and *very* self-centered, and that absolutely carries through to Paris."

When Rick and Kathy Hilton traveled and deigned to bring Paris along, they naturally stayed in Hilton hotels, where they demanded special services, including babysitting care for their daughter, despite the fact that Barron Hilton had a strict rule barring Hiltons from getting special treatment or favorable room rates.

"When they were in New York, and Paris was just an infant, Kathy and Rick would get one of the women from housekeeping at the New York Hilton to babysit for them," states a Hilton Hotels insider. "They would leave Paris on Friday and not come back for her until late Sunday. It was a known fact that Kathy and Rick liked to party, and when

Kathy was a young mother she had no qualms about flaunting the Hilton name and taking advantage of it. She'd let it be known that Rick was going to be 'the next Mr. Hilton,' so hotel executives were afraid to argue with her. None of Barron's [eight] kids were getting a free ride. The only one who ever took advantage was Kathy."

Kathy and Rick were prone to show up out of the blue without reservations at a Hilton hotel on a busy weekend and demand the best suite in the house, fine wine and food, and babysitting for Paris. One of their targets was the Hilton in Parsippany, New Jersey, which had a four-star restaurant and a hip discotheque. The hotel also housed a number of lavishly furnished suites leased by big corporations.

When Paris was just a toddler, Rick and Kathy appeared on a busy Friday with her in tow along with their two small dogs (which weren't permitted in the hotel unless they were Seeing Eye dogs). Though the hotel was fully booked, they made it clear they were Hiltons and wanted VIP treatment—the best suite, complimentary food, and a babysitter because Paris's parents wanted to spend the night boogying in the disco. The manager, who didn't want to get in hot water with members of the ruling family, broke the ironclad no-special-treatment rule and put them in a suite, vacant for the weekend, that was leased by the pharmaceutical company Warner-Lambert.

"I thought, 'What the hell, they're going to leave on Sunday so it will work out,'" he says. "But no sooner do I get back to my office, I get a call from Rick Hilton who says, 'It's customary that we get a welcoming amenity.' I told him, 'Oh, absolutely.' Then he says, 'We like a nice California red wine and something white, and my wife likes seafood.' And then he demanded a babysitter. I had to convince the hotel's elderly German seamstress to do the sitting."

The manager felt relieved when the Hiltons checked out Sunday night, because Warner-Lambert people were coming in the next morning. But then he got a call to return to the hotel posthaste because there was a major crisis.

"I go up to the suite the Hiltons were using, and there's dog shit and dog piss all over the place—I mean *everywhere*. They didn't walk their dogs for the entire weekend. It was a real nightmare. We ended up having housekeeping do a detailed, deep cleaning. After all that, I never heard a word from Rick or Kathy Hilton—never got a thank-you, nothing. But that's where their mind-set is. They act like the imperial court."

Kathy and Rick also threw their weight around at the Las Vegas Hilton, another place where they liked to party, and where Paris was spotted as a little girl wearing mascara and eyeliner painted on by her mother. (By then, Kathy was booking Paris into charity event fashion shows.) The Hiltons, including Paris and her sister, Nicky, quickly earned a reputation at the Sin City Hilton for "arrogance, threats, and intimidation," according to a number of present and former employees, such as Margaret Mary (Peggy) Cusack Yakovlev, who also served as a personal assistant to Eric Hilton and his second wife, Bibi.

"Kathy and Rick and the girls looked down their noses at the help and were very judgmental," states Yakovlev. "Paris and Nicky were running loose in the hotel, were always trouble, and the mother always seemed to be coaching them." She notes that the Hilton sisters usually were accompanied by hired help who looked like they were treated despicably.

When Paris and Nicky informed hotel employees who they were, the workers ran the other way. The philosophy was—if you run into Rick and Kathy or their daughters, just keep your head down and your mouth shut. "Kathy was absolutely pushy, arrogant, condescending, and presumptuous, and Paris picked that up from her," observes Yakovlev. "The spotlight always had to be on Kathy. It was always, 'Do you know who *we* are?' 'Do you know who *I* am?' Rick was usually like a bump on a log. He had a look on his face like he was taking a bowel movement."

However, Yakovlev remembers an incident in which Paris's father was shockingly outspoken. It happened some weeks after Kathy Hilton gave birth to one of their two sons, Conrad and Barron. Rick Hilton was smoking a celebratory cigar outside the main entrance of the Las Vegas Hilton's crowded celebrity showroom. Yakovlev, who was standing nearby, overheard another Hilton employee congratulating the proud father on having such a large and handsome brood. "She asked him what he attributed it to," says Yakovlev, "and he said, loud enough for anyone to hear, 'I like to fuck!' Guests were passing by and heard it and looked at him. I couldn't believe it." (Some detractors felt that Rick and Kathy did not measure up to the proud Hilton name. One, who personally knew the family, even put his feelings into print. Taki Theodoracopoulos, a controversial figure who wrote the "High Life" column for Britain's respected *Spectator* magazine, declared in a column that Kathy and Rick "are straight out of *The Beverly Hillbillies.*" He claimed, "They eat hamburgers covered with ketchup washed down with Chateau Latour." He called Rick "a hick . . . as thick as they come," and proclaimed that neither Rick nor Kathy would ever "win the Parenting of the Year award." Kathy and Rick also were among former CBS newsman Bernard Goldberg's 2005 diatribe *100 People Who are Screwing Up America,* for "raising the most vapid . . . twerp . . . maybe in the world.")

When Paris was about twelve and still on the innocent side, she had pet ferrets that she carried in her Prada purse. The cute little rodents accompanied her everywhere she went in the hotel, which caused headaches for the Hilton managers, who were afraid to challenge her for fear of her mother's wrath.

On one occasion, Yakovlev recalls, Paris and her sister showed up at the glitzy hotel showroom where the big acts entertained audiences of thirteen hundred at each performance. "The girls brought the ferrets in with them and Rick and Kathy didn't care. They could not see any further ahead than what their children wanted, while we were responsible for the safety of the guests. We did not want those little rodents escaping and rubbing up against customers' ankles."

One of the managers with gumption decided to confront the Hiltons. "You need to get your girls and your rodents out of here," he told the Hiltons. "They're *not* coming in. I am *not* allowing them."

Kathy Hilton put her hands on her hips and got in his face and said, "Well, their grandfather [Barron] will *certainly* hear about this! Their grandfather is going to know from *me* how *you* are treating his granddaughters." The manager's businesslike but emphatic response was, "You go right ahead and tell him. This is a publicly traded company and I am doing my job. I have a multitude of guests to worry about. You have to take the rodents elsewhere."

(There was considerable chatter that as Paris got older she made use of facilities at other hotels in Las Vegas where she demanded and received VIP treatment, just like her parents did. According to an insider, Paris and her pals "used the saunas in one hotel to go to the bathroom in because they were too lazy to get out of the sauna to use the actual bathroom facilities." Paris's purported urination problems became public in 2005 when a blogger, and then the *New York Post,* reported that "cleaning crews had to be brought in" at the opening of a Las Vegas club because Paris was "not able to wait in line for the bathroom." In early 2006, a Hawaiian taxi driver claimed she was inebriated and had urinated in his cab. He threatened to use her DNA in a court suit.)

**BEFORE RICK AND KATHY MOVED** their brood to New York City in the '90s, the Hiltons lived in exclusive Bel-Air, in Los Angeles, where Paris and Nicky attended a strict coeducational Roman Catholic school, St. Paul the Apostle, which went up to the eighth grade. The Hilton girls were required to wear uniforms and were given a Catholic education in addition to the reading, writing, and arithmetic. "It was more strict than a lot of schools," says a parent of a student who went there. "The principal was against having boy-girl parties until the graduation party."

Paris graduated from St. Paul's in June 1995, the only school from which she is believed to have ever received a formal diploma. But because of her increasingly wild behavior she was not seen at the eighth-grade parent-sponsored graduation party. She then went to Marymount High School in Bel-Air, but she didn't finish with her class.

Nicky, two years younger than Paris, was friends with another St. Paul's student, Diana Tangalakis, the daughter of an attorney. By an odd coincidence Diana's mother, Gini Tangalakis, had worked years earlier as a secretary in Conrad Hilton's offices and had experienced some amusing episodes with the old flirt who came on to her when she was twenty-one and engaged to be married and he was in his eighties.

On a number of occasions Diana Tangalakis was invited by Nicky to sleep over at the Hiltons', and that caused concern for her mother. "Back then Nicky was a very quiet girl, very polite and sweet, but it was hard for her to be accepted by the kids—kids that age can be tough," says Gini Tangalakis. "Nicky wasn't included in a lot because she was rich, because she had the Hilton name—you know, she was the first kid to bring a cell phone to school, so all of that made it difficult, and Paris already had a reputation at the school. She was off-the-wall even back then. I always thought that Nicky seemed to be a little more on the ball.

"When I would take my daughter up to Rick and Kathy's house to spend the night with Nicky, I always had to wonder—who's in charge here? Kathy and Rick were never around. There would be the house-keeper, who spoke very little English. That didn't ride well with me. I'd tell my daughter, 'If you feel uncomfortable, just call and we'll come get you if something doesn't seem right.' I'd drive away thinking, is this stupid of me or what?"

As Tangalakis observes, "It didn't appear to me that there was much parental involvement."

When the Hiltons decided to move to New York, there was much talk among the parents of St. Paul's alumni. "The scuttlebutt was that Kathy wanted to expose her girls to the social and nightlife world in Manhattan," says Tangalakis. "She wanted her girls to be in the limelight, and she certainly accomplished that."

**BY THE TIME PARIS** was in her midteens and becoming the reigning princess of the gossip firmament, she suddenly vanished from New York, where her family was ensconced in a thirtieth-floor penthouse at the exclusive Waldorf Towers. The Towers is the residential arm of the Waldorf-Astoria, one of the world's grande dames of hotels. Conrad Hilton had bought the place with much hoopla in the late 1940s. Now, several generations later, Paris Hilton was making all the headlines.

Not since the 1950s, when Paris's Hollywood playboy great-uncle, Nick Hilton—Conrad's firstborn, Elizabeth Taylor's first husband—was a constant boldface name in the columns for his narcissistic nights of broads, boozing, and brawling, had there been a Hilton so publicly outrageous and wicked.

At the time of her disappearance, Paris, who bounced from school to school because of her grades, her behavior, or both, was attending a hoity-toity private academy on Central Park West. While the Dwight School, founded in 1872, boasted that its mission was to "develop each student's unique capabilities by integrating mind, body, and spirit," rich-kid detractors from other fancy schools joked that Dwight was an acronym for "Dumb White Idiots Getting High Together."

When the whispering became a roar and questions about Paris's curious evaporation reached Kathy Hilton, she had a ready, albeit convoluted, explanation.

"Well, you know what? She never got friendly with anyone at Dwight. And Paris had a 3.8 average. She's very, very smart. . . . We left the school because we had a stalker. . . . It was the most frightening thing I've ever gone through," she explained in a piece in *Vanity Fair* that featured a full-page photo of Paris striking an arresting pose—legs teasingly spread, wearing a crotch-baring mini and a see-through mesh top for all the world's stalkers to drool over.

"It was so scary," continued her mother of the stalker situation. ". . . We pretended that we went here and there. We said, 'Oh, she went off there,' and the truth is, we spent some time in London, at the London Hilton. We brought the tutor with us."

She maintained that Paris graduated from high school "with home-schooling."

Curiously, however, Kathy Hilton's recitation of the circumstances surrounding Paris's disappearance differs substantially from the way Waldorf-Astoria management insiders remember it.

The hotel and the Towers, home over the decades to visiting presidents, potentates, and pretenders, have the tightest security. The insiders claim that if there had been a stalker, they never were made aware of him, and they would have been had he been a threat.

As one executive who, along with his father, had a long and storied history with the Hilton Hotel organization in New York, notes, "There are absolutely no secrets if you live in a hotel, especially if it's a Hilton Hotel and you're a Hilton. Employees are looking at the sheets and the underwear that go to the laundry every day. They have a proclivity to gossip. They relish in trying to find out what are someone's peccadilloes. It's like living in a fishbowl—your comings and goings are clocked. And if they've got a bone to pick with someone—and Paris's parents, especially Kathy Hilton, infuriated a lot of Waldorf people with their imperious manner—they'll make sure to bring them down."

According to the hotelmen, Paris had hightailed it out of the Waldorf for a fling with a cute trucker with a big rig whom she met while he was unloading goodies on the hotel's loading dock. Paris apparently wanted a taste of the simple life in the cozy cab of an eighteen-wheeler.

"I don't remember anything about a stalker *ever* surfacing in the hotel at the time," states Neal Schwartz, whose family ran the valet concession for decades at the Waldorf on a handshake between Schwartz's Hungarian-born grandfather, Harry, and Conrad Hilton himself. (The two men had bonded after Hilton scandalously married the Hungarian spitfire Zsa Zsa Gabor back in the 1940s. "Zsa Zsa would go off into rants and rages in Hungarian which no one but my grandfather could understand, so Conrad would say, 'Harry, find out what the hell she wants and just quiet her down.' Mr. Hilton liked and trusted my grandfather and that's how my family got the hotel valet business.")

Schwartz scoffs at Kathy Hilton's story about the stalker. "It sounds like something the Hilton spin machine would put out," he maintains. "Certainly there was no increase in security, and I'm sure Paris's grandfather [Barron Hilton, who ran the show at the time] would have made sure they would have done that. But there was no change in security at the hotel or the Towers. When Paris took off she had a bit of a wild-child reputation already."

Schwartz, whose family's company had offices at the New York Hilton and the Waldorf at the time of Paris's departure, was hearing about all the excitement from Waldorf managers who were sworn from talking publicly about the hotels' innermost secrets if they wanted to receive their pensions.

"There was a big to-do at the Waldorf—you know, how are we going to explain to Barron that we lost his grandkid?" says Schwartz, who was not a Hilton employee and therefore not subject to any Hilton gag order.

At the same time, there were whispers within the tight-lipped, low-key Hilton family circle of provocative and distressing behavior involving Paris and a group of young men, actions that had gotten her into a jam at school. There was chatter of Paris's sticky fingers, snatching everything from a relative's lingerie—"stupid things like panties," says a Hilton family insider—to an expensive car belonging to a girlfriend's parents. "She took it and was driving all over New York City. Of course, they hushed it up."

Whatever the reason for Paris's disappearance—deranged stalker, horny trucker, or some other shenanigans—one fact is crystal clear: Kathy Hilton shipped Paris off to stay with her own mother—Paris's maternal grandmother, Kathleen Mary Dugan Avanzino Richards Catain Fenton, known as "big Kathy." She lived in Palm Desert, part of Palm Springs, the sizzling California desert Babylon for the rich, famous, and infamous.

Kathy Hilton, known as "little Kathy," had high hopes that her mother—considered "a driven, ambitious stage mother from hell"— could straighten out the wild child.

Paris's grandmother adored her, called her my "Marilyn Monroe," and pledged she'd one day be world-famous. When Paris was still an adolescent big Kathy had tried to get her into modeling. At one point big Kathy called her close friend Jane Hallaren, who had been in the runway business years earlier, to secure Paris a catwalk slot at Eileen Ford's famed agency. "Paris was thirteen, fourteen years old and she was *breathtaking,* but she was kind of shy if you can believe it, and I didn't think she had the personality for it," says Hallaren.

"Paris was Kathleen's first grandchild, and they had a very special bond, and Kathleen thought she could take Paris under her wing, straighten her out, and make things happen for her," says Adele Avanzino, big Kathy's first husband's sister.

"Little Kathy sent Paris to live with her mom because Paris was *totally* out of control," states Michele "Mickey" Catain, the daughter of Paris's grandmother's third husband, Jack Catain, himself a real-life Tony Soprano–style mobster.

A young divorcée at the time, Mickey Catain had become like another daughter to big Kathy and had partied with little Kathy before she married into the Hilton family. A member of Kathy and Rick Hilton's wedding, Catain had seen Paris when she was just a baby and later when she was in her terrible twos. "She was *gorgeous*," she says. "Her face was incredible, like a porcelain doll."

But other than reading the burgeoning gossip about Paris's feverish frolics, Catain hadn't seen her face-to-face for some years until she was invited by big Kathy to visit her in the desert when the naughty teenager was under her jurisdiction. "I went and stayed for a weekend, and Paris was *such* a snot," Catain recalls vividly. "Even back then she thought her shit didn't stink. She was just a *very* spoiled girl."

However, Catain didn't get the impression that the change of environment had improved Paris's behavior. "I hardly ever saw her because she came into the house, changed her clothes, and disappeared again. She was always with a group of girls and they'd all go out together, which cracked me up because that's exactly what her mother [Kathy Hilton] used to do when we partied together. It wasn't New York nightlife, but it *was* Palm Springs. Paris must have had the town going crazy!"

After Kathy and Rick Hilton placed Paris in the hands of her grandmother to be tamed, the concerned parents took off for a much-needed breather from the stresses and strains of parenthood by going on a cruise aboard another wealthy couple's yacht. "They were gone for a long, long time," says a family insider. "And Mama [big Kathy] took care of Paris. And was *that* ever a trip!"

While staying with her grandmother, Paris was enrolled at the very fancy Palm Valley School in neighboring Rancho Mirage, where she had a reputation as a flirt who cared little about her studies, though she came prepared for algebra class in style, bearing a bejeweled calculator.

There were other schools on Paris's journey through secondary education. For a couple of months, she attended the Canterbury School in Connecticut, but was ejected when she left for a weekend without permission. For a time, she had matriculated at the Buckley School in Sherman Oaks, California, where her friends and classmates included Kimberly Stewart, the wild daughter of rocker Rod Stewart, and Nicole Richie, the equally wild daughter of singer Lionel Richie. "I just remember at Buckley all the guys loved her because, you know, we had to wear uniforms, like we had these proper uniforms, and there's a certain way you had to wear your skirt and everything, and I'd kind of lift mine up and she'd lift hers up a little further and our skirts would be a little shorter than everyone else's and we always used to get in trouble for that," recalled Stewart.

Paris also attended Professional Children's School in Manhattan, and spent some time at a school for troubled kids in Utah that featured behavior modification therapy. Because of her growing bad-girl reputation, Paris was said to have been refused admittance to a private Catholic school in New York. "Another family was considering enrolling their daughter but heard that Paris also was applying," maintains a knowledgeable source. "The parents threatened to send their daughter elsewhere if Paris was admitted."

Paris claimed years later that she had been diagnosed as a child with attention deficit disorder. As she got older, this led some to believe she was on drugs, which she denied using.

While big Kathy had serious concerns about her granddaughter's behavior, she was also extremely proud of Paris's growing fame. In fact, it was in a Beverly Hills condo owned by big Kathy where Paris struck the sexy pose for the *Vanity Fair* article in which little Kathy told the stalker story. Big Kathy thought her grandbaby's spread was *fabulous.*

"Big Kathy bragged about her and was so excited she was in the magazine," notes Catain. "She was looking at the layout and saying, '*This* is the vehicle to make Paris a star. She doesn't realize how much this is going to do for her. Her fame's just starting to take off.' I remember her telling me, 'This is the turning point for Paris's career, but we're not going to tell her.' She goes, 'We're not going to let it go to her head.' *Like it wasn't already there.*"

To her first husband's brother, Ken Avanzino, big Kathy predicted a most spectacular and grandiose future for her granddaughter. "You watch," she declared with the utmost confidence, "Paris is going to be bigger than Princess Di."

And to Linda McKusker, a friend from her high school days, big Kathy, referring to her granddaughter's uninhibited ways, asserted, "Paris really isn't like that"—that is, a poster child for exhibitionism—"she's just your sweet, average girl next door." Years later, Paris attributed her success to big Kathy.

Meanwhile, big Kathy threw the blame for Paris's bad-girl behavior on her very own daughter, Kathy Hilton.

"Big Kathy used to tell me, 'My daughter does not know how to be a mother. She's a good businesswoman, she's smart, she's beautiful, but she's *not* a good mother,'" maintains Catain. "She said Kathy never paid attention to those kids, Paris and Nicky, until they started to become famous. And that's because she had her own agenda, and because she's a very self-centered, selfish lady, just interested in how much higher she could climb. Big Kathy always said, 'Kathy's *the* worst mom.'"

# CHAPTER 2

**B**efore she bagged and tagged a scion of the Hilton Hotel family at the age of twenty, before she gave birth to the It Girl of the New Millennium, before she sold glitzy *shmattes* and art in her Sunset Boulevard boutique, before she hawked overpriced tchotchkes on her QVC home shopping network show called *Many Splendid Things,* and before she starred as the hostess of her own reality TV show, appropriately titled *I Want to Be a Hilton,* blond and perky little Kathy was as desperate for fame and fortune as would be her wild-child spawn.

Pushed by big Kathy, and discovered before she was two years old by a famous children's photographer who was knocked out by this perfect little creature's blond, all-American look, little Kathy's career was launched. But unlike her younger, very pretty and more talented half-sisters, Kim and Kyle Richards—who had had enormous success in TV sitcoms and movies in the '70s and '80s—Kathy never really made it and wasn't bankable.

During her fifteen minutes, however, she modeled in print ads and appeared in some three dozen TV commercials. By the age of thirteen she had made two appearances on her sister Kim's popular program,

*Nanny and the Professor,* and got mostly one-shot gigs on such network prime-time shows as *Marcus Welby, M.D., Family Affair, Bewitched, The Rockford Files,* and *Happy Days.* She appeared in a CBS movie called *Johnny Comes Home* and had a chance at a TV pilot, but it never got the green light. It was all downhill, career-wise, from there.

Based on her fancy-schmancy attitude teaching manners, style, and refinement to her supposed rube contestants as mistress of ceremonies on the ill-conceived 2005 NBC reality flop *I Want to Be a Hilton*—a program that had genuine Hiltons seeing red, and which Kathy herself famously declared "fucking sucks"—one would have expected the fabulous Mrs. Hilton to have been groomed at a proper finishing school, to have had matriculated at one of the elite Seven Sisters colleges, and to have done the grand tour of Europe in style, entering polite society as a refined debutante. After all, she had married into one of the planet's wealthiest and most powerful families.

But, as it turns out, Kathy Hilton was not to the manor born.

**THE FUTURE KATHY HILTON** was groomed for the stardom that eluded her by the overbearing, determined, and very outlandish big Kathy, who lived vicariously through her daughters' ups and downs. A materialistic diva, big Kathy was obsessed with accumulating money, diamonds, fancy cars, expensive homes—and husbands to pay for it all.

She was a mistress of manipulation who dominated and controlled little Kathy's and her sisters' every professional and personal decision, from the outfits they wore, to the jobs they took, to the men they dated and married. By the time the future Kathy Hilton was thirteen, her mother had made her take singing lessons, dancing lessons, guitar lessons, horseback riding lessons, swimming lessons, and ice skating lessons—all salable talents on the résumés she sent to casting directors and producers, hoping to make her daughter a star.

"She talked to her daughters every day, probably three, four times a day," recounts a friend. "She loved sitting for an entire day on the phone with her dogs around her *dictating* to her daughters. Even after little Kathy became a Hilton and was living like royalty in New York she'd be calling her mom every day, and big Kathy would give her orders."

Big Kathy's constant mantra to little Kathy, her firstborn, and to her other daughters—and later to her granddaughters, Paris and Nicky—was: Marry rich men and have lots of babies. And she made certain they did just that. (Besides the Hilton whom Kathy lassoed, Kim Richards tied the knot for a time with one of the sons of billionaire oilman and Hollywood mogul Marvin Davis and had two children with him. Kyle for a time was wed to the scion of a wealthy foreigner and had a daughter with him. Later, she married a well-to-do agent in Rick Hilton's hugely successful Beverly Hills real estate firm.)

"My daughters are married to men who have a total net worth of $13 billion," big Kathy once bragged to her friend Linda McKusker, as if she were hawking an IPO. "Big Kathy," McKusker felt, "had visions of grandeur. She really did drive her kids hard."

Friends jokingly compared big Kathy's mind control over little Kathy and her sisters to that of twisted '70s cult leader Jim Jones—sans the killer Kool-Aid. But more on the mark, they likened her to that famous-for-being-famous Hungarian hot mama Jolie Gabor, the Queen Mother who dictated that her glamorous offspring—Zsa Zsa, Eva, and Magda—marry rich and famous and live the high life draped in furs, diamonds, and rubies. (The drag queen RuPaul once described the Gabor girls as "guts, glamour, and goulash.") Zsa Zsa took her mother's advice to heart when she roped in and married the big kahuna himself, Conrad Hilton, the second of her many husbands.

**BIG KATHY'S MAIDEN NAME** was Dugan, and she never quite had much luck marrying *really* rich. Avanzino, Richards, Catain, and Fenton are the surnames of the serial bride's four husbands.

The first of her mostly horrific unions—essentially a shotgun wedding—was to a bad boy named Larry Avanzino, an Italian-American, who had gotten the pretty Irish-American Dugan girl pregnant in the backseat of her 1957 black Chevrolet convertible. The unplanned bundle of joy conceived in that cramped vinyl and chrome General Motors love nest would grow up to be none other than Kathy Hilton, Paris Hilton's mother.

The identity of Kathy Hilton's biological father and how her birth came about has been a long-held family secret. Says an Avanzino relative, "It's really made me angry that with all of Paris's fame the real identity of her [maternal] grandfather has been covered up. You only hear the name Hilton, never the name Avanzino. I guess it just doesn't have the same ring."

Big Kathy's third husband was Jack Catain, an organized crime figure, whom she is said to have married and divorced twice—turned on by the big diamond he gave her and by his tough-guy persona. When little Kathy was about to marry into the Hilton family, big Kathy split from the mafioso to avoid a scandal.

In her pantheon of husbands, number two, Ken Richards, and number four, Bob Fenton, were submissives to big Kathy's dominatrix. Richards, whom big Kathy had stolen from his wife and three children, raised little Kathy. Until she became a Hilton, she always publicly used the Richards name, never Avanzino. Richards also was the father of Kim and Kyle, whose careers he helped finance. Once Kim was bringing in a hefty revenue stream from her screen work, big Kathy gave Richards the heave-ho. As for Fenton, she boasted that she denied him sex throughout their marriage.

Big Kathy could be cruel—physically and emotionally—as a mother and a wife, the no-sex rule being just a minor bit of torture in the scheme of things. She had a frightening propensity for violent behavior such as physically abusing people. One eyewitness to, and target of, Paris Hilton's maternal grandmother's anger—a stepdaughter—says she was left "emotionally scarred" from their hellish relationship.

It was at the knee of this oddball of a matriarch that Kathy Hilton learned the good, the bad, and the ugly and later passed on her mother's philosophy and values to her own daughters, Paris and Nicky.

**BY HER MIDTEENS,** little Kathy's show business career was in the proverbial toilet. She lacked that elusive magical elixir for a successful run, and her mother's dream of making her into a star had all but faded. The kind of media that would rocket Paris Hilton to international celebrity status—the World Wide Web—sadly didn't exist back in the 1970s. Moreover, she was thought to be slothful by her stepfather, Ken Richards, who often complained, "Kathy's so lazy she won't get up—all she wants to do is party at night."

Studies were never Kathy's cup of tea, either. When she did attend classes, when she wasn't auditioning or working, it was at a small, curious private educational institution in the Los Angeles suburb of Encino—Valley Girl country. California Preparatory School, Cal Prep as it was known, attracted a mélange of child performers and wannabes, ranging from some of the Michael Jackson clan to *Partridge Family* star Danny Bonaduce, who assaulted a transvestite prostitute years later, giving him the proper credentials for his own reality show in 2005, when Kathy Hilton's was airing.

"Cal Prep was a joke," says a former student who went there and was a close friend of Kathy's. "It was just a place for rich kids and celebrities to go. Their parents paid the money and the kids went and hung out."

One mother, a close friend of big Kathy's, sent her daughter there because she suffered from dyslexia and possibly attention deficit disorder. "It was a good little school for more individualized attention, which is what my daughter needed," she says. "I got a letter from a teacher saying my daughter was never going to graduate with her class, but two days later she's up there on the stage—graduating. We paid the tuition and they just pushed her through."

If little Kathy wasn't academically inclined—and why should she be, her mother, big Kathy, was a high school dropout at sixteen, and Kathy Hilton's biological father, Larry Avanzino, turned out to be an alcoholic housepainter—one could blame her lack of interest on the school's odd methods of teaching. For instance, there was little or no homework, the philosophy being that "a student does not need to repeat for five hours after school what he should have learned in school." When one of the students was asked to name the days of the week, he replied, "Five school days and two days off." Learning history wasn't considered necessary, and tests were thought of as a big hoax. "The right answer isn't as important as the thinking process behind the answer." With no homework, no tests, little or no history, and classes in fencing and, oddly, Mandarin Chinese, Kathy thought Cal Prep was the coolest.

Having been indoctrinated with her mother's rules of mating behavior—*Marry Rich!*—teenage Kathy sought out suitors who were wealthy and well connected to show business. But one of the ones she picked early on didn't meet the profile developed by her mother.

Like big Kathy, little Kathy's first serious boyfriend was another bad boy, according to his public high school buddy and Kathy's close friend at the time, Pierce Jensen. He compared Kathy's steady to the pot-smoking, long-haired Jeff Spicoli, Sean Penn's character in the 1982 film about southern California teen life, *Fast Times at Ridgemont High.*

Kathy and her guy had four common interests—steamy make-out sessions, partying, hanging out . . . and steamy make-out sessions.

"Kathy was dumb as a nail," asserts Jensen, who at the time was a college-bound senior with Kathy's boyfriend in the class of 1974 at William Howard Taft High School in affluent Woodland Hills. Taft was a real-life Ridgemont High and, like Cal Prep, was attended by a number of child stars and the children of stars—among them Maureen McCormick, who played Marcia Brady on *The Brady Bunch.*

"Kathy's whole thing was going out and having fun," recalls Jensen. "And if we weren't going out to the restaurants in West LA, or cruising the Sunset Strip we would pretty much just hang out at her home."

Kathy lived in a pretty house that big Kathy's second husband, Ken Richards, had had built on Aqua Verde Drive on the edge of Bel-Air.

"At Kathy's we played paddle tennis or listened to music," says Jensen. "She never talked about anything except, you know, nonsense—going with this guy, going with that guy . . . 'he's cute, she's cute' . . . 'oh, I really like that song.' There wasn't a book in the house, no newspapers except for the trades and the tabloids. We never went to the beach, never went hiking, never did things that I would do with other girls that I would date. Just like her daughter Paris, Kathy was only interested in being *seen.*

"Her boyfriend was a partyer like we all were," says Jensen, chuckling years later. "We dropped acid, smoked pot, drank. He had a rattletrap car, and I know Kathy was embarrassed to ride in his clunker. I remember her mother saying, 'My God, *my* daughter—you're *not* riding in *that* car!'"

Unlike little Kathy's boyfriend, Pierce Jensen was much more acceptable to big Kathy, especially because his mother, Pat Priest, was a major mid-1960s TV star who played the role of Marilyn in *The Munsters* and had starred in one of Elvis's films, *Easy Come, Easy Go.* "Big Kathy gushed all over my mother when they met," recalls Jensen.

Jensen remembers Kathy's mother as being *very* overbearing and saw her as the epitome of the stage mom. "But by the time I knew Kathy the drive wasn't so much to get Kathy into acting—it was to get her a rich husband. Before we would go out her mom would say, 'Oh, you'll never get a rich man with *that* skirt on. Put *this* on,'" Jensen recalls vividly. "Big Kathy had an agenda. When we would go out and Kathy would see men in expensive cars, or men who looked wealthy, she'd make comments like, 'Oh, I'm going to bag me one of them one day . . . I don't have time for acting now, I'm busy looking for a rich guy.'"

Kathy's only known girlfriend at the time was homely and overweight, thus no threat or competition when she accompanied Kathy on her frequent outings looking for cute, rich guys. Also, she had a car and was Kathy's chauffeur.

Kathy's vanity didn't end there. In her room the failed starlet, who was jealous of Kim's and Kyle's success, kept stacks of eight-by-ten black-and-white publicity glossies from the days when she thought her career would blossom—sort of a contemporary teen version of *Sunset Boulevard*'s Norma Desmond reliving the glory days. She autographed the photos for friends or anyone who might have recognized her from her TV or modeling gigs.

Among the photos was one of her posing in a bikini—G-rated. Another was a shot of the wholesome blond teenager wearing a broad Pepsodent smile, her hands wrapped around a tree branch, the kind of photo *Seventeen* would run, sparking envy in girl readers with acne and baby fat. Kathy had given both to Jensen, inscribing one of them on the back with the words "Pierce, I love U! Kathy." Another note, on the back of the same photo, was inscribed, "Dear Pierce. You have been such a great friend and escort"—she underlined the word *escort* twice. "Maybe one day we will get 2-gether. Love ya, Kathy."

There was one other photo of Kathy that Jensen kept through the years, one he held dear to his heart—a Polaroid that he shot of her at a party.

"Everybody was fucked up," he remembers about that night. "We were all drinking, carrying on, smoking dope—although I never saw Kathy *ever* get high. I always got the impression that she was afraid to because she would lose control and be herself."

The photo looks like one you would see on an episode of *CSI: Crime Scene Investigation,* except Kathy eagerly volunteered to be the model. She never was, nor would she ever be, a victim.

Kathy is seen lying on a bare mattress with flower designs on it, her head propped on a pillow, her eyes wide open like a frightened deer staring into headlights. Her midriff is bare because she has the tails of her blouse tied, the sleeves rolled up, and her legs in jeans are spread wide and bent at the knees.

"She was just being her outrageous, flirtatious, outgoing, exuding-sexual-charm self," explains Jensen. "That night, at that party, she just plopped down on that mattress like, 'Come on, baby, do me. . . . Look at *me,* boys.' She was just being Kathy. But if I were to say, 'Come on, Kathy, take your top off,' she would say no. She would only go so far."

Back then Jensen and others in their crowd had a nickname for Kathy, who dressed "extremely provocatively and was the most flirtatious girl" they'd ever met. "We called her 'PT,'" reveals Jensen. "Everybody called her a prick tease. I've never met anybody like her since." (By coincidence her mother, big Kathy, had an X-rated nickname during her own wild teen years. She had been given the moniker "Pussy" Dugan.)

"Kathy flirted with every guy who crossed her path," maintains Jensen. "Even though she was involved with my friend, she flirted with me. She flirted with our friends. That's why it didn't surprise me the way Paris turned out, because her mother was the same way—although back then I don't think Kathy was sleeping with people. But you'd think she'd slept with every guy in the city by the way she acted.

"Me and my buddies always wondered whether she and her boyfriend were having sex—because the way she acted you would say, yes, *ten times a day.* They were just all over each other like cheap suits, making suggestive comments to each other, and rubbing and groping. I can imagine her mother telling Kathy all about sex—but also telling her you can please a guy in other ways, and string him along and you'll have him hooked.

"Her mother told her all her life that she was great and wonderful, so she had a *huge* ego, and you know that when you have a huge ego you don't act like yourself. You think you're better than everyone else and you act that way. She was always *on,* never a genuine person.

"I thought when she eventually hooked up with Rick Hilton that she must have pulled off the perfect acting job, that she nailed him with her fake personality, her false way of being. I thought, 'Well, she did it.' The prophecy is fulfilled."

# CHAPTER 3

In September 1974—well before Rick Hilton came on the scene—little Kathy focused her attentions on another young man who, for a number of reasons, caused consternation for her mother.

Jane Hallaren, who had been a confidante of big Kathy's since childhood, clearly heard the tension in her voice when she telephoned her in New York to discuss little Kathy's latest romantic travail. Jane and big Kathy's close bond had been formed when Hallaren, a street kid from Brooklyn, "beat the shit" out of big Kathy in the schoolyard of their Catholic parochial school after Hallaren had a *Heathers*-type confrontation with a clique of girls whom Kathy controlled. A onetime model's rep instrumental in Martha Stewart's brief commercial and print modeling career, Hallaren had later gone into acting—stage and film—receiving critical acclaim as a predatory lesbian college professor in director John Sayles's 1994 art film *Lianna*.

Over time, big Kathy had kept Hallaren in the loop on the goings-on in her life—"a book in itself," she states—and on little Kathy's various teen romances, all of which Hallaren thought "quite banal and superficial."

But the long-distance phone call on the night in question is one she has never forgotten.

"Kathleen said, 'Janie, Kathy's having an affair. It's with one of the Jackson Five. I don't know what to do.'

"Kathleen said she was allowing the relationship to proceed, rationalizing that the relationship was a step *up* for Kathy because it was a connection to a well-heeled show business family and celebrity. At the same time big Kathy didn't like black people, and here was Kathy involved with a black kid. It's the only conversation I ever remember having with her about any man in her children's, or her own, life, that she had trepidation about.

"I was sitting in bed listening to this, thinking, *'Oh—My—God.'* I thought, 'This is so absurd, so insane' that I said to her, 'I can't believe you're sanctioning this.'"

After that call Hallaren heard nothing more about the claimed romance until long after Kathy had become Mrs. Rick Hilton.

"It was when people started asking, is Michael Jackson straight or gay? When he was getting weird, and I said to Kathy, 'He's straight, right, being he had that affair with Kathy,' and she said, 'No, no, no, no—it wasn't Michael. It was one of his brothers.'"

Hallaren assumes big Kathy was telling her the truth about her daughter's relationship, but she also emphasizes that big Kathy was histrionic, an über drama queen who often exaggerated a situation to make it sound more intriguing and make her life appear more exciting.

Another bizarre situation arose when big Kathy's second husband, Ken Richards, learned that big Kathy had actually asked a young man to give little Kathy "sex lessons," according to Sylvia Benedict Richards, who married Ken Richards after his acrimonious divorce from big Kathy. "Big Kathy told Ken that she wanted Kathy to know all about sex, and how to perform sex, literally, the best way possible," asserts Sylvia Richards. "So she asked a young man to teach her in his van. Ken had a fit when he found out about it and confronted Kathleen. She told him to mind his own business, to keep his nose out of it, that Kathy was *her* daughter." (Years later, Paris received sex instruction from *her* mother, who warned her that performing fellatio would put "holes" in her face. "I totally believed her. She's, like, 'It's from sucking,' I'm, like, 'Ewwww!'")

Having watched big Kathy in action for more than two decades, Sylvia Richards observes, "She believed that rules didn't pertain to her. And this is the way she brought up the girls. There were no rules for them, either. And that's the way Kathy brought up Paris."

**AFTER LITTLE KATHY** finished high school there was a series of well-heeled, handsome, show-biz types whom she pursued. And she was known as a partyer—one of the pretty girls-on-the-make who frequented the bashes at the Playboy Mansion. As Sylvia Richards states, "Little Kathy partied all night, and slept all day."

For a time Kathy had "a big crush" on and "chased and dated" Dean Martin's son, Dean-Paul, discloses Jeanne Martin, Dino's widow, herself the 1948 Orange Bowl Queen. At the time, the handsome actor, who was a half dozen years older than Kathy, was ending a bad first marriage. "Kathy definitely wanted celebrity and wanted to marry somebody preferably in show business," recalls Martin. "She *loved* the limelight, *that* I know."

Kathy also chased and saw Lucille Ball and Desi Arnaz's son, Desi Jr. "She used to drop his name all the time," says Mickey Catain. "He came up to her mom's house a couple of times. She talked about him a lot." But that ended quickly because, as a well-placed observer notes, "Lucy would have none of it. She didn't think very highly of Kathy."

Dean-Paul Martin, who died in a plane crash in 1987, and Desi Arnaz Jr., who later married a dancer, fit perfectly the profile of the kind of man with whom big Kathy would have liked little Kathy to walk down the aisle—they came from money and had major show business connections.

"Kathy was desperate to chase them—not for her own sake but rather because her mother *wanted* her to. That's the *pathetic* part," observes Jane Hallaren.

After each and every date little Kathy, on instructions from big Kathy, would call her mother and give her an intimate description of what went on. "I was *there* at the house visiting when she called," says Sylvia Richards. "Mama wanted to know a blow-by-blow description of what went on. And little Kathy gave her a blow-by-blow description. Big Kathy didn't care what little Kathy did as long as she married somebody rich. She was that way with all of the girls. Kathy was out for the buck—as much as she could get."

When none of those relationships worked out, little Kathy trolled the trendy clubs and restaurants of Beverly Hills and the Valley. Riding shotgun on those manhunts was Mickey Catain, whose mobster father was married to big Kathy at the time.

"I was hanging out with her because our parents put us together," she says. "I was just divorced and I wasn't in that world of Kathy's with all the celebrities and with going out every night to the clubs. That girl *loved* to party. Kathy was very sophisticated when it came to that scene. She'd meet some guy and he'd call her for a date. A lot of them were foreigners, guys with money—Iranians, Persians, Asians. So she'd go on the date, but she'd invite like five other girls to go along with her and then we'd get there and the guy would go, 'Who are they?' I'd be *so* embarrassed. I'm like, 'Oh, Kathy, I can't stay,' and she's like, 'Oh, no, no, no. Stay, stay. It'll be fine.' And she'd make the guy take us to the most expensive restaurant and pick up the tab for all of us."

On one unforgettable occasion, big Kathy took the girls to meet the entire Dallas Cowboys team, apparently in hopes of securing dates for them. "She knew somebody with the Dallas organization and we showed up at their training session," says Catain. "First we watched them play and then we're limoed off to have dinner with them, the whole team. It was just to meet the guys and have fun and flirt. It was like one of the best nights I ever had."

Because big Kathy surrounded herself with gorgeous young women, wild stories and unfounded rumors circulated about her activities. Sylvester Stallone's mother, Jackie Stallone, a self-styled psychic, says she heard from her friend Eva Gabor that big Kathy "ran an escort service. Eva told me many times that the mother introduced girls to eligible men." David Patrick Columbia, who documents the Manhattan and

Hamptons society scene on a popular website called New York Social Diary, lived in LA for years, helped Debbie Reynolds write a memoir, and followed the movements of the contemporary Hiltons, says he had received reports from sources on the West Coast that one of the girls was connected to convicted "Hollywood Madam" Heidi Fleiss, who in 2005 was planning to open "Heidi's Stud Farm," a luxury brothel for women to have sex with male prostitutes. On the other hand, Fleiss claims she never heard of any of them.

At one point, big Kathy bought a used navy blue Cadillac limousine so she and her companions, among them Mickey Catain's mother, Marlene, could ride in style and meet affluent men. The car had a vanity plate with a portion of her name on it. At the time both women were divorced from Jack Catain, and the two had become friends.

"We went out together and I thought through her I could meet other people because I was married for so long," Marlene Catain states. "I would drive around with her in her limo while she was smoking grass, and she would have Arab guys in the car. We'd drive into Beverly Hills and everybody would look at us. She took me to the Playboy Club, which was very exclusive at the time. I had the impression she had connections there, or knew Hefner. I met some interesting people there through her. I thought it was fun. I felt like a voyeur."

Her daughter, Mickey, didn't think that Paris's grandmother took money in a play-for-pay sense from any of the men she encountered during her adventures. "She would pick them up and have them take her to dinner, or she would set them up with other women. She would hit on them, get them to take her out, take her on a trip—whatever she could get. And I think she always had in her mind the idea, is he marriage potential?

"She loved the idea of being married, of family. That's why she had her daughters' friends like me around her," Catain continues. "Big Kathy was just like a mother to everybody and she just loved all these girls to death and they just flocked to her. They hung out and talked and had sleepovers and got dressed to go out together. Kathy just kind of provided a shelter. It was fun and you'd get so wrapped up in it you didn't think of it as being really *weird.*"

Kay Rozario, a close friend of big Kathy's, points out that she was "very kind to a lot of young girls" and that she had "a lot of goodness in her." Among the girls who were in Kathleen's circle "were two who lost their mother," recalls Rozario, "and Kathleen practically adopted them and helped to raise them. The house was always *full* of young girls, and all those girls *loved* her. There was a great deal of kindness and love there that those girls weren't getting in their own homes, or from their own parents, so they were drawn to big Kathy."

When little Kathy wasn't out partying, she and her friends lolled by the pool or hung out in her enormous bedroom. Her clothing was piled everywhere—she had a *huge* wardrobe—and the decorating was very feminine—cute upholstered chairs and a king-size bed.

What little Kathy desperately wanted, though, was a car of her own. Big Kathy's brother, Chuck Dugan, had a used car lot in Encino, and he found an old Fiat and had it fixed up and painted black for his niece. For a girl who in the not too distant future would be chauffeured in Rolls-Royce elegance as a Hilton, Kathy was overjoyed with the little sports car. "But the first or second day she took it out, the thing blew up," remembers Mickey Catain. "Kathy just left it sitting there and walked away. I'm thinking, 'You just can't abandon a car like that.' But she says, 'Let someone else take care of it. I don't want it anymore.' That was always her attitude, and she never went back for it. She had no concern for anybody else. It was just what her needs were."

# CHAPTER 4

With no acting career, and no millionaire on the horizon, little Kathy received an offer she felt she couldn't refuse. Because she was a habitué at the Mansion, she was asked to pose in *Playboy* for $25,000, an awfully tempting proposition for a cutie-pie with no discernable future.

"Kathy was a pretty girl with a nice figure who hung around with that fast Beverly Hills–Hollywood crowd, and I guess it was Hugh [Hefner] or one of his people who made the offer—and Kathy wanted to do it," says Kay Rozario, with whom Kathy had discussed the proposition. "Plus she wanted to buy a new car and that offer of twenty-five grand looked good, and in those days that was like making a hundred grand."

The wife of Bob Rozario, the legendary musical director for Bobby Darin, Tony Orlando, and Donny and Marie Osmond, Kay Rozario was a longtime friend of Kathy's mother, and was like a surrogate mother to Kathy's half-sister Kim. Rozario's daughter, Leanne, was Kim's closest friend; they had met at Cal Prep. At the time Kim and Leanne were there, one of their classmates was said to have been Michael Jackson's brother,

Randy, and every so often his brother "The Gloved One" would come by the Rozarios' home to take the girls roller skating.

Kay Rozario says she was shocked—*shocked*—when Kathy, then about eighteen, told her of her plan to presumably take it *all* off for *Playboy.* "She said, 'They want me to do it and I can use the money and I can get a new car.'

"I begged her, 'Please do *not* do this.' I said, 'You are trying to catch a rich husband. What's going to happen if you find Mr. Right and he takes you home to Mother and somebody in the family says, 'You know what? Kathy was Miss October.' I said, 'Would you want that? They'll turn on you. You think they'll want a daughter who was a centerfold?' Kathy knew I was right, and she promised me she wouldn't do it. I talked her out of it."

Big Kathy, however, didn't think anything was wrong with the *Playboy* offer. "She said not a word. She may well have wanted Kathy to do it," notes Rozario. "That would not have been beyond the realm of her thinking, which would have been any way to the road to fame."

After Kathy reluctantly passed on the *Playboy* offer, she made another last-ditch effort for fame and riches: she cut a demo record with dreams of becoming a singing star.

Kay Rozario, who had been around major recording artists for decades because of her husband's position, felt big Kathy had a *good* voice, but little Kathy "had a *magnificent* voice—like Streisand."

Little Kathy took after her mother in the singing department as she did in many other ways. In fact, if it hadn't been for little Kathy's unplanned arrival in the world, big Kathy might have pursued a singing career of her own. As a teenager, with a few underage drinks in her, she had earned a reputation as a barroom chanteuse in the style of her '50s *Your Hit Parade* singing idol, Joni James, who had such hits as "Your Cheatin' Heart," "You're Foolin' Someone," and "Mama, Don't Cry at My Wedding."

"I always felt because little Kathy's sisters Kim and Kyle were famous, and she never got famous, that she felt empty," observes Mickey Catain. "And I always felt she had this, like, *thing*—not 'I'm going to *show* you I can make it,' but, 'I'm going to make *something* of myself.' I remember thinking when I heard her sing on that demo, '*Oh—My—God,* she's going to just soar. She's finally going to make something of herself. She's going to make her star that way.' It wasn't rock 'n' roll. It wasn't tacky. It was, like, mature music, like what Shirley Bassey would sing.

"Big Kathy had a great singing voice, they both had, and that's why when I heard Paris was going to put out an album it didn't surprise me because if she has half the voice her grandma and mom had, she'll be *amazing.*"

When Kathy was entertaining the idea of becoming a professional singer, she and big Kathy had asked the Rozarios for help. "At the time my husband was very hot in television, we knew a lot of people, worked with a lot of stars, and she wanted Bobby [Rozario] to write some arrangements for her," she says. "But my husband and I talked about it and we said, 'Look, this girl wants to get married into a jet-set wealthy lifestyle,' and that was her mother's aim for her, too, so we ended up not doing anything. We didn't think she was that serious about singing, but more serious about marrying someone rich."

The Rozarios were right on the money.

Kathy never pursued a recording contract because suddenly, seemingly out of the blue, she finally snagged that guy from money her mother had taught her to nab.

**RICHARD HOWARD "RICK" HILTON** was a cute guy with "a mop of blond, Shirley Temple curls and a laid-back West Coast manner"—the sixth of Barron and Marilyn Hilton's eight children, and a grandson of the patriarch Conrad Hilton in the genealogical tree of the enormously wealthy and powerful hotel chain dynasty.

For Kathy—and especially her mother—snaring Rick Hilton was like winning the Powerball jackpot. He was to little Kathy in 1978 what young, partying Greek shipping heirs Paris Latsis and Stavros Niarchos III would be to her daughter Paris decades later.

"Little Kathy was dating this one and that one and she was just trying to pick one that would marry her," states Sylvia Richards. "Mama [big Kathy] was pushing real hard—real, *real* hard—for Kathy to marry Ricky."

Mickey Catain agrees. "Oh, yeah," she says, "Ricky was Kathy's *big* coup."

Little Kathy had known Hilton since their high school years, and both ran in that same show business crowd that included Desi Arnaz Jr. and Dean-Paul Martin.

Hilton had essentially grown up on spectacular and exclusive Sorrento Beach, in Santa Monica, where his parents had an enormous home overlooking the Pacific, a house that Barron Hilton had purchased from the silent film star Norma Shearer. Among the Hiltons' famous and infamous neighbors on the beach were Peter Lawford, the druggy, womanizing "Rat Pack" actor, and his internationally known, politically powerful wife, Patricia Kennedy Lawford, one of President Kennedy's sisters.

Rick's childhood pal was the Lawfords' firstborn, Christopher Kennedy Lawford, who remembered the young Hilton as having "hair so blond it was white." He recalled in his memoir that the Kennedy girls "loved" Ricky, but he was "too shy to talk to them." Wrote Lawford, "Ricky and I went everywhere on the beach together. One day we snuck into his parents' bedroom so Ricky and his brother, Davy, could show me the gun their father kept under his pillow. It was a small .22-caliber revolver."

Awed as any boy would be by a real, live gun, young Kennedy asked his chum why his father slept with a loaded firearm. Rick thought the reason was obvious. "In case a robber comes in the middle of the night," he said. "But what if it goes off by accident while he's sleeping?" the Lawford boy wondered. "Doesn't it hurt the side of your dad's head when he puts his head on the pillow?" Rick's response was, "It's a thick pillow."

There had been a long connection between the Lawfords, the Kennedys, and the Hiltons, even though the Hiltons were staunch Republicans. For one, playboy Nick Hilton's best friend, Maxwell House coffee heir and Texas oilman Bob Neal, had served as best man when the Lawfords were married and had also arranged for their honeymoon yacht and cruise.

It was when the Hilton heir was nearing graduation in the class of December 1978 at the University of Denver that he and Kathy Richards started getting hot and heavy, friends say.

In the mid to late '70s, when Rick was matriculating, the university had a reputation as an expensive party school with a major social scene for "stuck-up," out-of-state trust fund babies and Eurotrash—many of them "very urbane Saudi Arabians whose parents bought them cars and clothes and gave them huge allowances for months ahead of time," says a very social member of Rick Hilton's class. "All they did was live in fancy apartments off-campus, drink Chivas, do quaaludes and cocaine, and party. One guy lived in a two-story penthouse filled with sixteen-foot-high plastic palm trees to give the Denver winter a Palm Beach feel. Another, a Brit, had her daddy fly in his private jet so she could take her classmates on day trips to Vail or LA."

At the time, though, the school was billed as "The Harvard of the West" and was one of the ten most expensive institutions of higher learning in America. The sons and daughters of chieftains of corporate America, like Rick Hilton, were well represented: a Royal Crown Cola heiress; the son of the president of AT&T; scions of Coors and Anheuser Busch; and, among many others, one of oil mogul Marvin Davis's daughters, Nancy Sue. Some years later her brother, Gregg, would marry little Kathy's half-sister Kim—Kathy is said to have introduced them. (A Davis grandson, Beverly Hills party dude Brandon Davis, would become a member of Paris Hilton's privileged posse and would accuse her in a supermarket tabloid of making racist and anti-Semitic remarks. But that was far down the road.)

There was a standing joke at DU when Rick was a student there that the only day a professor could give an examination was on Wednesday, because everybody would be off skiing the rest of the week. The perception among certain members of his class was that if parents had the money and could pay the tuition and expenses, a student could stay there forever. "We always laughed and said DU wasn't about academic credentials, it was about paying the tuition," a member of Rick's class notes.

During his college years, Rick may have had dreams of running the Paris Hilton after graduation—he took a French class and cut meat as a hotel and restaurant management school student. And he put to work the skills he was learning by throwing and catering the biggest and poshest parties DU had ever seen, charging each of the revelers a stiff $20 entrance fee. Clearly, the Hilton scion had inherited certain of his father's and grandfather's entrepreneurial skills and talent for making a buck. The bashes were held, naturally, in a ballroom at the family's Denver Hilton.

"Rick threw amazing—*amazing*—parties, really well done with great bands and great food—not potato chips like your typical college parties, and there were *hundreds* of people there," recalls Melanie Gelb, a classmate of Hilton's and a student in his sophomore sociology class. "It was *the* party to be invited to. Everybody knew he was a Hilton and a lot of women were attracted to him. He was cute then, with really longish, curly hair, and an easy, comfortable way about him—mild-mannered, not flashy."

Gelb's invitation to Rick's parties, though, may have been a quid pro quo in exchange for Gelb's hard work in class. "I got to know him because he used to borrow my class notes when he wasn't there," she recalls. "He sat on the far right and I sat on the far left, but the class was small and if you looked around, you knew who was taking notes. He borrowed mine a lot. I don't think he was embarrassed about it. Then, one day, he said to me, 'I'm having a party. Do you want to come?' And that's how I got to go to those great parties he threw."

Gelb remembers that Hilton was dating "a girl with blond hair who would hang on to him like a Christmas ornament, like she was protecting her turf. He didn't seem quite in love as she was. She just seemed more like she was pursuing him." At the time she thought the girl was from another school because she didn't recognize her from the campus. Looking back years later, she was convinced the young woman was Kathy Hilton.

Because of his famous family name, Hilton was well known at DU, and that's why a crazy plot to kidnap him was hatched by some staffers of *The Clarion,* the campus newspaper. Rob Levin, the paper's managing editor at the time, thought, "What a story!" He even could envision the headline: "Hilton Heir Snatched." His partner in the faux crime, he says, was Tom Auer, who later went on to found the *Bloomsbury Review.*

"We decided to kidnap Ricky from the student union as a prank because it was a slow news week, and we were not going to make news kidnapping somebody named Jones," says Levin who, looking back on the bizarre affair years later, thinks he must have gone off his bean. "We arranged to have somebody's Jeep as the getaway car, and the idea was that we would go into the student union and grab Ricky, stuff him in the Jeep, and then call campus security and report that he was kidnapped. We tried to drag him out of the union and into the Jeep, but he pitched up such a fit that we just let him go. I'm not sure Ricky was in a position to even know what was going on, what with various beverages he was drinking."

Years later Levin, who became a feature writer for the *Atlanta Journal-Constitution,* had been assigned to write a freelance piece for a business magazine about the new Hilton hotel that was opening at Hartsfield-Jackson Airport in Atlanta. "I was invited to interview Ricky's father, Barron, and when I got in there he was smoking a cigar and we chat and then I tell him, 'By the way, I kidnapped your son in college. I don't know if he ever told you that.' I told him the story and he thought it was the biggest hoot in the world, and I got out of there without him calling security on me, so I guess it was okay."

Aside from the parties he catered and the girls he dated, Hilton didn't leave much of a mark at DU, other than excelling at volleyball. He was a nonparticipant in extracurricular activities and a no-show at alumni functions. His only mention is in the commencement program as having graduated. "Rick Hilton appears to have floated under the radar," a school official says. However, the Conrad N. Hilton Foundation showered his alma mater in November 2005 with $3 million to create the Barron Hilton Chair of Lodging Management, as part of the university's Hotel, Restaurant, and Tourism School.

Not long after they started dating, little Kathy began bringing Rick Hilton home, viewing him as serious husband potential, and when she told big Kathy that he looked promising, she threw a house party that was like a victory celebration. One afternoon, Sylvia Richards had dropped by the house where she was met with a joyous scene—big and little Kathy and the mobster Jack Catain gloating over the possibility of marrying into the Hilton family. "We were talking and big Kathy said to little Kathy, 'Well, if you get pregnant with Rick before you get married, Jack and I will take the baby.'"

Everyone in their circle thought Kathy and Rick were a perfect match.

"Ricky was adorable, very well mannered, very pleasant, very quiet," says Kay Rozario. "He was always hanging around and they were in love and we were all *thrilled* for her. I said, 'Great, Kathy, now aren't you thrilled you got what you wanted?' I said, 'Aren't you glad you never posed for *Playboy*? Now you can buy *any* car you want.'"

At one point the two lovebirds snuck off to spend quality time together at a Hilton getaway residence. "Little Kathy would report to big Kathy from there every day," recalls Mickey Catain. "It sounded like Kathy and Rick played house, you know, just kind of got into it and they fell in love. It was all just so quick and then they came back from this trip and I remember they were sitting at my parents' kitchen table and they said they were getting married and we were like, *Wow!* Big Kathy was beside herself with joy. She had trained her daughter well."

**BEFORE AN ENGAGEMENT** could be announced, big Kathy had to take care of a major piece of monkey business, and that was to distance herself from Mickey's father, Jack. She rightly feared that her involvement with a gangland figure might be somewhat off-putting to the very image-conscious and extremely low-key Barron Hiltons and throw a wrench into little Kathy's long-dreamed-of nuptials to a Mr. Moneybags.

Around the time Kathy hooked up with Rick, forty-six-year-old Catain was the subject of a wide-ranging probe by federal organized crime prosecutors who had linked him to Mafia families in Chicago, Philadelphia, New York, and Detroit. Authorities viewed him as a clever criminal who hid his illegal activities behind legitimate businesses that included cosmetics, construction, and exotic-car sales.

The feds had started looking into his involvement in such nefarious doings as money-laundering, Super Bowl ticket scalping, counterfeiting, and extortion, and it would take the white hats almost a decade to secure a conviction under which he faced fifteen years in the slammer and $225,000 in fines. Big Kathy used to boast to friends like Jane Hallaren that "if you ever need someone taken care of," her husband had the muscle to handle it.

Mickey Catain clearly remembers big Kathy telling her, "'I can't have them [the Hiltons] finding out what your dad does.' She would laugh and think it was real cute, but she knew the rest of the world wouldn't approve. Kathleen was afraid that my dad, because of all his troubles, was going to give little Kathy a bad name. She was worried about that, about tarnishing little Kathy's image. She said, 'I've got to be careful with Kathy because of who she is marrying.'"

To avoid a scandal, big Kathy distanced herself from Catain, at least until things cooled off and little Kathy was safely married and in the Hilton fold.

According to Mickey Catain's brother, Michael Catain, their father and Paris Hilton's grandmother were married and divorced twice, though only one marriage certificate for the two could be found in California state vital records, leaving open the possibility that they were hitched the first time in another state.

What is on the record is that Catain and big Kathy tied one of the knots on July 4, 1980, taking the vows before a Unity minister in the Los Angeles suburb of Van Nuys. The witnesses were Michael Catain and Kathy's half-sister, the actress Kim Richards. "It was a very small wedding," recalls Catain. "Just a one-day thing at a little church—not *even* a church."

In her sworn marriage certificate, big Kathy listed her occupation as "Theatrical Manager." Big Kathy's marriage to Catain happened eight months after little Kathy married Rick Hilton—a wide enough window of time to separate the new Mrs. Hilton from a mob moll mama and her Mafioso guy, had anyone bothered to check.

"Dad liked big Kathy because she was the female version of himself—aggressive, a go-getter, a hustler, and he loved that," says Michael Catain. "I remember Kathleen telling me that she actually convinced Ricky that Kathy Jr. was a virgin. I just remember Kathleen laughing about that. She was really a female con artist."

One of the people who had been let in on Kathy and Rick's forthcoming nuptials happened to be a paid source of Barbara Sternig, the

*National Enquirer*'s veteran celebrity reporter in Hollywood. The source, Sternig says, was surprisingly another Hilton: Constance Francesca Hilton, Zsa Zsa Gabor's daughter with Conrad Hilton (who later reportedly denied paternity). "Francesca was the source for a number of *Enquirer* stories," states Sternig. "When I first joined the paper in 1975, she was tipping us. I used to talk to Francesca about stories all the time, and when I had something on Zsa Zsa I'd always call her, and she would tell me what I needed."

Sternig knew a bit about how the Hiltons operated. When she was a high school student at the Convent of the Sacred Heart, in Lake Forest, Illinois, Conrad Hilton had donated money to the school to build the Hilton Gymnasium. But the word among the nuns and students was that he had a hidden agenda. "There was a lot of buzz-buzz going around," remembers Sternig, "that he gave this money to prove he was a good Catholic even though he dumped one or two wives and was married to Zsa Zsa Gabor."

A smooth operator who once risked her life to infiltrate Frank Sinatra's inner circle in order to write an exposé about "Old Blue Eyes'" secret world in Las Vegas, Sternig knew a good story when she saw one. When she got the Hilton marriage tip, she remembers thinking, "There were good angles—Kathy's the sister who didn't make it in show business, but she sure made it in the marriage game. And Rick was known as a catch, but Kathy wasn't an heiress."

Because of the supermarket tabloid's notorious reputation, it was often difficult, if not impossible back then, to get people to cooperate on the record. Not so with the future Mrs. Hilton, who leaped at the opportunity to let "enquiring minds" in on her impending nuptials.

Knowing his ever-so-discreet parents would vehemently disapprove of him discussing his private life with a rag that had a reputation for touting space aliens and Elvis's ghost, the then very reserved Rick Hilton declined to participate, recalls Sternig, reluctantly letting his publicity-hungry future bride do the dishing. Moreover, Kathy agreed to meet Sternig for lunch at a restaurant especially chosen by the very savvy and ironic tabloid reporter for the interview: a place called Romeo & Juliet.

It was the first time Sternig had ever met Kathy, who also readily agreed to pose for photos. "Kathy talked all about the Hiltons and how daunting it was for her to be marrying into that dynasty, and I thought, 'She's a cute little nothing—nothing special, coming from a plain family. She was kind of a flibberty-jibberty little blonde—indistinguishable from many, many other little blondes in Hollywood, and that's what sort of struck me as incongruous, and made it interesting to me to see what was in her head, to see why he'd marry her over some other little blonde.

"My take on Rick was that he was enamored of show business and that's why he liked her—that she was an arm-piece who would happily hang out with him and do all the rich guy things that he wanted to do. I thought they were not the brightest lightbulbs in the chandelier, so it was a match made in heaven. I never heard anything about Kathy again until Paris became famous."

Kathy officially married into the Hilton family on November 24, 1979, in the Church of the Good Shepherd in Beverly Hills—"Our Lady of the Cadillacs," as it was known, because of its wealthy parishioners. It was the same Roman Catholic house of worship where Paris's great-uncle Nick—Kathy's new father-in-law's brother—had tied the knot some three decades earlier with Elizabeth Taylor in what the world press called "the marriage of the century." (Seven months of living hell later, their union was dubbed "the divorce of the century.")

Kathy and Rick's marriage took place some eleven months after Rick's grandfather, Conrad Hilton, died at the ripe old age of ninety-one. (Hilton family members say it's doubtful that the former Kathy Avanzino Richards ever met the patriarch.)

On November 27, 1979, the society page of the *Los Angeles Times* had a one-column headline reading:

## HILTON-RICHARDS
## RITE IS SOLEMNIZED

The four-paragraph announcement included a photo of "Miss Kathleen Richards, daughter of Mrs. Kathleen Richards of Bel-Air" wearing a virginal white gown and beaming into the camera of *Times* photographer

George Rose. Standing on her right, Rick Hilton had a pasted-on smile and was wearing a formal striped groom's outfit. The notice stated that the bride was a graduate of California Preparatory School in Encino and that her "attendants" included her sisters, "actresses Kim Richards (*Hello, Larry*) and Kyle Richards (*Little House on the Prairie*)." In a city like LA it is important to list screen credits in marriage announcements and obituaries. The bridegroom, the announcement continued, was a graduate of the University of Denver, and at the time was working as an associate with the Eastdil Realty Corp. in New York City. The bridegroom's father, it said, "is president and chairman of the board of the Hilton Hotel Corp."

Little Kathy's—and certainly big Kathy's—dreams finally were realized. Later, Kathy told her sister Kim, "If I hadn't married Rick, Mom would have taken me down the aisle with a gun in my back."

Not long after the wedding, Jane Hallaren recalled an evening when big Kathy was driving her home after a visit when suddenly she changed direction and headed for little Kathy and Rick's place. Hallaren had never before been there, wasn't that close to little Kathy, and was a bit embarrassed about barging in on them late at night.

"Kathleen takes me on a tour, shows me all their fancy furniture, and they had some beautiful pieces—a bit too much chintz, but their home was quite lovely. Then, she starts taking me up to their bedroom and I said, 'Kathleen, I don't want to go up to their bedroom,' and she says, 'Oh, you have to. They want to see you. They love you,' and I said, 'They don't really know me.' We walk in and Ricky's on the bed watching TV, and Kathy's walking around doing something, and she said, 'Hi, Jane,' and that was it. Kathy's sole reason for taking me there was to show me how well off little Kathy was living now that she was a Hilton."

Marilyn Hilton, a blond, blue-eyed looker herself when she married Rick's father, Barron, didn't think much of Kathy from the start. At the wedding reception she confided to her sister-in-law, Pat Hilton, Eric Hilton's wife, "She chased Rick until she finally got him." Pat Hilton, who knew Kathy slightly at the time, says, "She did not leave a very good impression with me, even before the wedding. I could look at her and see she was *determined* to be a Mrs. Hilton and wanted everybody in the world to know about it."

Another family insider asserts that Marilyn "had suspicions [little] Kathy was a gold digger. Marilyn thought Kathy was too pushy and brassy, and Barron couldn't stand being around that mother of hers. He didn't think she was stable. He used to call her 'The Madam'—as in bawdy house madam."

Barron Hilton banned big Kathy from visiting his home when he was there, according to Jane Hallaren. "She was only allowed there when he was not in residence. [Big] Kathy was always dying to get accepted by Barron, and there was *never* going to be any shot at that."

Kay Rozario, who knew about Barron Hilton's view of big Kathy— the Rozarios' daughter, Leanne, dated one of Barron's other sons, Ron— says that over the years Kathleen had become a heavy drinker, which Barron Hilton could not abide, probably because his own mother, Conrad Hilton's first wife, Mary Barron Hilton, had become an alcoholic.

"Barron couldn't stand big Kathy's drinking," Rozario asserts. "She got drunk and noisy and sloppy. You could call her a drunk. You could call her a lot of noise. You could call her all kinds of things—but not a madam," she says in her defense.

According to a longtime Hilton business associate, Rick secured his first after-college job, at Eastdil, through the auspices of his father, who was friends with Ben Lambert, who ran the real estate company and was on the Hilton Corporation board of directors. It is said that Rick spent part of his very first real estate commission on a new Rolls-Royce that Kathy wanted.

At the time of their marriage, the newlyweds lived in Rick's expensive rental in the nineteen-story white brick apartment tower at 420 East Seventy-second Street, in Manhattan's Lenox Hill neighborhood.

Some fifteen months after the wedding, on February 17, 1981, Kathy gave birth to the first of four children. They named her Paris Whitney. She was christened at St. Patrick's Cathedral on Fifth Avenue. Paris's first home was in a sumptuous penthouse at 220 East Sixty-seventh Street.

Friends and family members say she had all of the facial characteristics, especially the mouth and eyes, of her biological maternal grandfather, Larry Avanzino. "If you put a wig on Larry, you'd have Paris," notes

Jane Hallaren. "The only thing that Paris has that isn't Larry is her nose. That's Kathleen's nose."

**FROM DAY ONE,** Kathy—*and* her mother—had big dreams for Rick. Kathy saw him becoming the next Mr. Hilton, succeeding his father and grandfather as the Hilton organization's boss of bosses.

"Kathy's what we used to call the 'balabusta' of the family," says Mickey Catain, referring to the Yiddish term describing a pushy wife. "From the start she's the one that ruled the roost. Rick kind of just stayed in the background, never said much. Big Kathy would tell me that Rick wasn't focused on anything and that Kathy helped him focus. He could have cared less about high society and the social life, because he grew up with it his whole life. But [little] Kathy didn't and desperately wanted it. Rick's kind of come into his own and he's done real well for himself [in real estate]. But back then she pushed him into *everything*."

Like big Kathy with her husbands, little Kathy always would be the dominant partner in her "very long and successful marriage" to Rick Hilton, who amiably and affectionately refers to his loving spouse as "Mommy."

"Little Kathy's *big* dream was that she would be the next *the* Mrs. Hilton," states Sylvia Richards. "She wanted Rick to be the top dog and she would replace her mother-in-law, Marilyn Hilton, as the number one Mrs. Hilton."

Kathy and her mother, however, weren't aware that Barron didn't favor his children in that way. At his 500,000-acre Flying M Ranch, in Nevada, Barron kept a joke plaque by the fireplace that read: "*Money isn't everything, but it does tend to keep the children in touch.*"

It was well known within the upper echelon of the Hilton Hotel organization that little Kathy wanted to become "the reigning princess," says Tim Applegate, who served under Barron and Conrad Hilton as executive vice president and chief counsel through the 1970s and early 1980s.

On one occasion Applegate flew on the company plane from Los Angeles to New York with the two Kathys and other family members shortly after the engagement to Rick, and he recalls how they aggressively tried to impress him because they knew he had Barron's ear.

"I ended up in a limousine with the mother and Kathy on our way to the Waldorf, and the mother, in particular, was putting on airs about how wonderful her daughter was, how important she was, how big and successful she was, how Kathy was going to see that Rick became a big success. She was a real social climber. It was all supershallow, and I remember thinking, 'Kathy seems kind of like an airhead, and my God, I hope I don't have to do this again.'"

Applegate, who attended Rick and Kathy's wedding, recalls how "upset" Rick had made his father when the Hilton organization bought a new headquarters building in Los Angeles and his son wanted to benefit with a real estate sales commission for doing nothing. "Apparently Rick tried to get himself listed as one of the brokers on the deal—*after* the fact," asserts Applegate. "Barron was never very tolerant of such things. It was kind of like, 'Get out of here. We don't do things like that.' Barron thought it was improper. He always thought his kids were best off making their own way in the world.

"Conrad had given money to each grandchild (Rick among them) when they were born, so they all had enough money to get started in life. And Barron always believed, 'I'm not doing these kids any favors by throwing money at them.'

"When Rick was going to the hotel school at the University of Denver, he bought a BMW2002, not an expensive car. Barron called me up to his office and we had a conversation on the phone with Rick and we worked out a loan. After the call Barron repeated, as he did many times to me, 'I could give him the car, but I think it would be a disservice to him.'"

**FOR KATHY**, life as a Hilton wife was not an immediate bowl of cherries. She was instantly disliked by a number of Hiltons, especially the Hilton women, and the wives of top Hilton executives, who felt she was too pushy. Bibi Hilton, Eric's second wife, remembers Kathy declaring, "Once Marilyn [her mother-in-law] is dead, I'm going to be the queen, and I'll remember who in the family has been mean to me on the way up." (Years later, when early publicity about this book began appearing in the world press, the *New York Post* quoted Kathy Hilton as saying, "If

anyone participates in the book they will be banned from the family."
The *Post* said she had "even threatened people, telling them, 'I can make
your life very difficult [if you help Oppenheimer]. I am a very powerful
woman.'")

Kathy was shocked and angry when she realized that her father-in-
law, Barron, didn't give her husband special treatment. For instance,
Rick Hilton had the idea in the 1980s of going into the hotel business for
himself by developing a chic boutique hotel in trendy downtown Manhattan. But the deal with his backers was said to have been predicated on
having the Hilton name somewhere on the marquee, even if the hotel
was called "The Rick Hilton," because the Hilton name generated big
business.

Rick approached his father about the deal, bearing a special gift—
a bunch of his favorite cigars, Cuban Monte Cristos. Barron took the
cigars, but Rick didn't get what he had come for.

"Barron made it clear that there was no way in hell that he was
going to give Rick permission to use the Hilton name," maintains Neal
Schwartz, whose family ran the Hilton valet service in New York and had
a close working relationship with Barron. "Rick did want to be the next
Mr. Hilton, and I'm sure Kathy was stoking the flames. But I think Rick
finally came to realize that it was never going to be."

When Rick and Kathy and their brood moved into their huge suite
on the thirtieth floor of the Waldorf Towers, they threw the Hilton name
around in order to get an extremely favorable rate far below market
value, hotel insiders maintain. They were paying about $30,000 a year
for the apartment that would normally rent for seven figures annually.
"As far as I know, Barron was under the impression that they were paying market value. He was furious because he didn't want any of his kids
getting a break, and living off his name," contends Schwartz. "But Rick
got the deal because the manager was led to believe Rick would be the
next Mr. Hilton, and would want to be on his good side."

Kathy networked with the wives of Hilton executives, letting it be
known that she expected Rick to one day replace his father. "She was
very superficial—just interested in getting known as a Hilton, to be a

somebody—and was delighted that she married someone who had a foot in the door with money," says the widow of a top Hilton executive. "She was not to the manor born by any means. I'd see her at parties and she'd tell me about her shopping experiences in New York. This was just after they moved into the Waldorf. She said she had started shopping at a store called *Mar-Shalls.* She said, 'Well, I go to *Mar-Shalls.* It's wonderful.' And then it struck me. She wasn't talking about a fancy shop on Madison Avenue, but rather Marshalls, the discount store. Kathy just gave it a fancy name. I don't think Kathy would be caught dead today walking into Marshalls. That would be so below her. She kept telling me how she was Rick's wife, which, believe me, meant nothing. She got high and mighty and thought she was somebody because she has the Hilton name."

There were times when Barron was in New York on business and staying at the Waldorf, but in order to get in to see his father, even though they were in the same building, Rick had to actually make an appointment through his dad's secretary. Recalls a Waldorf insider, "Rick would call up to see what kind of mood his father was in before he'd try to get in to see him. His visits were always short."

Kathy was furious at the way her father-in-law treated Rick, which was generally the way he acted toward all of his children—none got special treatment. (In mid-2006, family superstar Paris Hilton was even refused a discount at the Glasgow Hilton and reportedly had to pay the full rate for a standard queen-size room.) It wasn't as if Rick had been singled out by his father, but that's not the way Kathy saw it.

"She had screaming matches with Barron," asserts Bibi Hilton. "She said, 'You are a bad father, a bad grandfather.' Oh, she was so mean to him. She treated him badly. At the Waldorf, she'd scream down the hall at him where other people could hear it. She's a mean woman. Kathy wants too much, and she's angry because Barron didn't give Rick the power."

Despite Kathy's ambitions for Rick, he never rose to the top of the Hilton organization. When asked by associates why his son wasn't involved in the Hilton family business, Barron Hilton's response is said to have been, "If he can't control his wife, how can he run my hotels?"

# CHAPTER 5

The story of Paris Hilton's colorful maternal roots begins in America's heartland, Nebraska, then shifts east to the tony town of Manhasset, on Long Island's "Gold Coast."

Paris's maternal great-grandfather, "Big Ed" Dugan, was an attorney in Omaha and during the Great Depression sought and won election to the Nebraska state legislature, where he later served as chairman of the judiciary committee, and sometimes sat in as Speaker of the House.

A gregarious politico and a shrewd lawyer, Dugan was a polished glad-hander who sported colorful suspenders. He was an avid golfer, a lusty drinker, a big, barrel-chested Irishman with a red face and a full head of sandy hair that turned white but never fell out. He had the deep voice and the enunciation of a screen actor. Everything about him was *bigger* than life. "He always looked like he was running against Huey Long," says a longtime family friend. "He had the body of Fredric March playing Williams Jennings Bryan and the big—*big*—head of Spencer Tracy playing Clarence Darrow in *Inherit the Wind.*"

Everyone adored his attractive, bright, and winsome wife, Dorothy

Callahan Dugan, nicknamed "Dodo," a fast-moving, quick-witted, petite woman—birdlike compared with her husband. "She dressed sharp, always had on a great hat, her shoes looked fabulous. She was chic," observes the family friend. Paris's maternal great-grandmother was a staunch Irish Catholic who went to every conceivable Roman Catholic mass and gave her husband four children: two sons, the kind of vanilla Ed Jr., the firstborn, and the mischievous blue-eyed Chuck, the youngest of her brood; and two daughters, the appropriately named, pretty and prim Madonna, the older of the girls by three years; and, of course, the family's flamboyant star, Kathleen.

Always vain, big Kathy lied about her age beginning in childhood, cutting off just one year, contending to lifelong friends that she was born on April 17, 1939, instead of her actual birth date of April 17, 1938. (Years later, in 2006, Kathy Hilton was shaving years off, too. She was heard to claim she was forty-four when she was really going on forty-eight.)

By the time big Kathy came into the world, her father had become a power broker as chairman of the Douglas County Democratic Committee, which encompassed Omaha, Nebraska's largest city, then known for a haunted former bordello and a famous insurance company, Mutual of Omaha.

When Dugan was up for reelection in the August 1938 primary, the *Lincoln State Journal* reported, "A number of fellow Democrats are out to get his scalp. . . ." A scandal of sorts ensued when cronies of one of Dugan's opponents charged that "steamroller" tactics had been used to secure his victory. He later expressed his "regret" that ballots had been handled in a highly questionable manner. Politically liberal, at least for the Cornhusker State, he once called for "a more progressive, wide-awake city government."

Several years after the Second World War ended, when Kathleen was ten, the Dugans moved east, settling in Manhasset, where Big Ed established a law practice, and he and Dodo were partners in their newly opened real estate agency. Their specialty was buying fixer-uppers, renovating then flipping them for tidy profits. The Dugans chose Manhasset because that's where the affluent Irish Catholics from the New York City boroughs headed when they had money, while nearby Great Neck had become the Promised Land for upwardly mobile Jews fleeing the Bronx and Brooklyn for the suburban good life.

A Manhattan bedroom community, Manhasset is among the fictional backdrops for F. Scott Fitzgerald's *The Great Gatsby,* a novel of decadence and excess. By coincidence, the protagonist, Jay Gatsby, had some of the same twisted values that possessed hotelier Conrad Hilton *and* career stage-mother Kathleen Dugan Avanzino Richards Catain Fenton throughout their lives.

The Dugans were drinkers and party people, so Manhasset was a perfect setting. Bars lined one of the main drags, Plandome Road, a half-mile stretch in a town that consisted of only four square miles. The place even had a drink named after it—"The Manhasset," which one wag described as a Manhattan with more alcohol. As Jane Hallaren, big Kathy's closest friend from childhood, observes, "There wasn't a parent in town that I can remember who wasn't an alcoholic. Parents were saying terrible things about each other. They had nasty, vituperative relationships. There was animosity and cleverness. It was *very* Irish."

The Dugans fit right in.

Dodo Dugan enrolled skinny, cute, precocious Kathleen, with her mop of spectacularly thick, frizzy-curly dark auburn hair, and her teasing green eyes, into classes at the newly opened grammar school at St. Mary's Roman Catholic Church on Northern Boulevard.

Always in control, always in everyone's face, the Dugan girl quickly became the leader of an A-list clique at St. Mary's—a small group of snarky, sanitized grade-school "Heathers" who sported a uniform of blue jackets and skirts, white blouses, and blue-and-white saddle shoes.

When little Janie Hallaren, whose parents had moved to Manhasset from the mean streets of Brooklyn, showed up for her first day of school in the fourth grade, Dugan made it clear to her who ran the show.

"I'll never forget our first meeting," says Hallaren years later. "The nun tells me to go down the aisle. Kathy was sitting in the first seat in the aisle and had organized some girls behind her and they fluffed their hair and eyed me as I walked passed them. Kathy turned around and looked at me like, 'You're not going to make it here,' and the four girls in succession behind her did the same thing. I was a very tough kid, so I waited for her outside after school and I said, 'You'll never do *that* again,' and I beat the shit out of her. That was that."

A few days later, Kathy, impressed with and respectful of Hallaren's toughness, invited her into her gang.

On one occasion, the two new bosom buddies met at the Dugan house, and another neighborhood girl showed up. All three went down into the basement and were listening and dancing to Kathleen's record collection.

"All of a sudden Kathy whispers to me, '*Look, Janie . . . look, Janie . . . Look . . .*' And she's pointing at the other girl's beautiful curly brunette hair. And I look and Kathy had *spit* all over this girl's hair. I could see *gobs* of spit. And Kathy was *giggling.* Still, today, I think of that scene and I get the willies. I went upstairs and said to Dodo, 'I have to go home now,' and I called my mother and told her to meet me at the top of the hill. 'I'm not staying here.'"

The curious incident foreshadowed acts even more bizarre and violent that Kathleen would commit later in life—even against loved ones. If there ever was a real-life Rhoda Penmark—the evil child in *The Bad Seed*—in the making, it was Kathleen Dugan.

Because she was not much of a student academically and had behavior issues, the future maternal grandmother of Paris Hilton bounced from one school to another. From St. Mary's the Dugans, who had a reputation as liberal parents—maybe too liberal—shipped her off to a Catholic girls' boarding school, the Academy of Saint Joseph, in Brentwood, a town on Long Island further east from Manhasset. But she couldn't abide by the rules or handle the rigid academic standards, so the next stop was Marymount, in Tarrytown, New York, where her sister, Madonna—called Donna—was also a student, though three years ahead. At Marymount, Kathleen's singing and acting talent came to the fore, and she began thinking of herself as a future star. She took speech lessons and joined the drama club.

"She loved the movies and she sang beautifully and she *loved* to doll up," says her sister. "We were both in *The Mikado.* Kathleen had a *very* nice voice and evidently mine wasn't that bad, but it wasn't as good as hers."

Aside from her love of acting onstage, and acting out in public, Kathleen Dugan despised Marymount. She missed being home and having unlimited freedom to do as she pleased. As her sister notes, "Kathleen was very unhappy being away. She wasn't used to being dictated to."

Back home she enrolled at Manhasset High School, an archetypal suburban 1950s teen scene where she was reunited with Jane Hallaren, who had just come into the school herself after being expelled from St. Mary's for participating in a beer party, an expulsion she claims was unfair. Kathleen was inducted into a tight-knit clique of Hallaren's friends—Christina Demaitre, and preppy Martha Hanahan. "Janie introduced me to Kathy, who was a *total* lunatic," says Demaitre, who was a cheerleader. "Kathy was different from everybody else."

In an era when girls wore circle pins, Peter Pan collars, crinolines, bobby sox, and penny loafers, Kathleen Dugan was a dyed-in-the-wool fashionista, just like her granddaughter Paris would be. She wore cat's-eye sunglasses and lucite and rhinestone Springolators with four-inch heels, the kind Marilyn Monroe wiggled on. Kathleen had even introduced boudoir wear into her style.

"She goes out one day and buys this pink brocade bathrobe that's zipped up the front and she bought a red waist cinch as a belt," recalls Hallaren. "It was something you would wear for lounging. But she wore it out. She said, 'Nobody will know. It looks like a gorgeous gown—and I'm wearing it!' Everything she did was ballsy."

Demaitre's European-educated, intellectual mother pegged Kathleen as a study in shallowness and narcissism. "Kathy thought she was so glamorous. She was very outrageous, self-involved, interested only in what *she* was doing," Demaitre says, still aghast years later.

Kathleen was invited to join Alpha Theta Alpha, the "Animal House" of sororities at Manhasset High, and most of the group's soirees were thrown at the Dugans' because no other rational-thinking Manhasset parent would have permitted a hundred or so beer-guzzling, scotch-swigging, hormone-seething teenagers to take over their gracious homes for an evening. "I'm sure many of us had too much to drink and were a complete danger to ourselves and the rest of the world as we drove away," notes Hanahan.

"Her parents were remarkable," says Demaitre, still dumbfounded at their permissiveness years later. "The whole house would be *full* of people, and they'd just go quietly up the stairs and go to bed. It was like Kathy was running the house."

Now that she was in a public high school, Kathleen was surrounded by good-looking, strapping fellows from fine Manhasset homes. She felt as if she had died and gone to heaven, although anything to do with sex was verboten. Despite her outrageous demeanor and provocative style of dress, friends like Hanahan and Hallaren contend that Kathy was strictly a tease with boys and extremely inhibited about sex. However, one young man had caught her fancy, and she would pursue Bob Conkey relentlessly, albeit unsuccessfully, into adulthood, even while both were in marriages, even to the point where he began to think she was stalking him, even causing his wife, who was CBS anchorman Walter Cronkite's secretary, to suspect hanky-panky.

# CHAPTER 6

**O**n a crisp, sunny fall afternoon the fire alarm sounded in the hallowed halls of Manhasset High School. The students and faculty were immediately evacuated and classes were canceled for the remainder of the day.

Within fifteen minutes, a beaming, gloating Kathleen appeared at the school's local hangout, overjoyed that classes were called off and hoping to spend the rest of the day with Bob Conkey.

"Kathy did it. They got her for it. I think they suspended her for a week," states Conkey, who, looking back years later, believes her motivation was to "make something, *anything* happen, to do something wacky, to get *attention*. She was a pistol."

And Conkey wasn't surprised by Kathleen's antics at school that day. He had experienced other such acts by her. "She'd call me in the middle of the night and wake up the whole family," he says.

Still, he found her fascinating. She was brassy, had an acid tongue, fired off the fastest and meanest put-downs, traits they shared in common. "Kathy was quick-witted, very flamboyant," observes a high school pal, Les Sutorius.

Moreover, Conkey found Kathleen a turn-on in her glam outfits. "'Cheap' is not the word, but she was a drama queen," he says.

Kathy was head over heels in love with Bob, but he didn't feel quite the same about her when she began chasing him when she was a sophomore and he was a senior.

The son of a corporate vice president, Conkey's favorite hangout was a bar called the Gay Dome—"gay" meaning "happy-hour gay" in those days, a place that served fifteen-cent beers to underage kids. He and his buddies would gather there after school, downing brews, talking cars and chicks. The front door had a round porthole-like window through which Conkey could see Kathleen anxiously staking him out in her idling, cool-looking Chevrolet convertible, one of two new Chevys her father had bought for the family. If he didn't take notice of her, one of his bar buddies would warn, "Uh-oh, Kathy's outside again."

Says Conkey, "She'd *always* be there. She'd wait until I finished drinking. Literally, when I walked out of that bar, she would be waiting. I didn't even have a date with her. Even though I had my car with me—I was hot shit with a '49 Ford convertible—I'd ride home with her. We'd make out for a while and that was it."

On those drives Kathleen Dugan fantasized about their future together. "Someday," he remembers her rhapsodizing, "we will meet again when you're a wealthy lawyer." He, however, had no such plans. In reality, his biggest concern was whether he could even get into college, let alone a law school.

Behind Kathleen's back Conkey and his pals joked about how she followed him everywhere like a hungry puppy. Kathleen's gal pals also got a kick out of her obsessive behavior. "When she couldn't find Conkey at the Gay Dome," recalls Hallaren, "Kathleen and I would drive all over town desperately looking for him, and if we found him, he wouldn't give her the time of day. She *always* made a fool out of herself—so she was a joke in those days when it came to him. She eventually had four husbands. She was *always* unhappy in love."

Kathleen's crowd also couldn't resist doing riffs on her nickname. From the time she was a child, the Dugans had called her "Pussycat," but that was shortened immediately to "Pussy"—Pussy Dugan—when Conkey and his chums got wind of it. They teased her incessantly.

Their dates, when he deigned to take her out, were at the Westbury Drive-In, and although she had Conkey in her clutches for the evening, Kathleen appeared more mesmerized by the movie. At home her only reading matter was movie magazines that featured gushy stories about Elizabeth Taylor, Natalie Wood, and teen heartthrobs like Troy Donahue. Little did she know back then that one day she would be linked to the Hilton family, whose members had intimate relationships with such stars. Otherwise, the Dugan house was devoid of any form of serious reading material, except for Dodo's Holy Bible.

After the movies and fumbling in the backseat, Conkey took Kathleen to the Gay Dome for a beer nightcap, and she would launch into impromptu renditions of her two favorite songs, "Summertime" and "Danny Boy."

After Conkey graduated from Manhasset High and was sent for a year to a prep school, which his father hoped would get him into a decent college, Kathleen's pursuit continued unabated, as it would on and off for many years to come. "She wrote me, literally, every day when I was at school," he says. "She'd write about what she did that day. She'd write about how much she missed me. She'd write about how she was looking forward to Christmas break when she would see me again."

With Conkey away, Kathleen and her posse had started going into Manhattan for fun weekends, cruising Greenwich Village and Times Square, flirting with guys, and going to bars. "I would want to go to poetry readings in the Village," recalls Hallaren, "but Kathy wanted to buy water pistols to shoot people."

Somewhere along the way Kathleen had met a young fellow who worked as a clerk, by coincidence, at a Hilton hotel, the Statler Hilton, the sapphire in a hotel group that Conrad Hilton had scooped up in 1954 for a record $111 million, then the largest real estate transaction in history. Kathleen had teased and flirted with the Hilton employee, leading him to believe there might be some action in his future, so he invited her to be his guest, which turned out to be a reverse con job.

"It was one weird, strange situation," notes Demaitre. "The guy said they were renovating a whole floor and we could stay for free. We went to the hotel and it was a beautiful room."

It was still early so Kathleen, the clothes horse, got all dolled up, and she and Demaitre hit Times Square. "We thought we'd pick up some guys," she says. They quickly met two cute fellows, one of whom was a Frenchman—and luckily Demaitre spoke French fluently.

"They were thrilled and must have thought, 'Maybe we can sleep with them,'" she says. "Of course, we were certainly *not* putting out, and they were completely freaked and stunned. Kathleen was so covered in rhinestones, it was hard to get to her, anyway; her outfits were so sort of forbidding, and she wore a girdle. She was absolutely determined nothing was going to happen."

Back at the hotel, the girls went up to the room that had been comped by Kathleen's acquaintance. Behaving like first-class guests who had won a weekend for two, they ordered wagons of tasty treats from room service.

"The next morning," says Demaitre, "the hotel caught us. They didn't know we were there, and they called our parents."

The Dugans were "remarkable" in their reaction, she says. Kathleen wasn't punished and was allowed to continue her madcap ways.

**KATHLEEN DUGAN'S HIGH SCHOOL** career skidded to a screeching stop near the end of her junior year when she was a not-so-sweet sixteen. She was furious that her parents had left her at home and gone off to Nebraska to visit a relative. Preferring to be on a school week jaunt rather than attending classes, she decided to show her parents just how angry she was.

"She called me and she said, 'You gotta come over. You can't believe what I'm doing!'" says Hallaren, whose jaw dropped when she arrived minutes later and entered the Dugan house. "Kathy had painted practically the whole house gold gilt—the toilet seat, the switch plates, the frames around the paintings, some of the walls, and she even painted her own portrait with gold gilt. I saw her doing it, and I said, 'Your parents are going to *kill* you.' And she said, 'If they're mad, they deserve it.'"

When they arrived home, Dodo Dugan hid any dismay she might

have had about her daughter's demon decorating. "She said, 'Kathleen, this is very pretty, this is very artistic, this is beautiful. You did a great job,'" recalls Hallaren.

Kathleen then quit school. "She simply just stopped going," says Hallaren. "The parents didn't make her go back. Kathleen was a *very* powerful girl."

Instead of working toward a diploma, Kathleen just hung out, cruising town in her convertible, having fun. Curiously, she continued going to Manhasset High School social functions as if she were still enrolled. Some classmates who weren't in her tight inner circle didn't realize she had quit and thought she was still a student.

Meanwhile, her girlfriends, who stayed close with her through the years, graduated in June 1957 and went off to colleges that fall before securing glamorous jobs. Hallaren became a top model's agent, working for the likes of Eileen Ford, then went into acting, winning her first audition on Broadway as Clara in *The Prime of Miss Jean Brodie.* Martha Hanahan also was in the fashion business for a time, as an art coordinator at *Mademoiselle,* and later raised horses. Christina Demaitre quit in the middle of her senior year at the University of Maryland to take a job as a reporter in the women's section of the *Washington Post* and later became a lawyer.

Kathleen still had her eye on show business, fantasizing about becoming an actress, or a singer like Joni James. She even considered testing her considerable talent as a vocalist against others on Ted Mack's *Original Amateur Hour,* the *American Idol* of the time, but she couldn't get past the fear factor of appearing on live television.

Instead, she went to acting school. Despite her lack of a formal high school diploma or an equivalency, Kathleen auditioned and was accepted in the fall of 1957 into the two-year program at the American Academy of Dramatic Arts in New York. One of her classmates, Robert Redford, graduated in what would have been Kathleen's class of '59. She, however, spent only one or two semesters before dropping out, because she'd fallen in love with a guy other girls considered an Adonis.

# CHAPTER 7

athleen had met Laurence K. Avanzino, two years older and a student and football player at C. W. Post, the recently opened campus of Long Island University, one glorious Sunday in October 1957, while he, his brother, Ken, and some friends were tossing the pigskin around on the front lawn of the Avanzinos' home in Manhasset's exclusive Plandome section. Always flirtatious, Kathy cruised by a few times with some girlfriends in her convertible before stopping and striking up a conversation with the blond-haired, handsome, well-built Avanzino, who, according to his sister, Adele, was "a cross between Steve McQueen with a little bit of Paul Newman's eyes." "Larry was *gorgeous*," notes Jane Hallaren, "and a *total* maniac."

The Avanzinos weren't strangers to Kathleen when she stopped by that fateful day. While she hadn't met Larry before, she knew Ken, whom she had set up with Martha Hanahan during one of his class breaks from Colgate University; he gave her his school pin and they went steady for a time. Kathleen also introduced another friend, Linda Eden, a younger sorority sister in Alpha Theta Alpha, to one of Larry and Ken Avanzino's close pals, John McKusker; the two later got married. Even back then big

Kathy was a matchmaker extraordinaire. And McKusker and Eden would play a key role in the Dugan-Avanzino romance.

Growing up together and attending high school in the Long Island town of Roslyn, the Avanzino boys and McKusker were known as "The Three Aces"—teenagers into fast cars, cute girls, and beer. Of the three, McKusker and Ken Avanzino would go on to become successful businessmen, while Larry would have a difficult and ultimately tragic life.

Of the two brothers, Ken, younger by a year, would have been the real catch for an ambitious, aggressive girl like Kathleen. Modest, amiable, very bright, and highly educated, he graduated from Colgate, went on to Columbia University, and later became extremely well-off. But Kathy could not have predicted back then that she had chosen a loser, albeit a handsome one. When she became serious about Larry—"It was pretty much love at first sight," observes Adele Avanzino—he was considered the family's "golden boy," according to Martha Hanahan. "The sun rose and set on him in the Avanzino house. He was very spoiled."

There were signs of trouble, however, such as his drinking, which started early and escalated through his life. Because he had "disciplinary problems" at Roslyn High School during his senior year, the future maternal grandfather of Paris Hilton was sent by his parents, Elizabeth, a housewife, and Laurence, a high-level executive at major corporations like Eberhard Faber and Olivetti, to live with an aunt in Boston where he was enrolled at Matignon, a strict and academically demanding independent Catholic high school. There, he became best friends with a classmate, Brian O'Riordan, who describes him affectionately as a "wild man" and a "con man."

"Larry was a big, handsome kid, and the nuns loved him," O'Riordan says. "But what a con artist he was! He was about as religious as the rest of us, which is to say he wasn't. But the nuns thought he was Saint Larry. He'd smile and lie to them—'Yes, Sister . . . No, Sister'—and I used to think, 'You *phony*!' A nun would say to him, 'Oh, you're living with your aunt?' And with a straight face he'd say, 'Oh, yes, Sister, we had some family problems and I thought it was better to come here,' and I'd think, 'You *liar*.' The aunt his parents sent him to was supposed to be tough, but he had her wrapped around his little finger within three hours of his arrival.

"Larry one time went to confession and the priest was known to be nutty as a fruitcake, so Larry started telling these things he did—like rape and murder. The priest pulled him out of the goddamn confessional and was yelling at him and Larry looks at me and says, 'I don't think he gave me absolution.'"

Though he was bright, he didn't study and never cracked a book. As Ken Avanzino observes years later, "My brother could get A's, or incompletes if he didn't like a course. The teachers loved him, or hated him. That's the way he was."

At Boston College, which he attended for about a year, Avanzino's dangerous and reckless side surfaced. In one incident, he is said to have crashed a boat into a bridge abutment and suffered injuries. Behind the wheel of his Ford coupe he was a speeding time bomb.

"The way he drove his car, it's amazing I'm still alive," O'Riordan says. "I bounced off the dashboard any number of times when he slammed on the brakes. There were a couple of guys from MIT who were giving Larry a hard time, and they stopped their car at a red light and Larry plowed his coupe into them and pushed them through the light. I said, 'Larry, for Christ sake, you're gonna get someone killed.' But those guys didn't do anything. They were afraid of him."

A snappy dresser who always carried a wad of spending cash, Avanzino was, and always would be, a ladies' man. But the girls he pursued back then had to come from money. In college, he fell in love with a very religious, beautiful, bright blonde from a wealthy family—her father owned a big trucking company—whom he met while cruising the campus at Regis College, a prestigious Catholic girls' school in the Boston suburbs.

"Larry *loved* rich girls. That's all he ever dated," says O'Riordan. "He was so blunt with them—'What does your father do? Does your dad make a lot of money?' Only Larry could get away with something like that."

The new girl in his life in the fall of 1957 was Kathleen Dugan, and the two seemed to have much in common: their wildness, their skewed values, their nonconformity. They were, and would be, a highly combustible mix.

Two tragedies of varying extremes brought Larry and Kathleen together in holy matrimony. The first was that he got her pregnant in the spring of 1958, some eight months after they had started going together.

"It was Kathleen's first time out [sexually], she was a total virgin, and she goes and gets knocked up in the backseat of her car," says Jane Hallaren, in whom Kathleen had confided. "It was the first time sex came into their relationship. She was horrified—*horrified*! She said, 'Janie, I'll have to kill myself! What am I going to do?' I said, 'Well, do you love him?' She was hysterical and said, 'I don't know . . . I don't know.' She knew something was not right with him, that there was something strange about the guy."

Or at least that's the way she made it seem to her bosom buddy.

Hallaren's dark view of Larry was that he "wasn't somebody you could even talk to, let alone think of starting a relationship with, especially when you were someone like Kathy who wanted to conquer the world."

But Kathy, others say, was madly in love with Larry, or thought she was, and one way to trap the elusive Adonis into marriage was to put aside her inhibitions and get pregnant. As Martha Hanahan suggests, "It might have been the first and only time Kathy and Larry had sex."

The second tragedy, which would be linked in a curious way to the first, happened on June 2, 1958. Larry's brother, Ken, was coming home to Manhasset from Colgate for the summer when the car in which he was riding, driven by a classmate and close friend, crashed not far from the university in the upstate New York town of Hamilton. The friend was killed, and Avanzino suffered a broken back that would keep him in a local hospital for three months.

Kathleen had gotten pregnant around the time of the accident. With Ken in the hospital, she and Larry decided to visit him, accompanied by their friends, John McKusker and Linda Eden, neither of whom had any inkling that she was probably with child and that the future father was about to make Kathleen an honest woman because of it.

Kathleen's Catholicism ruled out abortion. Moreover, abortion was considered dangerous back then. Horror stories abounded in the late '50s about abortion mills run by sleazy men and women using coat hangers as their operating tools.

While Larry could just as well have walked away from his pregnant girlfriend, Kathleen was adamant and demanded marriage. "She was madly in love with Larry," Martha Hanahan points out. "But I never got the feeling Larry was committed to marriage as she was."

Years later Ken Avanzino saw it another way. "Kathleen must have been a lot more intelligent than I gave her credit for in her younger years because she was a master at getting what she wanted—and she wanted to marry my brother."

As they were nearing the hospital near Cobleskill, New York, where Ken Avanzino lay bedridden, Larry Avanzino spotted a church and asked McKusker to stop. It was then that he and Kathleen announced that they were getting married. A minister who had been with the Congregational Church of Manhasset performed the brief ceremony, suggesting that the shotgun marriage had been prearranged without McKusker's and Eden's knowledge.

The next to know about the hasty nuptials was Ken. "They showed up at the hospital and they say, 'Guess what, we just got married,'" he recalls. "I was surprised, naturally, but Kathy and Larry were the type of people who would surprise you with whatever they did. My reaction? 'Let's have a beer!'"

Back in Manhasset both sets of parents went ballistic. The Avanzinos wanted Larry to stay in school and get a degree. "They didn't like Kathy," asserts Hallaren. "They were *very* much against Larry marrying her. They were unhappy and they kept her at arm's length."

The Dugans *and* the Avanzinos agreed that the newlyweds were far too young, irresponsible, and immature to be man and wife. With their parents' reactions so negative, Kathleen, twenty, and Larry, twenty-two, withheld the really big shocker—the impending arrival of the stork—for as long as they could before her bump showed.

"Kathy's mother was very religious and she wanted a big Catholic church wedding," says Adele Avanzino. "I don't know if Dodo knew her daughter was pregnant, but she knew her daughter eloped and she wasn't happy about that."

Plans were immediately put in motion for a second ceremony before a Catholic priest at St. Mary's, the Dugans' church, where Kathleen had once gone to school. The church nuptial was held on August 16, 1958. It was a big affair with dozens of family members and friends in attendance, followed by a reception under a tent in the Dugans' backyard. "Her parents, as I would have expected, put a good face on it," recalls Martha Hanahan, a member of the wedding party. "It was summer and the satin gowns we wore were lovely," says Jane Hallaren. "We all knew Kathy was pregnant. It just was unspoken."

Kathleen and the father-to-be moved into the Avanzino home temporarily, lying low to avoid the gossip until the baby arrived. Later, Dodo Dugan told a confidante, "I tried to talk her out of it, but Kathleen made up her mind she had to have Larry. Everything she saw that she wanted she had to have."

On March 13, 1959, almost seven months after the church wedding, Kathleen Dugan Avanzino, a month away from turning twenty-one, gave birth to a healthy and beautiful baby girl whom they named Kathleen Elizabeth Avanzino, Paris Hilton's future mother.

From day one, the Avanzino union was destined to fail.

"They had a volatile relationship," says Ken Avanzino. "They were both pretty high-strung, and one minute they'd be raising their voices at each other and the next minute they'd be embracing."

Raising their voices, however, wasn't the worst of it. Kathleen and Larry had knock-down, drag-out fights. One memorable bout occurred in the kitchen of the Avanzino home when, in the midst of a heated argument, with little Kathy screaming in the background, Kathleen hurled a bottle filled with milk at Larry, just missing his head. Incensed, Larry charged at Kathleen and punched her in the nose. "There was blood and milk all over the kitchen," recalls John McKusker. "They had some brawls, but that one was a classic. Larry was a very volatile, emotionally unstable guy."

While the Avanzinos and the Dugans helped the struggling young married couple financially, Larry also had to get a job to help support his bride and little Kathy. With just his street smarts, good looks, and brawn to go on, the only position Avanzino could secure was as the manager of an Esso gas station in the town of Wantagh, on Long Island. "Larry," McKusker points out, "was never a great provider."

Kathleen, who once had big dreams of becoming a singing star, was miserable. But she still belted out her rendition of "Danny Boy" when she and her husband would go to McLaughlin's, a piano bar on Northern Boulevard, in Roslyn, Long Island, to drink.

Visiting her one afternoon in the sad little bungalow the Avanzinos were renting in Long Beach, Long Island, Hallaren found her in tears. "Little Kathy was in a high chair and big Kathy was feeding her, and I remember her being *so* depressed. She said, 'This is not what I ever wanted for my life.' Kathy was angry because she was home feeding a kid in a high chair with a maniac husband while her friends were all having great times—and she had every reason to feel that way. The whole situation took her spirit away."

Kathleen's sister, Donna, witnessed the quick decline and fall of the marriage and says it broke Kathleen's heart. Still, she wasn't hanging on to Larry's ankles begging him to stay. "I know she was very much in love with him, but he was going a different route than what Kathleen had planned for her life," says her sister. "He had personality problems. He was a drinker."

# CHAPTER 8

**A** high school dropout, and with her dreams of becoming a singing star dashed by pregnancy and a shotgun marriage to a failure, Kathleen appeared to have no future. The only light in her life was her daughter. Everywhere Kathleen went people were enthralled by little Kathy.

"She was an absolutely *stunning* child," says her aunt, Donna. "She was *so* perfect with beautiful light blond hair and an absolutely gorgeous face like a China doll."

When little Kathy was in her terrible twos, big Kathy came to the conclusion that her baby had very marketable assets—her looks and cuteness—and that the darling child, if handled properly, could become a little walking, talking, moneymaking machine—a real life Chatty Cathy doll, only with a capital "K." At the same time, Kathleen, then working as a cosmetics salesgirl in a Long Island drugstore, had hit on a career for herself that didn't require a diploma—just lots of moxie: full-time stage mother and manager of little Kathy's seemingly bright future.

"Big Kathy was going to make sure little Kathy did what she didn't do—and that is become a star," observes Adele Avanzino, who would always have a close relationship with her ex-sister-in-law.

The self-styled mother-manager began schlepping little Kathy on the train into Manhattan, taking her from agent to agent, advertising agency to advertising agency, all of which was the last straw for her husband. Larry Avanzino thought it was wrong to promote his daughter like that, plus he was envious of his wife's drive and ambition.

"Larry didn't like it," asserts Adele. "Little Kathy was just a baby and Larry didn't like her being gone a lot of the time with Kathy running around, taking her here, and taking her there. Kathy worked *very* hard at it. She put all her energy into that child who she adored. And Larry was not happy about it." Adds their brother, Ken, "I think he felt inferior. The next thing I knew, they were separated."

After two years the marriage was formally severed. According to Kathleen's sister, Donna, "Larry did not keep up with the child. Kathy Hilton never really knew her father."

Enter Constance Bannister.

If anyone could be mesmerized by little Kathy's baby beauty—and do something to promote her big-time—it was Bannister, the photographer who invented the "pinup baby" concept. Bannister herself was a beautiful babe. Photographed in a bathing suit in a *Saturday Evening Post* wartime story, she became a "pinup girl" for sailors aboard a U.S. aircraft carrier.

Through the 1940s and 1950s, her world-renowned baby pictures— known as "Bannister Babies"—were published in dozens of books and calendars. Bannister Baby posters helped sell War Bonds during World War II. One of her baby photos, which had run in an American magazine, was even found in the pocket of a captured German soldier. One of her many books, *The Baby,* stayed on the bestseller list for two years, was reprinted in eight languages, and featured in *Life* magazine.

During the 1950s some of the more than one hundred thousand baby pictures she took appeared on popular TV shows—hosts such as Perry Como, Garry Moore, and Jack Paar adored her images and featured them with humorous commentaries.

Once Kathleen discovered that Bannister had a photo studio and home nearby on Long Island, she wasted no time making contact. Bannister saw star potential with the toddler, and Kathleen eagerly put her signature on the photographer's Model Release for Minors, which assigned all rights of twenty-eight-month-old little Kathy's image to Bannister.

One of the many photos of little Kathy shot by Bannister shows the child wearing a skimpy diaper and a halter top. Another cute one shows her in a child's rocking chair talking on an oversize telephone; she's wearing a frock, Mary Jane shoes, and white socks, and her blond hair is up in bows. A caption on a little Kathy headshot, apparently for an advertisement, reads, "Smart girls wear seat belts." Another is of her in profile—on her knees in prayer.

Because of the charming pictures, and with Bannister opening doors for her—the famed photographer had contacts ranging from advertising in New York to TV and movies in Hollywood—little Kathy appeared in a Dial soap advertisement, the first of a number of such modeling assignments.

As the years went by, Bannister also played a key role in the TV and film careers of Kathleen's other daughters, Kim and Kyle, from her second marriage to Ken Richards, according to Bannister's daughter, Lynda Hatcher. "Mom took one look at those girls and fell in love," she says, "and she took them under her wing. Connie had a knack of picking the ones who had it. Kim landed a major role—Prudence on *Nanny and the Professor,* and that was *huge*—due to Connie's contacts. They were nothing when Connie met them. She did not receive one dime in commissions or management fees; not one red cent was paid to my mother. My mother (who died at ninety-two in August 2005) did it out of sheer belief in what these little girls were capable of doing."

**AROUND THE TIME** little Kathy's modeling career was taking off, a new man came into big Kathy's life, one far different from her first husband.

Kenneth Edwin Richards, the son of a Methodist minister, was already married with three children. A successful business executive, he was two decades older than Kathleen. He served as a lieutenant colonel under the army's surgeon general during World War II. In 1942 he married blond, pretty, and petite Evelyn Henderson, part Scottish, part American Indian, who brought three children into the world—Kenneth Alan Jr., Diane, and Grant Benson Richards.

For a fellow who grew up in very modest circumstances and whose father just squeaked by financially as pastor of the Valley Stream Methodist Church on Long Island, Richards was a genius when it came to developing and marketing ladies' clothing. No-iron cotton? Credit Ken Richards as its codeveloper. "The Skort," women's shorts with a flap or panel across the front to make them resemble a skirt? His idea. Mix-and-match sportswear? Richards's concept. He was, as they say on Seventh Avenue, a *macher*—a mover-shaker who got things done.

He had started as a junior buyer at J. C. Penney and within a decade had become the department store chain's head of women's and girls' sportswear apparel. By 1960 he had become director of S. H. Kress & Company, an iconic but fading chain of five-and-dime stores located in the downtown areas of many American cities. When he was appointed, the company's president optimistically noted he would "play an essential role in the company's progressive policy of entering the junior department store field." Less than two years later, though, Richards was ousted at a time when Kress faced diminishing profits and was under attack for refusing to serve blacks at its lunch counters in the South.

Around the time Kathleen landed him, he was earning a princely salary as special consultant to the president of Mohasco Industries Inc., the world's largest carpet manufacturer. Besides a fancy home on Long Island, he had a beautiful apartment in Manhattan and had purchased a lovely family farm upstate in Claverack, New York, and he was in partnership in a motel and restaurant venture nearby. All in all, the Richards family lived a very high life—the kind of life Kathleen wanted for herself and was determined to get.

Richards was tall, slim, handsome, sophisticated, bright, and well-off, but there was a catch—and a big one. He was still married, although his union of some two decades was on rocky ground, mainly because his wife, Evelyn, had a serious drinking problem.

Kathleen met Ken Richards for the first time at a party she attended at Richards's sumptuous home on Whitehall Boulevard in Garden City, Long Island. Long after she had snagged him away from his wife, leaving the family devastated, Kathleen boasted to her stepdaughter, Diane, "I knew at that party your father was the man I was going to have."

The two, however, actually began an intimate relationship some-time later at a Long Island restaurant and bar where Kathleen, when not in her stage-mother persona, was working as a hatcheck girl while someone babysat for three-year-old little Kathy at home.

It was at that nightspot one horrific night when Kathleen perpe-trated the first of a number of bizarre and violent acts—emotional and physical—that punctuated what would be a long and stormy relation-ship with Ken Richards and his daughter.

Diane Richards, sixteen, and her older brother, Ken Jr., were at home watching television late one evening when a policeman, accom-panied by a shouting and angry Kathleen Dugan, a woman the Richards children had never seen, or even heard of, before that moment, appeared at the family home, then on Stewart Avenue in Garden City.

"We answered the door and she started ranting and raving, going on and on, making incomprehensible accusations about my mother, try-ing to make it seem like my mother had done something to her," says Diane.

The police officer had accompanied Kathleen to the Richardses' home because of an altercation that had just happened involving her and Evelyn Richards, who had been rushed to the hospital.

Arriving at the emergency room, Diane and her brother found Eve-lyn in agony—one of her ankles had been seriously injured—and she was in a foggy state. "It was very hard to understand her speech," recalls Diane vividly. "She was in a state of shock and a great amount of pain and she was drugged."

Richards's wife had gone to the restaurant-bar that she and her hus-band frequented, most likely to confront Kathleen Dugan about the affair. The two women had words. Another restaurant employee later told Mrs. Richards that she saw Kathleen "put knockout drops in [her] drink." Ear-lier in the evening the coworker had warned Richards's wife, "Be really careful when you're dealing with Kathleen."

What happened next at the restaurant remains a dark memory for Diane. "Kathleen drugged my mother and then followed my mother, who was staggering, trying to get away, out to her car, a Lincoln Continental, that had heavy, heavy doors. As my mother was getting in the car Kathy purposefully slammed the door on her ankle and crushed it. The whole thing—the knockout drops, slamming the door—was intentional.

"When we got to the hospital her ankle was horribly mangled. After we got home and my mother came out of her drugged stupor, she said, 'Who was that maniac?' She couldn't believe what had happened."

In a cast for weeks, her mother's injury eventually healed, but the assault has remained with Diane ever since. "I believe Kathy came to the house with the police officer to try to turn around what really happened, to put the blame on my mother. She was going on and on, trying to make it look like my mother had done something to her. As I later learned, Kathy was good at doing that sort of thing. My mother most definitely was the victim."

Kathleen never apologized and showed no remorse. "I think there was a part of her that was missing," observes Diane. "She had no conscience."

Meanwhile, Kathleen aggressively pursued Ken Richards, even showing up unexpectedly at out-of-town hotels when he was on business trips. Richards later told his third wife, Sylvia, that Kathleen "was all over him because he had money and she was determined to get it."

Kathleen "deliberately got pregnant" around January 1964, in order to rope Richards into marriage, just as she appeared to have done with Avanzino. When she told Richards that she was with child, he secured a Mexican divorce from his first wife. Diane Richards asserts that Kathleen "contributed heavily" to her parents' breakup, even though the marriage was already in trouble.

Ken Richards and Kathleen Dugan began living together, at first in the home of her parents, who had moved from Manhasset to Wantagh, and then in the small town of Lynbrook, Long Island, home of Ken's mother, the widow of the Methodist minister.

Because Diane "worshipped" her father, because she "adored the ground he walked on," because she "couldn't bear growing up not being with him," and because she was having problems at home with her mother, she decided to move in with her father and Kathleen—this despite "a lot of strain. . . . We didn't get along at all. My brothers and I all had problems with . . . exposure to Kathleen."

Diane's brother, Grant, who became a successful rancher, supports all of his sister's allegations and attests to Kathleen's violent behavior. The night of the assault on his mother, he had been the first to arrive in the emergency room to find her in agonizing pain, and years later he harbors enormous resentment toward Kathleen, who he describes as "some lady my father met in a bar in Long Island. It caused a great deal of grief for my family."

When Richards moved into his mother's home with Kathleen, it sparked a tense living situation, especially for his mother, a religious woman who questioned the morality of him living in sin and who held Kathleen, his pregnant mistress, in contempt. Moreover, "Maunie," as she was called, was elderly and suffered from osteoporosis.

Returning home from high school one afternoon, Diane found Kathleen alone in the kitchen, laughing hysterically. "I said, 'What's so funny?' And I was starting to laugh, too, and I again asked, 'What are you laughing about. What's so funny?' And when she stopped laughing, she said, 'I fed Maunie dog food for lunch!'

"I was horrified. I don't know whether I told my father because anytime I tried to tell him things Kathleen did, she'd start accusing me of being a troublemaker. I was so afraid of her that I just finally withdrew into a complete shell. She had a violent disposition and she intimidated me and she *knew* she intimidated me and she enjoyed it. She had a sadistic streak. She needed help."

On another occasion, Richards's mother got out of the house and was wandering around the neighborhood, essentially a cul-de-sac of several homes. "When Kathleen discovered she was missing, she was furious," asserts Diane. "When she found her, she dragged her back to the house and threw her down on the concrete floor in the garage. It was terrifying."

Richards later claimed that Kathleen once "tried to kill his mother" by purposely allowing the elderly woman to wander off into frigid winter temperatures on Roxbury Hollow Farm, the property he owned in upstate New York.

Not long after his divorce, Richards married Kathleen. His children weren't present, and friends and relatives of Kathleen apparently didn't learn about the quickie service until afterward. Their marriage sparked more anger. Richards's children viewed Kathleen as "a gold digger."

"She wanted fancy sports cars and big homes and expensive jewelry and expensive clothes and expensive furs," states Diane.

Diane confronted her father. "I was so upset at the things that were happening that I told him, 'Kathleen's the most materialistic person I've ever known in my life.' I said, 'She just married you for your money.' I'm afraid it didn't set well with him."

On September 19, 1964, in a hospital in Mineola, Long Island, big Kathy gave birth to her second child, another beautiful baby girl, the love child whom the now-married Richardses named Kimberly. She was called Kim for stage and TV and was known as Kimmy to friends and family. Ken Richards had wanted to adopt little Kathy, but big Kathy adamantly refused his loving gesture "because she wanted complete control of her," maintains Sylvia Richards, his third wife. However, Richards would raise the future Kathy Hilton as his own.

Kim was just a few months old when Kathleen, with the help of her husband, got the baby her first job, a Firth Carpet commercial. Richards was in a business meeting with the Firth executives when big Kathy un-expectedly showed up with Kimmy in her arms; she believed in direct marketing. The agency that handled the account "fell in love with her," and Kim was hired to crawl around on one of the company's plush rugs. Like little Kathy, Kim would be driven hard to become a star by her de-manding and enterprising stage mother.

Meanwhile, for Diane Richards, the only bright light in her increas-ingly hellish teenage life was little Kathy. "Having her around brought me happiness," she says. "She was just so sweet, and I thought she hung the moon. Having had two brothers growing up, I felt I finally had a beautiful little sister. She was just so precious. I used to take her with me all over the place, even to parties. I was so proud of her."

At first the newlywed Richardses, with little Kathy and baby Kim, rented a beautiful home in Lloyd Harbor, on Long Island's North Shore, where Diane Richards finished high school. But Kathy wanted more than just a rental.

Kathleen picked out a new car for herself, a green Jaguar XKE convertible, and chose a large, gorgeous home with a swimming pool behind an exclusive golf course in the tony Long Island enclave of Old Brookville, about twenty-five miles east of Manhattan and close to the Sound. Like Manhasset, it was home to captains of industry and socialites who built mansions along what was known as the Gold Coast.

But despite the fancy address and opulent lifestyle, life was not sweet in the Richardses' household. "There were," as Diane Richards asserts, "assaults on my father by Kathleen."

Very late one evening, for instance, Ken and Kathleen Richards arrived home from a night on the town and got into the kind of heated arguments that had become commonplace—so loud was it that Diane and little Kathy, a toddler of about five years old, and baby Kim, were awakened and frightened by the yelling and screaming.

Diane, then eighteen, raced downstairs in time to witness a scene that is etched in her memory. "They were really fighting, and the next thing I knew it escalated and one of them had opened the basement door and Kathleen tried to literally push my dad down the basement stairs. He was holding on for his life, and I was in the middle of it because I was trying to defend my father. I was scared to death that he was going to be killed right there. I was trying to get her off of him.

"When that incident happened, my father kept saying over and over, 'She's crazy! She's absolutely crazy!' And I think he realized at that point he was in over his head."

# CHAPTER 9

Around the time Kim was born, Ken Richards began hunting for a new job, this time on the West Coast.

There are some, like Diane Richards, who believe it was Kathleen, her "very manipulative and demanding" stepmother, who "encouraged" him to find a position in Los Angeles "so she could pursue the children's acting careers in Hollywood."

Fortunately, Kathleen's wish came true. Richards was appointed president of a big discount store chain headquartered in the entertainment capital of the world.

Richards went ahead to make arrangements for a temporary rental home on Veteran Avenue in the lively Westwood section of LA, and the family immediately trekked to sunny La-La Land, *Beverly Hillbillies* style, traveling across country in a caravan of fancy cars—unlike the TV Clampetts, who piled into a pickup truck. Also making the trip besides Kathleen and the girls were Kathleen's stepdaughter, Diane, Dodo Dugan, and Adele Avanzino.

En route, Kim fulfilled a lucrative assignment in Philadelphia. Just four months old, she'd been hired to do a commercial for the relatively new disposable diaper, Pampers—a deal that was brokered by Kathleen through contacts of Constance Bannister. Like little Kathy, Kim would do a number of commercials as a baby, including one for Ivory Snow.

"Kathy was *thrilled* moving to California. I don't think she left New York with any sorrow," says Adele. "Ken was going to have a very good position and they were going to have a great house and things were going to be wonderful. And, best of all, Los Angeles was where entertainment was made, and Kathy had big dreams for her kids."

For about a year the Richardses lived in Westwood while their new home with a pool was being custom-built on Aqua Verde Drive in the more modest San Fernando Valley side of the exclusive and gated community of Bel-Air. Kathleen decorated the home in blood reds and icy blues.

But life wasn't as "wonderful" for the Richards family as Adele Avanzino had envisioned. Like the thick smog that often enveloped the Valley, a toxic cloud hovered over the Richardses' marriage. Kathleen continued to instigate fights with her husband. She constantly berated him for not making more money. "Ken Richards was a very nice man, a gentleman," Adele notes. "But Kathy had the dominant personality."

She wanted more and more things, and her clothing obsession spiraled. "She was like Imelda Marcos. Kathleen had dozens and dozens of expensive pairs of shoes," notes Jane Hallaren. On one occasion Kathleen had an exclusive Beverly Hills furrier drop off for her approval and subsequent purchase by her husband a selection of "very expensive, very, *very* beautiful" mink and sable coats in different styles. She luxuriated in the furs and modeled them in front of a mirror for hours until she chose the ones she wanted. "My father always tried to please her," says Diane Richards. "Maybe he tried too hard."

Big Kathy, who would train her daughters how to snag and marry rich men, offered up the same advice to Diane, who was now at the right age. "I was starting to date, and she told me I should *only* go out with rich men—lawyers or doctors—men with a *lot* of money," she says. "I didn't agree with that philosophy. What she tried to teach me reinforced my beliefs that she was just after the material things in life. Kathy was behind all my sisters marrying wealthy guys."

While big Kathy's twisted lessons in love and marriage grated on Diane, it was her continuing abusive and violent acts that eventually caused the young woman to flee the household permanently in fear for her life.

"She did show affection for her children when they were real little, but then there was a rough side to her," maintains Diane. "She could be abusive to little Kathy and Kimmy—and she was to me. If she thought they were misbehaving, I saw her pull their hair—I saw her slap. My father would jump in all the time. He couldn't stand what she was doing."

One incident especially stands out. The Richardses had an Irish maid who was also the children's loving nanny. She and Diane got along well, and on one occasion she telephoned Diane to say she knew a nice young man with whom Diane might want to go out. "She was going to set me up on this date with this friend of hers," says Diane, "and it inflamed Kathleen that Marie, who was this really nice person, was calling *me*. Kathleen said, 'You don't associate with the hired help!' And she grabbed hold of my hair and started to pull me across the room, and my father just had to pull her off of me."

The violent denouement came in the kitchen of the Richardses' home when Kathleen served up a very special treat to her then-twentysomething stepdaughter—a snack consisting of a bun, chopped beef, American cheese, and one other ingredient that only Stephen King could have imagined as part of the recipe.

"Big Kathy just got angry at me one day, so she put a little screw in the cheeseburger she made for me," says Diane. "She always told me I had pretty teeth and I guess she wanted me to break them. I bit down on it. Fortunately, I didn't hurt my teeth."

The incident was the "last straw" both for Diane and Marie, the nanny. "She had witnessed that and that's why I think she quit her job," states Diane. "That was just more than she could abide. I was just terrified of my stepmother. I wish I hadn't been so afraid, but I was. She had a way of staring right through me. When I left that time after the cheeseburger incident, it was for good. It was just a cumulative effect, and I just realized it was too much for me to take anymore. I felt I was going to go under if I didn't get away."

She says Kathleen's action had the same impact on her father. "He was just pulled down further and further and further. He had gotten in so deep and he was not thinking how to get out, or maybe he didn't think he *could* get out after a while."

**IN APRIL 1968,** having turned thirty, Kathleen had a third pregnancy, and this time it was unplanned by her. With their marriage in tatters, the Richardses decided to go away together for a weekend to see if they could patch things up. They slept together for the first time in many months, and she conceived, and when she found out she was pregnant "she was livid," a family member says.

Being pregnant, however, didn't stop her from hitting the bricks again with dreams of seeing one of her daughter's handprints on the Hollywood Walk of Fame. This time, though, she focused on Kim rather than little Kathy. And of her daughters, Kim would be the most famous, career-wise. The child did have enormous acting talent and charisma, far more than little Kathy.

"All the girls had the knack and the ability. They were good around people and around strangers. But Kim was *extra* special," observes Kathleen's sister, Donna. "We used to play games with Kim—let's make believe—and we'd say make believe you're this, or you're that, and she would start acting. And then we'd say, okay, game over. But she'd keep on going. She just had that special talent."

As she was marketing Kim, Kathleen gave birth to her third daughter, another little doll, whom the Richardses named Kyle, and who looked more like her father than her mother, with a thin, long face and dark hair, unlike her blond, blue-eyed sisters.

It was Ken, not Kathleen, who awoke to handle the 3 A.M. feedings and generally play nursemaid when the girls were babies. Moreover, Kathleen couldn't and didn't cook very much, but for some reason she loved to clean and was famous for vacuuming. "She did nothing," Richards later claimed. Observes Sylvia Richards, his third wife, regarding Kathleen as a mother, "I don't think she really cared about the kids—except for the money they made."

Kathleen was working on turning Kim into another Drew Barrymore or Tatum O'Neal, both of whom would have troubled private lives, as would Kim down the road. Like her big half-sister, little Kathy, Kim had the all-American looks and attitude that Hollywood admires—blond bangs, hazel eyes, husky voice, and a bouncy and bubbly personality.

She was about to turn five when a new family sitcom was being readied by a bright, ambitious Brooklyn-born producer, David Gerber, who had an amazing track record as a packager of prime-time series for 20th Century–Fox Television. Around the time big Kathy was shopping her daughter, the entertainment division of the American Broadcasting Company was planning to air Gerber's independently produced *Nanny and the Professor,* as white bread as any half-hour of prime-time television could be.

Then the number-three television network, ABC, scheduled the series, mainly because of the viewing public's interest at the time in anything and everything British—and *Nanny* starred a pretty, perky English actress. Juliet Mills was the daughter of the actor Sir John Mills and older sister of Disney star Hayley Mills. She had been cast in the part of the nanny, Phoebe Figalilly, who uses her psychic magic to bring calm to a chaotic American family, the Everetts. That, in a nutshell, was the high concept that Gerber had pitched and ABC and the sponsors had bought. The show would be popular, although not a blockbuster.

When Kathleen heard about the casting call, she was virtually first in line with Kim at her side. "It was like a stage-mothers-from-hell convention," recalls a veteran casting director. "They were elbowing each other out of the way. Hair-pulling and eye-scratching were not out of the question. We looked at hundreds—*fucking hundreds*—of little girls with sparkling blue eyes and blond hair and brilliant white smiles, and cute mannerisms, and we were tearing our hair out and then Kim Richards and that bitch-on-wheels mother of hers came in and we said, 'We have a go.' Whatever magic we were looking for, Kim Richards had it. Plus, I remember the mother had some good connections in town."

Kim had been well trained by big Kathy. The child had only just learned to read when Kathleen began teaching her how to memorize dialogue, something she'd also done with little Kathy and would do with Kyle. "To keep it natural, I would just play a game, skipping words, which she'd fill in," big Kathy explained years later. "I'd do that until she memorized it."

That might have been a bit of an exaggeration on big Kathy's part, because Kim had inherited a trait of her father's—a photographic memory. When Richards was in college he had been accused of cheating, but his professors changed their mind after watching awestruck as he read a chapter of a book and repeated it verbatim. Kim had the same talent.

Kay Rozario, who described herself as a "second mother" to Kim over the years, observes, "She was a kid who took direction and was very precocious, very cute, and that got her by. She'd walk into a room and everybody would stop and listen. She was very bubbly, very up, though not the brightest bulb in the lamp."

Big Kathy, meanwhile, had become a fearsome figure on the sets where her daughters worked, because she was a diva. Ted Bessell, a Manhasset boy who starred with Marlo Thomas on *That Girl* and knew Kathy Dugan from the old days, had problems with her on programs he later directed and produced, shows that had either Kim or Kyle in the cast. Jane Hallaren says Bessell described Kathleen as "a horror show" and that he considered her "impossible to deal with as a stage mother."

Rozario, who had been a part of show business for years with her musical director husband, says that with *Nanny*, Kim's career started to fly. "So big Kathy put more emphasis on her. She did it with a lot of love, whether it was misguided or not. Kimmy did very well in those early years and Kathy got a lot of satisfaction out of that. Kim was so dependent on Kathy and that's the way she wanted it. She controlled all of her daughters, but particularly Kim, who was the big moneymaker."

Big Kathy also often pitted her daughters against one another. When Kyle eventually began generating more work than Kim and scored a key role at the age of eleven in the 1980 Disney family horror film *Watcher in the Woods* (starring a bored-to-death Bette Davis), big Kathy heaped praise on Kyle.

"She'd say about Kyle in front of Kim, 'Well, this is *my baby.* This is *my little sweetheart.* Kyle's working and what are *you* doing?'" recounts Sylvia Richards. "Big Kathy did this *constantly* to those kids. I don't know what she thought—whether she was going to get more production out of them by doing that, or what. But I do know it was devastating to them. Looking back, I don't know how *anybody* survived in that family.

"Kim so wanted to please her mom because I don't think she ever really felt that her mother loved her," continues Richards. "*All* of them— little Kathy, Kim, and Kyle—were always trying to please Mama. They knew their father loved them. They didn't have to prove anything to him. It was absolutely *pathetic!*"

After the first episode of *Nanny* aired, Kim Richards received huge national publicity and developed an enormous following. Fans followed what she wore and whom she dated and all the gossip about her that appeared in teen magazines. And there was a lot of it. Of course, it was nothing like the blizzard that would surround Paris years later, of which Kim was said to be hugely envious.

As she moved into her teens, and with more credits under her belt, Kim became a staple of the fanzines. One fashion spread had her at fourteen when she weighed ninety-one pounds and stood just five feet in a "soft velour, long-sleeved maroon top of cotton polyester. About $21." She was often photographed with other young stars such as *Diff'rent Strokes* cast members Dana Plato, Todd Bridges, and Gary Coleman.

According to family insiders, little Kathy was "jealous" of Kim's success and all of the attention and adulation she received both from the public and from their mother because, as one close observer notes, "little Kathy wasn't making any money for her mother, and Kim was."

*Nanny* had a short run of two seasons, and the show's cast seemed to be jinxed. The TV family's patriarch, Richard Long, was an alcoholic who died of a heart attack four days before his forty-seventh birthday. Trent Lehman, who had played one of Kim's two brothers, committed suicide by hanging himself from a belt looped through a chain-link fence behind an elementary school near his North Hollywood apartment.

Kim, who had just turned eighteen, was devastated. "When I heard what had happened I cried. . . . We were in, like, *Teen Beat* and *Tiger Beat,* and all those magazines, and *People* magazine. It had been like that our whole lives," she observed on a "Whatever Happened to . . ." segment on *Entertainment Tonight* about the mostly has-been cast of *Nanny and the Professor.*

After *Nanny,* Kim Richards had recurring roles on such bland, short-lived sitcoms as ABC's *Here We Go Again,* starring *Dallas* star Larry Hagman, and NBC's *Hello, Larry,* featuring *M*A*S*H* costar McLean Stevenson, and she made numerous guest appearances, playing cute-young-girl roles, on popular prime-time series such as *CHiPs, Magnum, P.I., Diff'rent Strokes, The Dukes of Hazzard,* and *The Love Boat.* With her clean-cut Abercrombie and Fitch looks, she became a regular on the Walt Disney lot, appearing in more than a dozen TV and feature films. Next to Hayley Mills, she was only the second child actress to be offered a highly lucrative contract with the Disney organization.

Kim had fulfilled big Kathy's dream. She finally had a box office star in the family.

Kim was working constantly, and the money was rolling in. It seemed like a dream life, according to the fan magazines, but it wasn't.

For one thing, she never had a real childhood; her days and nights were spent on sound stages and in TV studios. She once told *People* magazine, "I remember driving home and seeing people in windows having dinner, wishing we were doing that. And I didn't have a whole lot of friends at school because I wasn't there enough to make any."

Most of her acquaintances were other young, ambitious, and troubled actors she met on sets, such as Dana Plato, who would die of a prescription drug overdose, and Todd Bridges, who also would have a drug problem and run-ins with the police. When Kim was fourteen, Plato and Bridges convinced her to sneak into the Magic Mountain amusement park, even though they had celebrity passes. Ashamed, Kim confessed what she had done to big Kathy. "Dana and Todd laughed at me," she said later, "but I respected my mom and never wanted to let her down."

Kim thought of her mother far differently than others did. She saw her as her moral compass.

**RICHARDS FAMILY INSIDERS** contend that big Kathy was out of control, drinking heavily and cheating on her husband.

Richards came face-to-face with her adultery on his return from a business trip. Big Kathy was supposed to meet him at the airport, but she wasn't there. He took a cab home only to find her in their bed with another man. Not long after, he suffered his first heart attack.

Another of big Kathy's affairs resulted in a pregnancy, which she confided later to Sylvia Richards. "She told me that she had fallen in love with a car dealer and had gotten pregnant, but that she lost the baby. She told me about him, and how much she loved him, but that he was married."

Big Kathy also seemed to have a thing for professional athletes. Her husband learned that she and some girlfriends had been sleeping with members of the San Francisco 49ers football team at their training camp.

At a Christmas party, Sylvia Richards was introduced to a basketball player who was a star of the Harlem Globetrotters team. "He was sitting with big Kathy," recalls Richards. "I came over and she introduced me and out of the blue he said that every time he and Kathy got together they had sex. He said to Kathy, 'Well, I haven't been around for a while and I kind of miss being with you.' I almost fell out of my seat!"

During that time, Kay Rozario was sometimes asked by Kathleen to be her designated driver. "Kathy was a wild, wild lady," observes Rozario. "I didn't drink, but sometimes when my husband was on the road I went out with her so I could drive her home to keep her safe because she couldn't drive—she *loved* that booze."

Other times Kim had to pick up her mother, and sometimes she and her sisters were made to perform for big Kathy's men friends, according to John Jackson, a former boyfriend of Kim's and father of one of her four children. "The way she controlled Kim was just unbelievable," says Jackson. "Kim used to tell me stories of when she was twelve and thirteen and fourteen years old and how she'd drive the family car and go pick up her mom at different bars," he asserts. "Her mom would have men over *all* the time on different nights of the week and she'd make Kim perform for them—do her little skits and dance. Her mom would have her basically perform on cue. She was that typical frustrated mother of a child star living through her children."

Jackson's assertion is supported by Sylvia Richards, who heard similar stories from the Richards girls, and even from big Kathy herself. "Kathleen was always having men to the house," she states. "One night she had some black man in her bed and Kim and Kyle went in and Kyle had a fit and ran him off. They didn't tell their father this stuff was happening because they were too embarrassed."

Another problem had to do with the enormous income Kim was generating, estimated to be in the seven figures at the height of her career, and how that money was being spent, and by whom.

Around the time Kim started earning star salary, her father's career was tanking. Richards had lost his job with the discount store chain that had originally brought the family to California, and he had gone through a series of lesser executive positions and gotten into a variety of small-time business ventures, such as selling plumbing fixtures, albeit gold plumbing fixtures. His daughter, Diane, attributes his career decline and fall to "the instability in his home life with Kathy."

At that point, according to Adele Avanzino, "Some of the children's money was going toward things like the family's living expenses. Ken wasn't working and I don't think that made for a happy marriage."

The money issue resulted in a lot of finger-pointing. A number of close Richards family friends felt the main culprit was Kathleen.

Larry Avanzino's close friend John McKusker had been involved in some business ventures with Richards in California and considered him "a hell of a nice guy and very talented." He says, "To the best of my knowledge Kathleen took *all* the money that Kimmy was making—and Kathy was living off it."

Kathleen indicated to her friend Jane Hallaren that she was investing the money in jewels. "She wouldn't know her way around the stock market if her life depended on it," she asserts. "But she invested in gems. She had a *tremendous* amount of gems."

Others, like Kay Rozario, were aware that Kathy was dipping into the girls' money pot, but she points out that Kathy probably deserved what she took. "She was Kim's mother and she taught her everything she knew and that's who gave Kim her career, and Kathy worked very hard at it. Who's to say whose money was whose?"

In the Richardses' home there were recriminations, loud arguments, threats of divorce. Big Kathy had started bad-mouthing Richards to her friends like Jane Hallaren. "Kathy said she hated him, that he was no good, that he couldn't do anything right, that he was worthless. Kathy had beaten Ken down to nothing. She said, 'I'm getting rid of him,' and then 'I got rid of him,' in that order. She gave me the impression the girls did not keep up a relationship with their dad."

By 1970, after six turbulent years, Kathleen claimed she had had enough of Richards and gave him the boot. Along with the money issue, they also were battling over their children's future in TV and the movies.

An ugly nine-year battle ensued. Ken Richards wound up sleeping alone in the maid's quarters. "Kathleen wouldn't give Ken a divorce because he wanted at least 50 percent custody of his daughters, Kim and Kyle, and Kathy wanted full control," says Sylvia Richards. "At the time Kim was making a lot of money, and Kyle was starting to make money, and this is why Kathy wanted complete custody."

Ken Richards eventually moved out of the Bel-Air hell house and into an apartment in nearby Encino where, on July 4, 1978, he met Sylvia Benedict, a divorcée, who lived in the same complex with her daughter, Cyndi, and her little boy, Bobby. Richards, who by then had gone into the real estate business in the Valley, pursued Sylvia, and they began living together while his divorce and custody fight continued unabated. Kathleen alone went through a half dozen lawyers.

Kim and Kyle loved their father despite their mother's efforts to alienate them, and they became close to Sylvia when they visited Richards on weekends. "After Ken and I had gone together for a while, the girls *begged* their father to marry me—they didn't want him to lose me," says Sylvia Richards.

Then Richards faced the toughest battle of all. He had a family history of high blood pressure and heart disease, and in early 1979 he was admitted to Ventura Hospital in critical condition, facing open-heart surgery. His life was on the line.

In order to protect his assets from Kathleen should he not survive the operation, he had given Sylvia power of attorney. "Just before Ken went into the operating room," recounts Sylvia Richards many years later, "our lawyer called Kathleen's lawyer and told him that if she didn't

sign the divorce papers *before* Ken had the surgery, and if Ken didn't survive, that he would sue her on my behalf and take everything for myself
and the children. I don't think Kathleen, who was in the hospital room,
thought Ken was going to live, so when the call came in from her lawyer
she literally tore out of the hospital room and finally signed the divorce
papers after nine years."

Their divorce was final on May 17, 1979.

A day after Richards's successful heart surgery, as Sylvia was sitting
vigil in the intensive care unit, praying for his full recovery, little Kathy,
who by then was engaged to Rick Hilton, telephoned her. Sylvia, who
had come to view little Kathy as a clone of her mother—"in every
way"—thought she was calling to wish well the man who had raised her.
Instead, she teased and taunted Sylvia. "She told me that her mother had
been going to the hospital when I wasn't there, and that Ken had told her
how much he loved her—that he loved her more than me, that he would
never stop loving her. She said other things that were very hurtful—and
untrue. Little Kathy and big Kathy *loved* hurting people."

Sylvia Richards has never forgotten another traumatic incident that
occurred in New York on the occasion of Paris's christening at St. Patrick's
Cathedral. While Kathy and Rick had not invited Sylvia and Ken Richards to the sacred event—Kathy all but ignored the man who had raised
her from the age of three—Barron and Marilyn Hilton had generously
flown them to New York in their private plane and put them up for a
week at the Waldorf. A celebratory dinner after the christening was held
with family and friends at a fancy restaurant when Kathy Hilton once
again began attacking Sylvia.

"All of a sudden she said in front of everyone, 'I'd sure like to see
you and Mom and Ken go to bed together. I know who would win *that*
game.' I was so embarrassed I could have died," states Sylvia. "She was
just trying to hurt me by insinuating that her mother was better in bed
than I was. Ken was mortified. Kathy's a *very* mean person. They are very
bizarre people."

It was shortly after his divorce from big Kathy was final that
Richards was hit with another big Kathy shocker. From his attorney he
learned that she had illegally sold a piece of valuable land he owned

where he planned to build a home. She had forged his signature on the required property sales documents and pocketed the money. "He could have sued her," says Sylvia Richards, "but he held off because of the girls and was worried about hurting them. Of course, afterwards, Ken said if he had to do it over again he'd have thrown big Kathy's little tush in jail."

As part of the divorce settlement, Kathleen received the Bel-Air house—Richards decided to let her have it because he didn't want to up-root Kim and Kyle. Some years later, however, when big Kathy sold the house, she was supposed to give part of the proceeds to her daughters. According to Sylvia Richards, "They never saw a dime, and Ken kicked himself for letting her have it."

Ken and Sylvia were married in a small ceremony at a Methodist church in the Los Angeles suburb of Ventura in November 1979. Ken wanted his daughters there, but big Kathy barred them from attending, which devastated Kim and Kyle and deeply hurt their father.

Just days later little Kathy and Rick Hilton had their big wedding in Beverly Hills. Richards demanded an apology from little Kathy for the hurtful things she had said to Sylvia at the hospital after his surgery. She laughed in his face and refused. "She wouldn't apologize, and we didn't go to her wedding," says Sylvia Richards.

# CHAPTER 10

**W**hen Kim Richards was nineteen, she began a relationship with gawky, curly-haired George M. Brinson—called Monty—scion of a wealthy supermarket chain family from the South. He wasn't a Latsis, or a Niarchos, but the young man's family did have big money.

Brinson had left the family homestead in High Point, North Carolina, to make his mark as a producer in Hollywood. With a Ferrari and a penchant for action and high-stakes gambling, he was instantly welcomed into a glitzy, fast Hollywood crowd. It was through a friend of Rick and Kathy Hilton's that Kim was introduced to Brinson, and after a blind date dinner at the trendy Palms restaurant in Beverly Hills "we were basically together every day," he says.

It was not an easy courtship. While she was living with Brinson, Kim started seeing other men, he asserts, rich boys from even wealthier families. One was John Davis, son of billionaire oil and entertainment mogul Marvin Davis.

"Kim would say she had to go babysit Paris and Nicky and, really, she was being fixed up with John, and I found out about it," claims Brinson. "She was being *influenced* to do it. She was being pressured because of the billions of Davis dollars." The pressure, he's certain, was coming from one influential source—big Kathy—"who was looking for the best for her daughter, and those guys had megamoney."

At the time, though, Kim would marry Brinson. Like big Kathy with Larry Avanzino, Kim's was a shotgun wedding because she had become pregnant. "We found out and we did the right thing," states Brinson years later. "It was Kim's choice to have the baby. They [Rick and Kathy, and big Kathy] didn't believe in abortion because they were Catholic. It wasn't even an option."

With marriage arrangements being rushed, Brinson gave Kim an engagement ring, but big Kathy didn't feel it was suitably large. "She told Kim to give it back to him," recalls Mickey Catain. "Kathy told me, 'I'm not letting her take *that* ring.' She made him give her a bigger one."

The Brinson-Richards nuptials took place in July 1985 at the same house of worship where Kathy and Rick took their vows—the Church of the Good Shepherd in Beverly Hills. One of Kim's wedding gifts was a watch and a pair of earrings worth about fifty thousand dollars. It was from one of her other very rich former suitors.

Photos of the Brinson-Richards reception appeared in a celebrity monthly called *Teen Favorite Superstars* with a story that was headlined "Here Comes the Bride (At an All-Star Wedding)!" It declared that Kim "... now has a new role—as the real-life blushing bride."

The article disclosed that one of her bridesmaids was her sister, Paris Hilton's other aunt, Kyle Richards, already at sixteen a veteran of six years of Hollywood work; she'd been one of the recurring cast of *Little House on the Prairie* and had appeared in a slew of cheesy movies and TV series, but nevertheless was a high earner for big Kathy, who now had two star contenders and one Hilton wife in her brood.

Kyle's date at Kim's wedding was teen actor Tommy Howell, a member of the Malibu rat pack of Rob and Chad Lowe and the Emilio Estevez–Charlie Sheen brothers. *Teen Favorite Superstars* asked the burning question, "Hmmm ... is there another wedding in the future for the Richards family?"

The other bridesmaid was Moon Unit Zappa, who had introduced the whole "Valley Girl" concept with her 1982 song. A year later *Valley*

*Girl,* the movie, was a box office smash, and "Valley Girl Speak" had spread across the country. The film's tagline was: "She's Cool! She's Hot! She's from the Valley!" It satirized the whole vapid "gag me with a spoon . . . *fer sure*" Valley Girl zeitgeist of which Kim and Kyle Richards were a part and little Kathy was an alumnus.

The Brinsons bought a spectacular two-story apartment in one of the ritzy condominium towers on Wilshire Boulevard. Kathy and Rick were so impressed with the place that they bought one as an investment, one floor below Kim and Monty's place.

Some seven months after their nuptials, Kim gave birth on February 21, 1986, to a beautiful baby girl whom the Brinsons named Brooke Ashley.

A month later, they started a production company, Brinson/Richards Entertainment, with big Kathy, who envisioned herself a movie mogul, playing an active role. The company, however, produced just one film— the forgettable and pedestrian *Escape,* released in 1990—with Brinson as the cowriter, Kyle as a cast member, and Kim as the heroine, Brooke Howser, who comes to a small town where everyone and everything is "strange." The film was made on a million-dollar budget, the money a gift from Brinson's parents.

Like their film, the Richards-Brinson union tanked.

At a Christmas party at Marvin Davis's, a curious incident foreshadowed the eventual end. "I actually lost my wedding ring because it was too big. It just fell off my finger," recalls Brinson, laughing at the memory. "So it's me, Britt Ekland, and her boyfriend, Slim Jim Phantom, from the Stray Cats, crawling around on the floor looking for the ring. We never found it."

Not long after that party Kim went out for an evening to a private club in Beverly Hills with some girlfriends. Around 2 A.M. Brinson drove up in his Ferrari and discovered his wife leaving the club, walking hand in hand with Marvin Davis's other son, Gregg. "It was the final straw," Brinson declares.

The two got divorced but shared custody of Brooke, and the exes remained friends. Years later, Brooke and her cousin, Paris, became close pals, traveled together, and Brooke even roomed with Paris and Nicky in the sisters' West Hollywood home.

Brinson, who became a professional poker player, maintained a close friendship with Kathy and Rick and continued to think of himself as "the brother-in-law."

His ties to the Hiltons were so tight, in fact, that Brinson, with Rick and Kathy's enthusiastic support, put together the 2005 first annual Nicky Hilton's New Year's Eve Poker Tournament, in the new poker room at Caesars Palace in Las Vegas. "Rick and Kathy don't play," notes Brinson, "but Paris is learning and Nicky's pretty good."

**BIG KATHY REJOICED** when Kim Richards Brinson's next future husband came into her life—this one via an introduction by her half-sister Kathy Hilton, who was prompted from behind the scenes by their mother. All big Kathy had to hear were the three words "Marvin Davis's son" to realize that, like Kathy with Rick Hilton, Kim with a Davis son was hitting the marital jackpot. Or so it appeared at the time. "Big Kathy was *thrilled*!" declares Kay Rozario. "And why not? She saw Kimmy marrying a son of one of the richest men in America."

Aaron "King of Prime Time" Spelling loosely based his '80s network melodrama *Dynasty* on the family into which Kim would marry. The saga of the fictional Carringtons, a wealthy Denver family in the oil business, was Spelling's view of his friends the Marvin Davises, a *super*wealthy Denver family in the oil business. (The Davises eventually relocated to Beverly Hills, where Davis turned his entrepreneurial skills to lucrative real estate investments, and even more bankable entertainment.)

The Davises, naturally, lived like royalty, with servants, expensive cars, private jets, yachts, and mansions, such as the Knoll, a 45,000-square-foot Holmby Hills palace. They were running neck and neck with the Hiltons in terms of big, *big* money when Kim Richards came into their lives. However, Kathy Hilton had her own thought on which was the superior tribe, one that she openly communicated to Sylvia Richards. Rolling her eyes about the Davises' ostentatious lifestyle, she once declared, "*I'm* married to the Hiltons and they're *old* money. *I'm* old money. The Davises are nothing but *new* money."

The Davises, meanwhile, thought the Hilton bunch were trailer park trash.

Rick Hilton had gotten to know the family when he was enrolled at the University of Denver with Nancy Davis, Gregg's sister. Their parents had rubbed shoulders in Los Angeles's tight-knit, upper-stratosphere party and high-society circuit. Socially ambitious Kathy Hilton had become part of that orbit when she propelled herself into high-profile charity and committee work and elite, celebrity-driven fund-raisers as a reinvented young LA society matron. Kathy became involved in Barbara Davis's glitzy fund-raisers, including one for multiple sclerosis; a spectacular event was held on the grounds of Kathy's father-in-law Barron Hilton's fabulous estate. (Barron's wife, Marilyn, had been stricken with MS.)

So it was to no one's surprise that enterprising Kathy—looking out for her newly divorced half-sister, Kim, a single mother with a jones for the high life—would through all her society connections and friendships introduce Kim to the immensely wealthy, most eligible bachelor Gregg Davis.

For big Kathy, the Davises were even bigger fish to fry for Kim than the Hiltons were for little Kathy—mainly because the Davises represented to her the embodiment of Hollywood glitz and glamour; they were flashier and more flamboyant and more fun than that stuffier, low-key hotel family who had refused to accept her into their elite fold. But she ran into the same kind of wall with the Davises. Big Kathy would later confide to Mickey Catain that she believed the Davises suspected "her daughters were gold diggers, so they didn't like her because they knew the influence she had over the girls."

The wedding of Kim Richards to Gregg Davis was "elaborate and humongous," according to Sylvia Richards, who attended with her husband, the father of the bride. The ceremony was held at the Davises' opulent estate. The Olympic-size pool had been covered and an enormous canopy placed over it, and that's where the bride and groom exchanged their vows. Afterward, there was a sit-down dinner for some two hundred guests.

The newlyweds' home, a gift from his parents, was in affluent, tree-lined "Little Holmby," so named because of its nearness to the massive estates like the Playboy Mansion and the Knoll in ultraexclusive Holmby Hills. "Gregg was born with a gold spoon in his mouth," says Kay Rozario, "and now Kim had a lot of money, and those two spent like there was no tomorrow; *whoa,* did they spend, with no concept of the real world and how people live."

In the garage, they had a couple of Ferraris and Mercedes-Benzes, and a few other cars, which were detailed weekly by the staff. They had dune buggies and Ski-Doos—expensive snowmobiles—and had had trailers custom-built to carry their fancy toys when they went on trips. It wasn't considered unheard of for Kim to go shopping and spend $10,000 in an afternoon as she prowled from one exclusive boutique to another on Rodeo Drive. "I'd shop with Kim and we'd go into a store and she'd see things she wanted and say, 'I want every color in this, I want every color in that,' and she just bought, bought, and bought some more," says Sylvia Richards, who, with Kim's father, were frequent guests of the young Davises, who had set up a special suite for them in their home. "She was like little Kathy—she *loved* to spend."

It didn't matter how much money they spent, because Marvin Davis kept doling out more. Every time he made a deal, such as when he sold his exclusive California golf resort, Pebble Beach, he lined up Gregg and his siblings and each one of them got a slice of the proceeds.

"When Marvin made that deal," says Monty Brinson, who had kept up a friendship with the Davises and Kim, "Gregg gave her a check for a million dollars and told Kim to go out and buy whatever she wanted."

When Brinson bet and lost $50,000 on a Los Angeles Lakers game, he only had $10,000 in his pocket to pay off his bookie. Gregg, at Kim's request, loaned him the rest.

Kim had two children with Gregg, a daughter, Whitney, and a son, Chad. Now the mother of three, she had decided to retire permanently from acting, though she would work on and off over the years. "I thought

I'd have my baby [with Brinson] and go right back to work, but when I held her, I'm like, I'm not putting her down, she's mine—and then I had another one, and I had another one, and I had another one," she once said, verbalizing big Kathy's incantation to her daughters to have lots of kids.

While Kim was having fun spending lots of money, her husband, Gregg, was under his father's thumb. If Marvin Davis made a deal, Gregg just had to watch. When Gregg talked about moving out of town with Kim and their children, Marvin would have none of it. "I want all your credit cards right here on my desk," he told his son. "If you're going to leave, we're not going to support you." Apparently the plastic meant more than the independence: Kim and Gregg stayed.

At the same time, Barbara Davis "was like big Kathy, but with money," in that she dominated Kim, according to Sylvia Richards. "She would call Kim and say, 'We want you at our house. *Now!*' And Kim would say, 'But my mom and dad are here.' And Barbara would yell, *'I don't care! You get up here in a half hour!'* Barbara Davis was doing this to them constantly. Whatever Marvin and Barbara wanted, Kim and Gregg had to jump."

Big Kathy had come to despise the Davises because they had snubbed her like the Hiltons had, and she resented how they treated her daughter. "Kathy kept saying, 'Oh, someday we're going to write a book about them. They're *horrible,*'" says Mickey Catain.

Meanwhile, the marriage of Kim and Gregg Davis began to rapidly deteriorate. "Marvin and Barbara Davis broke that marriage up," Sylvia Richards asserts.

John Jackson, who became the new man in Kim's life after she and Gregg Davis separated, maintains the two split up "because Barbara and Marvin said, 'Enough's enough!'" They gave their son an ultimatum: either leave Kim or face being cut off from the family fortune. He chose the former.

Meanwhile, big Kathy, whom Jackson describes as "money-driven, amoral, and would in a moment backstab you," tried desperately to keep her daughter's marriage from falling apart. "I heard plenty of stories about big Kathy chastising Kim," he states. Kay Rozario maintains that big Kathy's hidden agenda was to keep her daughter's marriage together because of the Davises' money.

According to Jackson, "Kim finally pissed it all away and Gregg went in a different direction—and then it was all about money. For big Kathy it was all about how much money Kim could get from Gregg, which cars she could get, getting the house, all that crazy stuff."

An acrimonious divorce and child custody battle ensued. Kim is said to have gotten a settlement and child support from the Davises, ranging between $20,000 a month that continues until the year 2009 and $23,000 a month for life, or until she remarries, and shared custody of the daughter and son she had with Davis. The divorce and custody battle also was said to have caused a major rift in the friendship between the Hiltons and the Davises.

"When Kim and Gregg split up, Kathy Hilton took sides with her sister," maintains Jackson. "Then Nancy Davis [who went to the University of Denver with Rick Hilton] and Kathy were at each other's throats. I could not believe the amount of shit that was going on."

**AFTER THE DAVISES DIVORCED,** big and little Kathy set up Kim with other big shots with big money. Big Kathy, for example, arranged for Kim to go out with an Arab prince; big Kathy also borrowed his Mercedes and totaled it, apparently while under the influence.

Kathy Hilton, meanwhile, sought out wealthy men who ran in her Manhattan social circles. One was a Revlon cosmetics honcho. Another was Donald Trump, who once viciously declared that Kathy's father-in-law, Barron Hilton, was "a member of the lucky sperm club"—a snarky dig that Conrad, not Barron, started the Hilton fortune. (But in March 2006, when Trump's model wife, Melania, gave birth to a boy, The Donald named him William Barron in honor of the Hilton bossman.) Rick and Kathy socialized with Trump, and Kathy figured he and Kim might be a match made in heaven.

"Kathy couldn't run around anymore because she was married, so she lived vicariously through Kim, just like big Kathy lived vicariously through little Kathy," observes Sylvia Richards. "Kim told me that Kathy kept setting her up with Trump, and Trump would call—I was there when he telephoned—and wanted her to come to New York. He would give her the money and she would go. But I don't think Kim was really too keen on him."

**A USED HARLEY-DAVIDSON** motorcycle and an execution-style murder were the curious catalysts that brought Kim together with the next new love of her life, John Jackson, an aircraft parts supplier, who fathered her fourth child.

Immediately after her separation from Davis, Kim dated a bad egg, a twenty-nine-year-old securities broker and high roller with a house in Malibu. John Collett was a central figure in one of the country's largest scams, involving eight thousand elderly investors and nearly $150 million in losses. He was under investigation on suspicion of illegally selling partnerships in oil and gas leases.

A former stereo salesman, Collett was talking to Kim on a phone outside of Brent's Deli, in the San Fernando Valley community of Northridge, during lunchtime on October 28, 1991, when, as Jackson put it, "someone walked up to him and popped a cap in his head."

Moments later Kim called the deli asking, "Have you seen my boyfriend, John Collett? He's a nice-looking guy."

Collett had been shot twice in the head at point-blank range by a hit man who had been paid $30,000 to bump him off.

"The killing devastated her, but I don't know for how long," says Kay Rozario. According to Sylvia Richards, Kim was "supposedly in love" with Collett, and "I know she was very shook up about that episode. But Kim was *so* dramatic all the time. And, of course, the killing was *very* dramatic, so she hung on to the story forever."

Jackson learned the sordid story from the dead man's mother, Jan, when he responded to a classified advertisement offering to sell her late son's Harley. When Jackson bought the motorcycle, she suggested he call Kim "because it was her favorite bike. I thought it was kind of morbid, but one night on a fluke I dialed her number, we met and then from about that day on we started dating."

Kim was still living in the Davises' Little Holmby house when she hooked up with Jackson in the spring of 1992.

"We were living in the fast lane," Jackson says. "We were jet-setters and bounced all over—Paris, St. Tropez, Orlando. And we were taking the kids with us most places. Kim was always very kid-oriented."

While the two never married, they had a child, Kimberly, Kim's fourth, and her third daughter.

Eventually, Kim moved out of the Davis house and into a home she had purchased in Calabasas, a rustic community that is home to a number of TV and movie celebrities in northern Los Angeles County. By that point the honeymoon period had ended, and Jackson states his relationship with Paris Hilton's aunt became "the worst nightmare of my friggin' life."

Jackson blames many of Kim's issues on big Kathy. "She was 100 percent the problem," he observes. "Kim's a spittin' image of her mother in every way. The amorality, and the drinking, the revolving door of men who she [big Kathy] had in her life when Kim was with me, and just the conniving craziness about her, and the way she [Kim] spent money like water. Kathy was that typically frustrated mother of a child star who lived through her children." And Jackson believes "without a doubt" that Kathy Hilton was the same kind of mother with Paris.

Jackson got an up close and personal look at the Hiltons—Kathy and Rick, and Paris—during the five years he spent living with Kim, and he came away with a bad taste. He got to know Paris, who frequently spent a week or two hanging out with Kim at the Richards-Jackson house, and he and Kim attended parties thrown by the Hiltons. He says that one of the things that struck him about little Kathy, big Kathy, and Kim and Kyle was how bitchy they could be.

"They always speak so derogatorily about people behind their backs," he says. "It's unbelievable, because they get *joy* out of making fun of people. They'll be out shopping and they'll be making fun of some other woman's shoes or outfit."

He says he also heard occasional racial and anti-Semitic slurs. "There were always those kinds of jokes," he claims. (Paris would be accused publicly of making such remarks by Marvin Davis's grandson, Brandon Davis, a member of Paris's privileged posse.)

While Jackson attended a number of parties with Kim at Rick and Kathy's, one of Kathy's more intriguing ongoing theme bashes occurred during the sensational 1995 murder trial of O. J. Simpson. Only someone with the prestigious Hilton name like Kathy could have the key players in the O.J. drama over for private dinners to dish about the case. "It was wild," observes Jackson.

Kathy had been a friend of O.J.'s wife, Nicole, and was part of the circle that included many of her friends. "Big Kathy told me that Nicole once told little Kathy that O.J. was violent and that she feared he might kill her someday," recalls Jane Hallaren.

When O.J. went on trial, Kathy invited virtually all the key figures, as Jackson remembers, from prosecutor Marcia Clark to Simpson houseboy Brian "Kato" Kaelin. "Every time Kim and I went, there was a new person on the O.J. end—[Simpson 'Dream Team' attorney Robert] Shapiro, [Simpson pal and defense attorney Robert] Kardashian." Another trial player who became a friend of Kathy Hilton's was Faye Resnick, victim Nicole Brown Simpson's so-called best friend—a onetime cocaine user who parlayed her role in the case into a nude layout in *Playboy* and a book deal.

"It was just so Kathy could get the scoop on what was going on behind the scenes—and also so she could feel important," Jackson declares. "It was quite a show."

# CHAPTER 11

**P**aris Hilton's maternal grandmother's third husband was far different from her second. While Ken Richards was a mild-mannered, beaten-down-by-big-Kathy businessman, Jack Catain was a hot-tempered mobster who had the connections to put out contracts.

Short—five foot eight, round—190 to 200 pounds, and hunched over, he was not the healthiest of gangland types. "We called him the six-million-dollar man," referring to all the money he spent on his numerous surgeries, says his daughter, Mickey.

In a 1969 U.S. Senate investigation into organized crime headed by then–Arkansas senator John L. McClellan, Catain, son of a Chicago produce market worker, was identified as a member of the Mafia. In a subsequent probe involving a major extortion case, Catain was linked to Philadelphia Mafia godfather Angelo Bruno, who was murdered the same year big Kathy and Catain said "I do."

To this man, Kathy Hilton's mother was married—twice, according to his son.

It took years for the government to nail Catain. They finally won a conviction in 1987, after he was divorced from big Kathy, for his part in a

$3.3 million counterfeiting operation, though he claimed the government used liars to convict him. According to the prosecutors, Catain conspired to sell part of a multimillion-dollar cache of counterfeit $100 bills.

Catain had been linked to a number of major cases, including a wide-ranging, national headline–making Internal Revenue Service probe into alleged ticket-scalping at the 1980 Super Bowl in Pasadena. There was testimony in that case that Catain "was aware" that a key witness "was to be killed" because he "was to testify against Catain" in his counterfeiting case.

Catain also figured in the case of charismatic financial "wonder boy" and convicted "con man" Barry Minkow, who ran a $100 million Los Angeles–based carpet-cleaning and building-restoration business called ZZZZ Best. It was all one huge Ponzi scheme in which early investors were paid off with money thrown at the twenty-one-year-old Minkow by later investors hoping to make a fast buck. At one point, Minkow reportedly borrowed $400,000 from Catain at interest rates between 2 and 5 percent *a week*. Catain would later sue Minkow for failing to split with him certain of ZZZZ Best's profits.

Among those who lost money to Minkow was big Kathy's and Kim Richards's close friend Kay Rozario, whose daughter, Leanne, dated Minkow briefly and says he was smitten with Kathy Hilton's sister Kim. "She was beautiful and she was such a talent," he says. "Back in the day I was trying to hit on her when I was this jerk who was a lying, cheating thief. I pursued her in the sense that she was good-looking and I was a sleazeball."

He recalls one evening when he pulled up in front of famed chef Wolfgang Puck's tony West Hollywood restaurant, Spago. Sitting beside him in his Datsun 280ZX was the lovely Leanne Rozario. Stopped just in front waiting for the parking valet was the couple with whom they were having dinner—Rick Hilton and his sister-in-law, Kim Richards. "Leanne looks at me and says, 'See, *they* drive a Ferarri.' So the next day I went out and bought a Ferarri."

But he claims he never even got to first base with Paris Hilton's aunt.

Big Kathy and Jack Catain were introduced by a mutual friend, Los

Angeles produce king Chet Frangipane, who says he picked up Paris's grandmother on the Hollywood freeway one afternoon when she flashed by him in her black Corvette convertible. "Kathy was not a bad-looking lady and I pulled her over in my Mercedes, gave her my business card, got her number, gave her two pounds of fresh mushrooms, and made a date," says Frangipane years later.

The two went out for about a month, but then he lost interest. "It's like a piece of food," he explains gruffly. "You want it, but the more you look at it you say, what the fuck do I need this for?" It was then that he introduced big Kathy to Catain, whom Frangipane had met at a golf tournament in Palm Springs that was sponsored by an organization called the Italian-Western Golf Association. "It was like an Apalachian meeting. There were more FBI than golfers," he jokes, referring to the infamous meeting of all the top crime bosses back in the '50s in upstate New York. He says that Kathy and Catain "hit it off" immediately and about a year later got married.

With all of Jack Catain's wise-guy attributes, big Kathy could still "break my balls," as he used to intone, and make his life miserable. But she was intensely attracted to him.

"My dad was a tough guy, and Kathy just loved that image of a guy being tough and kind of treating her rough. She liked that mafioso thing," observes Mickey Catain. "There was just a lot of energy between them."

Kathy raved about Catain to friends like Jane Hallaren, who was among the first outside of her immediate family who learned they had gotten hitched. "She called and said, 'Janie, you are not going to believe this but I got married, and you can't tell anybody that he's mafioso, and he's *fantastic*.' She was nuts about him—and liked the danger. She talked about him all the time, how she was really taken with this guy, that he had given her a lot of jewelry. Kathy's one of those people who was just absolutely *addicted* to chaos and drama."

Moreover, Kathleen saw dollar signs when she looked at Catain, even knowing that most, if not all, of his wealth—the roll of dough in his pocket, his cars (a Rolls-Royce Corniche and a special edition Cadillac convertible), all the jewelry he gave her, his 8,000-square-foot house high on a hill in Sherman Oaks—had come from the proceeds of criminal activities.

"Kathy was a gold digger, no doubt about it," concludes Mickey Catain. "And so were her daughters. She trained them that way."

Her brother, Michael Catain, who, like his sister, had become close to big Kathy and got to like her despite her avarice, nevertheless agrees that her agenda always was their father's money. "The funny part was she made no bones about it," he offers. "It wasn't as though she hid the fact. She would laugh, and she would kid, and she would literally say, 'I'm here just for the money,' but in a joking way. In the end, though, she wasn't joking."

One of Catain's big calling cards was the flashy ring he gave Kathleen—a *huge* fifteen-carat rock, most likely "straight off the truck." Behind Kathleen's back he snickered about the stone because it was yellow, and far from a pure specimen.

(Years later her granddaughter Paris beat big Kathy by nine carats when she reportedly received a $4.3 million, twenty-four-carat diamond engagement ring from the young Greek shipping heir Paris Latsis. However, the authenticity of the ring, whether it was actually given to her, and what happened to it, was in dispute.)

The ring Catain slipped on big Kathy's finger had had a number of wearers. According to Catain's son, his dad gave the same ring to many women in his life and always made certain he got it back when they were through. One woman to whom he was married for a short time, Joan Parnello, widow of Frank Sinatra's orchestra conductor, Joe Parnello, returned the ring to Michael Catain in a park "stuffed in a stuffed animal's ass," he recalls, chuckling at the memory. Big Kathy, however, is the only woman in Catain's life who refused to give back the rock when their marriage was over. "Kathy ended up with it," says Catain's son.

He says his father married Parnello after his first marriage and divorce from big Kathy and then remarried big Kathy before they divorced a second time. "Kathy probably had something to do with his marriage to Parnello breaking up." Chet Frangipane says Catain decided to divorce Kathy the first time because "they were always fighting. She'd get drunk and he'd tell her to get the fuck out. Why'd he remarry her? What the fuck does a guy do for a good blow job? So Jack went back and forth with her."

Of all of her many bizarre relationships with men, big Kathy's involvement with Catain was surely the oddest. After all, what couple would enjoy spending a weekend at a Hilton Hotel in the San Fernando Valley getting injections of lamb's urine, or some other odd potion, from a La-La Land New Ager in hopes the shots would make them healthier, prolong their lives, and rejuvenate them? His daughter, Mickey, recalls, "We did have some guy come to our house and we got these strange injections. I took them also. I remember turning red and becoming very hot after receiving them. They were expensive. We would have numerous people at the house in line for those shots."

Big Kathy may have got the idea for the shots from Hilton family chatter. The patriarch, Conrad, was known to have made trips to Switzerland to get injected with urine from a sheep that he was told would help him stay healthy and keep up his stamina sexually.

Hilton, though, was in far better shape than Jack Catain, who desperately needed rejuvenation. He had a long history of medical problems, including a bad heart that would eventually do him in, and he got about on artificial hips, often using a walker.

Big Kathy tried her best to keep up his heart rate. For instance, she *never* permitted Catain to see her without her makeup on, even going to bed with her face fully made up. Once Catain started snoring, she'd tiptoe into the bathroom and take off the makeup. In the morning, she'd wake up before him and put her makeup back on.

"She always cared about how she looked, always had to be dressed up for my dad," says his daughter. "She used to yell at me, 'Put lipstick on! Put makeup on! What's the matter with you?'"

Despite how hard big Kathy tried to make herself look beautiful, Catain still chased other women, or at least big Kathy suspected he did. She was so jealous that one night she climbed over the wall that surrounded his house to spy on him to see if she could catch him with another woman, but it was so dark that she fell on her backside and limped around for a few days. "It was funny, the stupid things she did," says Kay Rozario, who heard about the incident from Kathleen.

Around the time big Kathy became involved with Catain, nineteen-year-old little Kathy was starting to get serious with Rick Hilton; Kim Richards, about thirteen, was making appearances on TV shows like *Hello, Larry, Kraft Salutes Disneyland's 25th Anniversary,* and a sitcom called *Why Us?;* and ten-year-old Kyle was in one of the first big scary teen flicks, *Halloween,* appeared in the Disney feature *The Watcher in the Woods,* starring Bette Davis, and was on TV's popular *Little House on the Prairie.*

By that point in their lives the girls were so shell-shocked by their mother's freaky lifestyle that her involvement with a mobster was something they just shrugged off. "Little Kathy was not happy, and after she married Rick she was even *more* unhappy because now she thought she was upper crust, and just look who Mama was with," notes Sylvia Richards. "Kim and Kyle were kind of numb with everything because they had gone through so much with their mother that her relationship with Catain just seemed to roll off. After a while it was just, 'Oh, well, it's somebody else.'"

Because of little Kathy's impending marriage into the Hilton family, and Kim's and Kyle's very public careers, big Kathy had kept her relationship with Catain low key even to the point of not actually sharing the same residence with Catain *after* they married. Incredibly, the odd couple lived in separate domiciles *throughout* their marriages—big Kathy in her Bel-Air manse and Catain in his immense home on Royal Oak Road in Sherman Oaks.

Early in their relationship, when things were going well, they began house hunting, looking at multimillion-dollar properties together. But when it came to signing the papers, big Kathy balked.

"My dad wanted the house to be in both their names and Kathy said, 'Oh, no you don't! *You* buy the house, but it's *all* in *my* name!'" states Mickey Catain. "Kathy was very adamant about money. Kathy came to me and she said, 'Look, I don't want to split the ownership with your father because if your dad dies, I'm *not* going to split the house with you. I want the house in my name.' She was real open about it."

Most of the time big Kathy brought her lap dogs, her luggage, and Kim, Kyle, and little Kathy before she married Rick Hilton, to stay for a weekend or longer with the Catains. "We used to all party together," says Mickey. "Every night there was something going on. Kathy would bring her brother, Chuck, and his wife, Jane, and her mother, Dodo. She'd bring her friends. We had a wild time."

On other occasions they hit the bar, nightclub, and disco circuit— Jimmy's, Pips, or The Daisy in Beverly Hills, which catered to the rich and famous, or a tony club Catain liked on Ventura Boulevard in Encino. Once Kathleen started drinking, though, she got wild and would begin flirting with other men, which infuriated Catain.

"She used to love to make my dad jealous," maintains Mickey. "She would flirt with any guy, even with just a friend of ours, someone she had no interest in whatsoever, just to get my dad jealous. Then they'd yell and scream at each other. It was never physical, he never hit her or beat her or anything, and because they had separate houses, he'd scream at her to go home."

Big Kathy got turned on by professional athletes, and one she knew from her teenage years was Jim Brown, who had played at Manhasset High School and with whom she sometimes hung out in Los Angeles where he lived after retiring from the Cleveland Browns as a Hall of Fame star running back.

"She was friendly with him and she used to brag about it and she used to try to make my dad jealous because my father was kind of a little bigoted," recounts Catain. "She'd see Jim Brown at this one club we'd go to, and she'd go sit on his lap and put her arms around him and flirt with him in front of my dad, and that used to drive my father *insane.* They'd have some big fight and then they'd go home and make love. That was kind of their pattern."

**SOMETIME AFTER CATAIN** and big Kathy were married, an explosion and fire destroyed his Sherman Oaks home. A number of years later Kathleen turned over to Mickey Catain a suitcase filled with irreplaceable Catain family photos and memorabilia. Mickey was thrilled because she assumed everything had been consumed in the flames.

When Catain expressed surprise upon seeing the items, Kathy told her a deep, dark secret. "'I collected all those pictures and your father and I got them out of the house the night before it blew up.' She said that my father blew up the house for the insurance money because he was in trouble. I literally had no idea my father did this."

In the end, it was Catain, in ill health and using a walker, who wanted a divorce from Kathleen; when she balked, he threatened to sue her—or worse—to get back all of the expensive jewelry he had given her.

"He gave her a *lot* of jewelry. I saw it. I mean *lots* of jewels, like some big ruby and emerald deal," says Jane Hallaren. "She told me that if she gave him any trouble, or asked for any kind of alimony, or wanted the jewelry back, he would make her life miserable. I got the feeling he was threatening her life. She said, 'Listen, this guy is Mafia, he's involved, he's a gangster. He'll kill me.' Whether that was drama or not I tended to believe that it was true. She said, 'He's crazy.'"

According to Kay Rozario, Catain also "took Kathy for some dough. He wiped some money out of her. He told her to invest in God knows what. Part of it might have gone to ZZZZ Best. But I think Jack just took it and that was it. She dumped him, and she told me, 'That no good bastard. He stole all my money.' I don't think he took everything, but he took a big chunk. He was a royal piece of work."

Big Kathy and Jack Catain were divorced in 1982, and a year later he remarried, this time to Phyllis Sherwood, a onetime showgirl who had been divorced from Bobby Sherwood, a popular big-band leader from the '40s.

Catain told Sherwood, who also got taken for a lot of money in the ZZZZ Best scam, that big Kathy had pushed him into marrying her. "It was one of those things where she said let's get married real quick—bap, bap, bap, and he was, like, well, okay," says Sherwood, who met Catain at a wedding and was married to him for five years until he died. "Jack made it sound like he wasn't really serious about marrying her. When Kathy married Jack she was looking for exactly the same as what she wanted for her daughters—she wanted the money. That was the most important thing in her life. And I guess it worked out pretty good because Kathy Hilton did very well for herself by marrying Rick. I mean, she's no brain trust. And big Kathy's the grandmother of that *charming* child, Paris. Oh my God, the whole bunch of them are idiots!"

Jack Catain died on February 21, 1987, in the cardiac intensive care unit at Encino Hospital. He was fifty-six years old. At the time he was free on bail, waiting to begin a fifteen-year federal prison sentence. No one remembers big Kathy being one of the mourners at his funeral service.

# CHAPTER 12

**A**round the time Jack Catain died, big Kathy, low on dough, sold the Bel-Air home that Ken Richards built for her and used the proceeds, along with money she is said to have borrowed from a wealthy Middle Easterner one of her daughters was dating, to buy a two-bedroom condominium apartment in the déclassé flats of Beverly Hills, a first-floor unit in a "modern, characterless" building, as Jane Hallaren described the place.

Though only in her midforties, big Kathy was "at a stage in her life when she was cutting back and trying to make life a little simpler," contends Adele Avanzino, sister of Paris's maternal grandfather.

For a woman who was downsizing, big Kathy made a curious decision—she wanted to again play mother to an infant. To Hallaren she revealed, "I'm going to get another baby." Hallaren, who had heard a lot of wild stories from her childhood pal, was stunned. "I said, 'What do you mean, another baby?' And she said, 'There's this horrible woman who doesn't want her baby, and I'm going to get it. I met this woman in a parking lot and I told her, 'You better get me that baby.'

"She was crazy about babies, but what she was telling me was all so grotesque and illegal," continues Hallaren. "She was so casual about it and I asked her, 'Kathy, how are you going to bring up a baby at your age with your lifestyle?' And she said, 'Well, if I can't do it, the girls will take it. They want another baby, we all want another baby in the family.' I thought to myself, how much control does she have over her daughters?

"I didn't talk to her for a few months and then I called and said, 'So, did you get that baby?' And she said, 'No, no, no. I can't go into it, but that horrible girl didn't let me have the baby.'"

But, in fact, there *was* a baby. The girlfriend of a Dugan family relative had gotten pregnant and wasn't prepared to care for the baby, so big Kathy volunteered her services. "Kathy got the baby and kept it for a while," says Adele Avanzino. "Kathy didn't want the infant to go to a foster home, or an orphanage, or a Catholic charity. Eventually, another Dugan relative took the baby, which was fine with Kathy."

**WITH HER DAUGHTERS** essentially on their own, and needing a money-making venture, big Kathy went to real estate school with dreams of becoming "a realtor to the stars," but she found getting a real estate license an effort and quickly lost interest.

She took up art instead. During the day she set up her easel on her patio and turned out oils and watercolors of landscapes and animals, and had a built-in outlet for her work: Kathy Hilton's boutique on Sunset Boulevard called Elizabeth's Staircase. Big Kathy usually signed her paintings using an assumed name because she didn't want her wealthy daughter's customers to question why her mother needed to earn a living. Little Kathy also stocked children's tables and chairs on which her mother had painted cute designs.

By night, big Kathy shed her *artiste*'s smock and got dolled up to crawl Beverly Hills bars, clubs, and discos frequented by high rollers. She played the Hilton card to the max, using her connection to the famed hotel family to impress men. In her hunt for another husband with money, she made it appear she was a rich Hilton heiress looking for a long-term relationship.

"She was always at one of the good restaurant bars, sitting out front, and she always seemed to be buzzed," says the former actress Carole

Wells Doheny, who was married to one of the scions of the oil-rich Beverly Hills Doheny family dynasty and had been a close friend of Paris Hilton's playboy great-uncle, Nick, and other Hiltons. "You'd walk in and there she'd be just hanging on the bar and she'd be trying to pick up any guy who had any money and who would pay her tab.

"I always felt sorry for her because she seemed to try too hard. She would glom on to you. You could never get past her at the bar. She would always tell you who she was, and who she was related to."

With a little scotch in her, Kathleen did what she did back in Manhasset when she was a teenager, which was to launch into song, belting out such standards as "Danny Boy," "Summertime," and "My Funny Valentine." At places like the world famous Polo Lounge in the Beverly Hills Hotel, a bar crowd could find her singing with the piano player. "She liked the schmaltzy stuff, and she was very dramatic, so she could pull it off," notes Avanzino.

Hallaren says it was during that period that Kathleen had started pursuing wealthy members of the geriatric set—men in their seventies and eighties. And then there was her "Seabiscuit" period when she chased little fellows with big money—racehorse jockeys whom she met at bars and at the tracks.

One of big Kathy's social acquaintances at the time was the niece of a man once dubbed "the scourge of Hollywood," a flamboyant character who in the '50s conducted a reign of terror against some of Hollywood's biggest stars and made a bundle in the process.

Her acquaintance was Marjorie Meade Roth, niece and confidante of Robert Harrison, the founder and publisher of *Confidential*, the big daddy of the sleazy celebrity exposé magazines that had their garish golden age in the '50s and '60s. In Conrad and Nick Hilton's heydays as Hollywood men about town, the father and son were often targets of blaring *Confidential* headlines, such as "The Strange Role of Zsa Zsa in Conrad Hilton's Life."

By the time big Kathy met Roth, she was married to TV writer and producer Marty Roth, the brain behind such popular TV sitcoms as *Three's Company* and *I Dream of Jeannie*. Some seventy episodes of *The*

*Dukes of Hazzard* came from his typewriter, and he was the hit series' executive story editor.

The Roths had met big Kathy through their friend Gary Stein, a wealthy Beverly Hills bachelor who owned a metal-plating company in the San Fernando Valley.

Stein was dating Kathleen who was, according to Roth, "his partner in drinking. She was a *very* heavy drinker, and Gary liked to drink so they had that in common. She was wild, and there was something about her that was *not* endearing. She was sort of like a con artist.

"It was around the time her daughter Kim married Marvin Davis's son, and I used to say to Kathy that she was better than Jolie Gabor because all her daughters married so *unbelievably* well. I said to her, 'You know people talk about Jolie Gabor and what she did with the Gabor girls, but you beat her by a *mile.* You should write a book for women on how to get their daughters into wealthy marriages.' I was teasing her, and she just ate it up."

Through big Kathy, the Roths also met and socialized with Kathy and Rick Hilton.

"We really liked them," Roth says. "They were young and fun. When I knew Kathy back then, she was an absolutely lovely girl and I found it hard to believe she was the daughter of *that* woman.

"One night Marty and I had dinner with Rick and Kathy at the Bistro Garden in Beverly Hills and we were sitting at a table outside and there was this horrible crash. Ricky had just bought a brand-new Porsche and he said, 'I'll bet it's my car.' And we said, 'Oh, no!' And he said, 'I'm going to go look,' and he ran out and his Porsche was smashed. He came back and we laughed and we finished dinner and we had a fun time. He didn't seem to mind."

Years later Roth, whose husband had died, looked back on their friendship with the Hiltons and wondered whether their interest in keeping up a social relationship was because Marty Roth was a big wheel in TV and might be helpful to Kathy's sisters, or even her daughters. "It's possible," she says. "Marty absolutely was a connection to TV."

• • •

*FOR YEARS BIG KATHY* had been partying in Palm Springs. The California desert playground was an oasis of rich, divorced men ready for trapping by predatory females. It had been for generations a getaway for the rich and famous, and rich and infamous, who lived and died there—from the likes of Presley, Sinatra, Liberace, Monroe, and the Gabors to Alan Ladd, who overdosed in his hideaway on Camino Norte after a week of nonstop drinking and popping pills.

Looking for a new life and a new man, big Kathy decided to take her show to Palm Springs, ridiculed in hipper quarters as "God's Waiting Room" because of the old stars who hung out there.

"She used to go there a lot," says Halleren. "She scoped out the scene, liked what she saw, and that's why she decided to move there. She'd been through everybody [in Beverly Hills], every bar, and her reputation was too crazy, and she knew she was old news."

Adele Avanzino essentially agrees. "Kathy just got tired of the whole LA scene," she says, "and just thought life would be a little easier down there, a little simpler."

Big Kathy planned her move with military precision. Her strategy was to buy a house on a golf course, sit out on her patio armed with cocktails and dressed provocatively, and flirt with the duffers passing by, hoping to score a hole in one with a rich daddy.

Just before she moved, and as part of her strategic planning, she made a change in her appearance. "Her idea was to first get a face-lift and then make the big move to Palm Springs and marry a billionaire," recounts Hallaren, in whom big Kathy confided her plan of attack. Hallaren recommended a top plastic surgeon who had done reconstructive work on her own face after she was in a serious automobile accident, Dr. Steven "Doc Hollywood" Hoefflin, who was best known for his work on Michael Jackson's face. His other celebrity patients included onetime Hilton wife Elizabeth Taylor, so big Kathy felt she was in good company. Moreover, Kathleen thought there was a chance of romance with him because she thought he was single—and definitely well-off.

Big Kathy came out of surgery "looking exactly the same, only younger, so it was a great job," Hallaren says. "I *loved* her nose. It's the same nose that Paris has, and Kathy Hilton has it, too. It's got a marvelous kind of different bump on it, which I think is wonderful. She had just gone to him for the face-lift, and Dr. Hoefflin talked her into the nose job." She also hoped to lose weight; because of her drinking, she had blown up to about 170 pounds.

In Palm Springs, she bought a modest house at 195 Club Drive overlooking the Indian Ridge Country Club. Her new abode was in the section known as Palm Desert. Bob Hope, who held his celebrity Bob Hope Chrysler Classic there, once quipped, "There's so much loot in Palm Desert they could give Texas food stamps."

# CHAPTER 13

*T*hey called Robert C. Fenton Jr. the "Silver Fox." For a man nearing seventy, the six-footer who once played college basketball was in great shape. He had a full head of gray hair and was known as a dapper dresser. As one of his two daughters, Barbara Frank, says, "Dad was a *big* person, with a *big* personality, and had *lots* of charisma. At his age women were just coming at him. It was *amazing!*"

One of the women who would land him—and make his life and the lives of his daughters a living hell—was big Kathy.

At the time she snagged Fenton one boozy night at a Palm Desert drink and dance joint out on Highway 111, the former aerospace marketing executive was "spinning out of control." Earlier that year his former dental hygienist and homemaker wife of thirty-five years, the mother of his two married daughters, and the grandmother of three girls, had died of uterine cancer. Her death had come not long after they had moved from the Los Angeles suburb of Northridge to a "spectacular" home in Palm Desert.

"It was like everything was awesome in their lives," says Barbara Frank, a nurse. "My parents had a *really* amazing relationship. A typical

Saturday night for them was barbecuing steak, and I'd walk in to look at them dancing and listening to Frank Sinatra, having a cocktail. My mom was the quintessential housewife—the cook, the cleaner, the entertainer. My dad didn't even know how to make a sandwich for himself. My mom's death was brutal for him."

While his daughters always knew that their very charismatic father was "a partyer" and "definitely loved it all—food, wine, music, and women," they believed he never strayed during his marriage. However, there was another side to Bob Fenton that knocked them for a loop. As a widower he had become a serial Casanova.

Out of the blue, some six months after his wife was buried, Fenton met and married a flashy singer who worked at a popular Palm Springs lounge called Melvyn's. "She didn't wear any underwear so when she sat on the bar and crossed her legs she would give everybody a free show," according to Fenton's other daughter, Judy Goldstone. "They called her 'The Black Widow.'"

The marriage between the Silver Fox and the Black Widow lasted several months and was dissolved in 1998. "Dad realized, 'Oh my God, what did I do?'" asserts Frank. Her sister adds, "She got the wedding ring. That's it."

Fenton's daughters were so shocked by their father's behavior that they convinced him to go into grief counseling at the Betty Ford Center in nearby Rancho Mirage. He went a couple of times. Two to three months later he met Paris Hilton's grandmother, and the two moved in together.

"I was freaked out!" declares Goldstone. "I shared a housekeeper with my dad and she started telling me that he had photographs of the Hiltons in his house—Kathy and Rick Hilton and Kathy Richards—the whole deal."

In that same time frame, Goldstone was shopping in the local Target store one afternoon when a pretty woman approached her and asked her whether she was Bob Fenton's daughter. Goldstone thought she recognized the good-looking blonde as a girl who had gone to high school with her sister. "I said, 'Oh, you're Barbara's high school friend, right?' And she said, 'No, I'm Kim Richards,' and I said, 'Who are you?' because I didn't know who Kim Richards was. And she just glared at me and said, '*Your* dad is living with *my* mother.' And I went, 'Ugh!' and just turned and walked away from her, and that was the end of *that* conversation."

Fenton had asked Kathleen to marry him on several occasions, but she played hard to get. She changed her mind, however, when he presented her with an enormous emerald ring surrounded by diamonds one glittery evening at Morton's, a fancy steakhouse in Palm Desert.

Fenton had waited until his beloved had gone to the ladies' room and then called over the waiter and plopped the rock into a fresh martini. Kathleen discovered it when she took a gulp. "Oh, yeah, she was thrilled," says Adele Avanzino, who had accompanied them to dinner. "It was a big, *big* ring, and it was all very exciting."

Certain friends of big Kathy's were against the marriage. They felt that Fenton was a gigolo who was out to get *her* money. Moreover, they suspected he wanted to marry her because of her access to the Hilton wealth through her daughter. Never once did they look at the other side of the picture—that she thought Fenton was loaded and wanted to unburden him of some of his green.

Six days before Christmas 1999, Fenton and big Kathy, with her daughter Kyle as a witness, stood before the Reverend Daniel Rondeau in St. Margaret's Episcopal Church in Palm Desert, and were married. On the marriage certificate, the bride listed her occupation as "Artist/ painter" and her usual kind of business as "Theater."

Fenton's daughters were angry—and catty—about the latest development involving their father. Furious at his actions, they refused to meet his new bride. *Ever.* But they soon learned what kind of woman she was, or at least heard the gossip.

"I was showing a girlfriend of mine some pictures of my mother and father and telling her how I couldn't understand what my father was going through, and I said he's married this woman Kathy Richards and this girl's eyes popped out of her head and she said, '*Kathy Richards?!* You've got to be *kidding*!!!' and I said, 'No, why?' And she said, 'She is a *pig*.' That's what she called her, and she said she goes to the 'nasty' Nest—that's what we call it in Palm Desert, the 'nasty' Nest—a club for people who are really old and go there to drink and sing and dance.

"My friend was there giving a bachelor party for her father, and Kathy was there and she had on this top that was really low cut and her boobs were hanging out and she was French kissing all these men. I said, 'You have got to be *kidding.* Oh my God.'"

After hearing her friend's story, Goldstone immediately telephoned her father.

"I said, 'Dad, this girl told me about her being at the bar with her boobs hanging out and French kissing these men,' and he said, 'I don't want to hear about it.' I said, 'Dad, what are you doing? Why are you with her?' And he said, 'I love her, Judith. She's my wife now. You are just going to have to accept this.'"

At that point, big Kathy declared war on her husband's daughters. The first volley came in a phone call to Barbara Frank from her father. At the time Frank was going through a costly divorce and custody battle, but she had been getting financial support from her father, who was helping to pay her attorney bills. That all changed after he married big Kathy.

"Kathy might as well have called me because it came from her telling my dad what to do," states Frauk. "He said, and I'll never forget his words, 'Under no circumstances am I going to continue helping you in any way financially.' I said, 'Dad, I'll pay you back. I'll refinance my house. I really need help.' And he said, 'Barbara, I'm with Kathy now. She won't allow me to help you anymore.' I thought, this isn't my dad. Who is this man?"

Beyond cutting off financial assistance to his daughter, Fenton went along with another, even more disturbing maneuver instigated by his bride. Big Kathy convinced him to sell his house, the one he had purchased with his wife before she died, and put all of the proceeds, about $250,000, into renovating *her* house.

Still, big Kathy tried to ingratiate herself with Fenton's daughters, if only to please him. Or so it appeared. At one point, she telephoned Judy Goldstone and said she had her mother's ring and jewelry box and that she wanted Goldstone's little daughter, Emily, to have it in memory of her grandmother. Shortly afterward, Fenton arrived at his daughter's home without his bride and left the ring in the mailbox, since his daughters weren't speaking to him. "I had my mother's engagement ring and I was really happy about it," Goldstone recalls thinking at the time.

Several years later, after Kathleen was out of the picture, Fenton was sitting at his daughter's dinner table when he said, "Judith, I want Emily to have Mother's diamond ring." When Goldstone replied that he must have forgotten because he'd already given her the ring, his response left her shaken. "He said, 'No, not *that* diamond,' and I asked, 'What do you mean?' And he said, 'Well, Kathy made up that story about the ring to make you come around to like her. The ring you got was never Mother's ring.'

"Kathy had made up a whole scenario," continues Goldstone, still incredulous years later. "She actually kept my mother's real ring. My father was so crazy in the head and just trying to get along that he never balked at anything Kathy did. He told me he didn't come to the door the day he dropped off the [phony] ring because he was embarrassed.

"That night my father gave me a ring and said, 'This is your mother's *real* diamond, and I want Emily to have it,' and I said 'Fine,' and just let it go. Kathy didn't like me because she couldn't control me, because I refused to ever meet her. I never actually came face-to-face with her in my whole life."

Fenton's daughters believe that the single biggest reason for Kathy's spell over their father, and his obliviousness to what she was doing to him, had to do with the Hilton family. They are certain he was "blinded" by the Hilton fame and wealth. "She played that up," says Goldstone. "He would always tell me, she's part of the Hiltons, her daughter is Kathy Hilton, her son-in-law is Rick Hilton, his father was Conrad Hilton's son. He was completely impressed. He told me, 'I enjoyed going to the Waldorf with them in New York, I enjoyed spending time with Rick—Rick and Kathy were very nice to me. I enjoyed babysitting the boys for them.' He was impressed with Kim being a child star and Kyle being in the movies, and he really wanted me to meet Rick Hilton and make dinner for him when he came to the desert."

On his birthday, and on Father's Day, Fenton always got a nice card from Kathy and Rick. In the envelope was a check, usually for five hundred dollars.

Others, such as Adele Avanzino, saw how "enamored" Fenton was of the Hiltons and how he adored being in their exclusive orbit. "He loved the connection," she says, "until Kathy would say, 'I'm Kathy Richards and I'm Kathy Hilton's mom.' Then Bob would say, 'No, you're not Kathy Richards, you're Kathy Fenton.' He liked the Hilton connection up to a point, but he wanted her to always remember that her last name was Fenton, not Richards or Hilton. He reminded her of that all the time, but she mostly used the name Richards, except if they went someplace like the Waldorf in New York—and then she threw the Hilton name around."

Meanwhile, Kathy began treating Fenton like dirt. She refused to have sex with him and made him sleep in a guest bedroom. When he bought her a gift—an inexpensive Movado watch at the local Costco discount store—she laughed in his face and threw it at him. "What am I going to do with this piece of crap?" she bellowed. "Take it back and buy me a barbecue."

To friends, she boasted, "I don't do *shit* for Bob. I won't travel with him. I won't cook for him. I won't do anything for him."

# CHAPTER 14

**A**round the time that she met husband number four, the Silver Fox, big Kathy learned that husband number one, the Italian Stallion, was dying.

Larry Avanzino, Paris Hilton's maternal grandfather, was in a near vegetative state in a long-term-care nursing facility, mostly for the poor and destitute, in Providence, Rhode Island. He had suffered serious brain injuries when he was viciously assaulted and smashed in the head with a baseball bat and knocked down a flight of stairs. The slugger was believed by family members to be someone close to him, someone to whom he might have been abusive. But nothing ever was proven.

Avanzino had lived a narcissistic and hard life after he and Kathy had gotten divorced, one far removed from that of the Hiltons' glamorous world. Mostly, he worked as a housepainter, drank, pursued women, and made more babies.

When he was in poor financial straits, which was most of the time, he received help from his loving and loyal successful brother, Ken. "Ken owned the building that Larry was living in," says John McKusker, who had witnessed Larry's elopement with Kathleen and was a guest at Paris

Hilton's christening. "Ken was always bailing Larry out of shit. Larry was an alcoholic, a drug addict, whatever."

After his marriage to big Kathy failed, Avanzino had two more wives with whom he fathered three daughters and two sons, who are distant half-sisters and half-brothers of Kathy Hilton's. One of Avanzino's sons, Laurence Jr., was in the Providence, Rhode Island, news in December 1995 when he was a witness for the prosecution in the case of his best friend, who was accused of beating and stabbing to death a girlfriend in an argument over her earnings as a stripper.

Avanzino rarely if ever had contact with his daughter Kathy Hilton as she grew up, or with any of her children, Paris included. As his second wife, Diane Campisi, whom he married in 1964, points out, "Larry didn't bring Kathy up, so nothing in her life had anything to do with him, other than the fact that Kathy Hilton has his genes."

When Campisi first met Avanzino at a cousin's wedding he appeared to have potential, and "anybody would have fallen in love with him," says Campisi's mother, Josephine. "Larry had a Mercedes, a two-seater, with a canvas top, and at that time he was in sales, starting a new job with a company in New York. When Diane was dating him, all the waitresses paid so much attention to him. But his life went downhill. It was very sad."

After the beating, Avanzino was comatose for about two years. His brother, Ken, had advised friends like John McKusker not to visit because of the terrible shape he was in. But when big Kathy learned of his plight she told a friend she had gone to see him and that her onetime Adonis "was toothless. That was all she had to say."

On February 20, 1997, Paris Hilton's maternal grandfather died in his hospital bed at the age of sixty-one. His obituary described him as a "self-employed painter." There was a funeral mass for him in the Most Blessed Sacrament Church in Wakefield, Massachusetts, and he was buried in Oak Grove Cemetery, Medford, Massachusetts.

In the very public world of Kathy Hilton and her most famous daughter, Paris, there has never been a mention of Avanzino. It is as if he had never existed.

· · ·

**SOME TWO MONTHS** after Larry Avanzino died, Ken Richards, big Kathy's second husband, was stricken with cancer of the kidneys that had metastasized to his lungs and his bones. The doctors gave him a year to live.

Richards, who had raised the now-prominent Kathy Hilton from the time she was three years old and was the father of the moneyed and successful Kim and Kyle Richards, was just scraping by, living on his social security and the small salary Sylvia, his wife of almost twenty years, was drawing from her job as personnel manager of a discount store in Boise, Idaho, where the couple lived in a small condominium.

Richards, who was eighty years old and could no longer work, had been virtually abandoned by the Hiltons and by his daughters. With mounting medical bills, Richards, against the advice of his wife, who was "too proud," contacted Kathy and Rick Hilton in New York, explained their dire straits, and asked to borrow some money.

At first the Hiltons made excuses. "Rick told Ken, 'I have kids to put through school. I have party dresses to buy for Paris and Nicky, blah, blah, blah,'" recalls Sylvia Richards, still incredulous and emotional some years later at the Hilton heir's response. "It was very humiliating because Ken had to *beg*. He *literally* had to beg."

Finally, the Hiltons, living in a Manhattan penthouse with a spectacular home in the tony Hamptons, agreed to loan Richards ten thousand dollars. But there was a proviso.

"He made us pay back the loan," states Sylvia Richards. "And they never *once* came to see Ken. Never *once* called and said how are you doing? Are you starving to death? Are you getting your medicine? This is the man who raised Kathy Hilton, but she was in the upper crust now and she didn't need Kenneth."

Choked with emotion, she adds, "Kathy Hilton's just like her mother. She had a very good mentor, and she learned well. Kathleen, the mother, had no soul, and the daughter doesn't either."

With her husband becoming increasingly ill—the cancer had spread to his hips—Sylvia Richards sold their condominium and paid off Hilton, and the Richardses moved in with Sylvia's daughter, Cyndi, from her first marriage, and her husband, who lived in Las Vegas.

"We sold everything, and by the time I paid off Rick I had, I think, one hundred and forty-nine dollars left," says Richards. "We had maxed out our credit cards to pay for Ken's medications."

She says she didn't ask for any more help from Kathy and Rick.

Things only got worse for the Richardses. At her wit's end, Sylvia Richards telephoned her husband's youngest daughter, Kyle, who lived in Beverly Hills, to see if they could stay with her while her father was being treated at the VA hospital in Los Angeles. Kyle and her second husband, Maurico Umansky, a broker at Rick Hilton's high-end real estate agency, Hilton & Hyland, readily agreed.

But when Richards got to the hospital, accompanied by his wife and daughter, he was shocked to learn that the VA had made no room arrangements for him. "Ken was in a wheelchair in terrible pain," says Sylvia Richards. "Kyle called her mother-in-law who is a psychiatrist, and she said to bring Ken to Cedars Sinai and she'd make sure he was admitted." He was there for three weeks, and the cancer had spread throughout his bones, requiring daily radiation treatments.

By then Sylvia Richards had accepted an invitation—one she would come to regret—to stay at Kim Richards's home in suburban Calabasas. "Being at Kim's was just beyond belief," she asserts. "Her father is dying and he's hurting and she would get drunk and jump on the bed, bring the kids in, and could *care less.* Because she was a little girl TV and movie star, she'd been doted on all her life and was very selfish. She thought whatever Kim wanted, that's what should happen."

Richards couldn't take it anymore and told his wife he wanted to return to her daughter's home in Las Vegas where he could have some peace and quiet as death neared, but Kim and Kyle demanded that he stay in California.

"This way," maintains Sylvia Richards, "if they wanted to see him they didn't have to travel very far. They were *that* selfish. One day we were in the room with Kenneth and he was telling Kim we were going to go home, and she *flew* at me, came at me with hands and fists, and physically attacked me. She was screaming that I was trying to take her father away. She called the security patrol and tried to get me removed from her house. She told me that Rick and Kathy were going to do things to me. I said, 'Let 'em come on!' It was a terrible mess. Ken wanted to go home and I was going to take him one way or another."

Kim finally consented and arranged for a plane to fly the Richardses to Las Vegas. The next morning, Ken Richards suffered a heart attack and was rehospitalized for a week. Shortly after he arrived back home, extremely weak, Kim showed up.

"It was midnight and she was drunk on her rear end and blubbering," maintains Sylvia Richards. "She had two strangers bring her to our house in a pickup truck, and she didn't know who those guys were. I refused to let her come in and wake up her father. Later, she told me she had gone to the Las Vegas Hilton and gambled all night."

The next day Ken Richards, in critical condition, was taken to the Nathan Adelson Hospice in Las Vegas. That night his wife slept in a chair next to his bed, knowing he was dying. In the morning, when she went to get breakfast, a nurse found her. "He's fighting to stay alive because he doesn't want to leave you," she told her. "You've got to tell him he can go."

She did, and a short time later Kenneth Richards died. The date was April 28, 1998. His daughters, Kim and Kyle, didn't show up until after he was gone.

Meanwhile, someone at the hospice had notified the Hiltons in New York. While the widow was still in the room with her husband's body— he would be cremated—Rick and Kathy telephoned. "Rick is on the phone and Kathy is in hysterics in the background," says Sylvia Richards, who has never forgotten the moment. "Rick says, 'Kathy needs to talk to her dad.' I said, 'Rick, he's gone.' But he insisted. *'She's got to talk to him.'* Kathy got on the phone. 'Oh, Dad, I love you so much and I miss you. You've done so much for me. . . .' I didn't say anything. I just let her ramble. And I was thinking maybe somebody else was there besides Rick. I thought Kathy was putting on an act because she *never* gave a *damn.* She never showed him *any* love. If she loved him, she would have been there. None of them lifted a finger to help."

Sylvia Richards's daughter, Cyndi, who lived through that horrific period leading up to Richards's death, still sheds tears remembering those events.

"Why didn't Kathy Hilton help him out, because he might have lived longer if she had helped?" she asks, her voice choked with sorrow and anger. "Where the hell was Kathy Hilton when her father died? Getting them to help him was like pulling teeth. By the time they paid back Kathy and Rick for that loan, my mom and dad had no money. The Hiltons are a cruel family."

# CHAPTER 15

**A**s a cancer-riddled Ken Richards was dying in 1998, big Kathy discovered a lump in one of her breasts. It was malignant and would later spread to a lung and then to her brain. Her daughters, who lived on her every word, who were so dependent on her, were devastated.

The Dugan family suddenly seemed cursed by cancer. Both of big Kathy's brothers would be stricken not long after her diagnosis. One would die of cancer of the liver, the other would require treatment for bladder cancer, according to their sister, Donna. Because of the genetics, fear of breast cancer would hang over Kathy Hilton, her daughters, Paris and Nicky, and Hilton's half-sisters, Kim and Kyle.

Big Kathy's initial reaction to the diagnosis was "Oh, no, not me," according to Adele Avanzino. "But then in her next breath it was, 'You know what? I'm going to fight this thing until the end,' which she did. She was unbelievable through the whole thing."

Among the first of her friends she called to break the terrible news was her childhood pal Jane Hallaren. "She said, 'I have cancer and I think this is it.' I burst into tears and she burst into tears. She said, 'I thought I would have so much longer,' and I said, 'I thought you would live forever, too, honey.'"

She also telephoned the man who got away—her first teenage love, Bob Conkey. Big Kathy wept and said, "We never did get together after all these years." She talked about "all those missed moments in life."

Despite her suffering, she also took the opportunity to bad-mouth her caretaker husband, Bob Fenton. "She told me that he basically bull-shitted her when they met, telling her that he had a lot of money, and she said he didn't have any money, and that basically he was living off of her," says Conkey. "It's funny because she thought she was going to live off of him. It was one of those classic—you mean *you* don't have any money, *either*?"

Bob Fenton, who once again would have to care for a wife with can-cer, accompanied her, along with Adele Avanzino and a couple of Kathy Hilton's friends, to the doctor's office in Palm Desert. Big Kathy was adamantly against having a mastectomy, so her course of treatment would involve having surgery to remove the tumor, and then chemo-therapy and radiation. "Nothing is going to put me down," she confi-dently told her husband and companions after the visit. "I'm going to fight this as hard as I can. I have too many things to live for." Always con-cerned about how she looked, she seemed more worried about losing her hair as a result of the chemo than about losing her life.

Ken Richards's widow, Sylvia, who had forged a modicum of a friendship with big Kathy years earlier when they shared his daughters, Kim and Kyle, also had had breast cancer and had decided to have a dou-ble mastectomy in order to survive. "I told Kathy, 'You better have them removed,' but she wouldn't hear of it. She said she had this wonderful doctor who patted her on the butt and pinched her on the boobs and said the way he was treating her was the way to do it. She didn't want to lose her breasts."

However, Kathleen may have had second thoughts mastectomy-wise after she started her treatments. She had another friend who had had the surgery and was then living a normal life. Kathleen's sister,

Madonna, remembers her complaining, "*She's* now on a cruise having a good time, and here *I* am getting chemo and radiation, and dying.' She had a rough ticket with the cancer."

Despite how shabbily big Kathy had treated him, Bob Fenton became her devoted, around-the-clock nurse. Even those in Kathleen's camp who disliked him and believed all the nasty things she had to say about him attest to how concerned and compassionate he was during her illness.

According to Adele Avanzino, Kathleen "felt terrible" that Fenton would have to go through the same trauma he did with his first wife. "I remember her saying, 'Bob, you don't have to go through this with me.' She suffered in his grief, too. He went from one grief to another."

The situation, however, infuriated Fenton's daughters, who saw a completely different picture. "I really felt sorry for my dad because I think he was used," declares Barbara Frank. "Here was this man who was totally vulnerable, who really wasn't thinking clearly, and had just gone through the most horrific, unimaginable loss of my mother to cancer, and then here he had to do it again."

By late 2001, big Kathy's cancer had spread to her brain, and she had to undergo surgery in Los Angeles. It was at that point that she knew she didn't have much time left.

On one occasion, Judy Goldstone called the house hoping to speak with her father, but Kathleen answered. "She started screaming at me," recalls Goldstone. "She told me how much she hated me and what a horrible person I was, and that her cancer had now spread to her brain and that she was going to die, and that I was nothing but 'a cunt.' Then she hung up."

Some six months before she died, Kathleen prepared her will. A relative of Fenton's who was staying at the house at the time had warned him, "You better get in there and listen to everything that is going on, Bob, because she's going to screw you." Fenton's response was "No, she isn't. She loves me."

During Christmas 2001, Adele Avanzino and her brother, Ken, visited Kathleen. "When we got to her house in the afternoon, she opened the door and she was using a walker and she didn't have her wig on. We asked if we could take her to dinner and she said that would be great, that she hadn't been out at all. When we got back to the house, she had her wig on and she was all dolled up and ready for some fun. That was Kathy."

On March 2, 2002, some six weeks before her sixty-fourth birthday, Kathleen Dugan Avanzino Richards Catain Fenton, Paris Hilton's maternal grandmother, died.

She succumbed peacefully in her daughter Kim's home where she had been moved a week or so earlier. Her obituary in the Palm Springs *Desert Sun* newspaper, which was prepared by her daughters, described her glowingly as "a homemaker for twenty-five years."

Kathy Hilton, the first of big Kathy's brood, and son-in-law Rick flew in. Accompanying them was Paris, who arrived with her latest arm candy, hunky model Jason Shaw (with whom she would later appear in a steamy video, reportedly answering the door naked.)

Because a number of friends and family couldn't get in at the same time there were several services for big Kathy, who was cremated. Two small services were held in Kim's home. Fenton is said to have missed the second one because the widower was out playing golf. A larger, private service was held at the Palm Springs Mortuary in nearby Cathedral City, and Kathy Hilton arranged for another in Los Angeles.

In the wake of her death, now two-time widower Bob Fenton quickly came to the stark realization that he should have heeded his relative's warning about monitoring his late wife's will. Aside from the urn containing her ashes, which he kept by the side of his bed, he wound up with nada. The way his daughters saw it, their father had been taken to the cleaners. "Financially, my dad was screwed over big-time," claims Barbara Frank. "He sold his home, gave her the money, moved in with her, and ended up with nothing."

Big Kathy's house, in which Fenton had invested a quarter-million dollars of his own money to fix up, was left to Kathy Hilton, Kim Richards, and Kyle Umansky.

Even from the great beyond, Paris Hilton's devilish maternal grandmother would make life a living hell for her fourth and final husband. According to a stipulation she is said to have made, Bob Fenton was permitted to stay in the house for a year after her death. However, he could not have any female company, or he would be evicted. To make certain that he was abiding by that condition, Kim Richards had been instructed to check to make sure there were no ladies on the premises.

Actually, big Kathy, in one of her last acts in this life, might have been doing a good deed for Fenton by barring women from the house.

Once he got back on his feet he again fell into his serial Casanova persona, met a sexy middle-age babe who his daughter said lived in a trailer park, and married her. The union didn't last very long.

Almost three years to the day that big Kathy passed on, Fenton, who had been battling pancreatic cancer, died. His cremation took place at the Discount Cremation and Burial Services of the Desert in Palm Springs.

Some years after big Kathy's death, her childhood pal, Jane Hallaren, observes: "All Kathleen ever wanted out of life was to see her daughters become stars and marry rich men. Her favorite granddaughter surpassed them all. Whether Kathleen's in heaven or hell, I'll bet she's thinking of Paris and saying, 'You go, girl!'"

# HILTON

## BOOK II:
## PATERNAL ROOTS

# CHAPTER 16

**A** couple of years before his death at ninety-one in 1979, Paris Hilton's great-grandfather, Conrad Hilton, went to the hospital for his annual checkup. He always was as particular about his health as he was about the cleanliness and service in his worldwide chain of hotels. He thought of his thousands of annual guests as his extended family, though actual Hilton family members attest he was perhaps more concerned about his customers than his own brood.

Rarely ill a day in his life, the broad-shouldered, six-foot-two extrovert who often sported a Stetson and cowboy boots would rather walk than ride, and his long legs gave him an Olympian stride.

In fact, it was by fast-stepping up and down Fifth Avenue for days, discreetly scoping out the comings and goings of the then down-on-her-heels Plaza Hotel, that he assured himself she was well worth buying and giving a makeover. He always referred to his hotels in the female form as if they were his mistresses, and he described his love affair with hotels as "a series of romances in which girls played little part."

Affectionately called Connie since childhood, Hilton had enormous charisma and tremendous energy. As the many women in his party-loving, party-giving life noted—such as (almost) Miss Hungary of 1936, Zsa Zsa Gabor, his second wife—Connie was as amply endowed physically as he was financially and had amazing stamina and staying power.

Besides walking, Connie Hilton also got his exercise by dancing the Varsoviana, a waltz done up Texas style, which he learned secretly and on the cheap at an Arthur Murray studio near his Beverly Hills headquarters. He instructed his administrative assistant, close confidante, and rumored onetime sweetheart, Olive Wakeman, to interrupt even his most important business meetings to remind him if he was running late for dance class by whispering, "You have an appointment with Mr. Murray."

So Connie, who in his late eighties had married for a third time, was naturally mighty concerned when the doctors conducting his physical concluded that it might be wise to remove his prostate, the loss of which could severely impact his highly vaunted and much praised boudoir calisthenics, or so he feared.

"The old man stuck his head up and says, 'Well, now, doc, how's that gonna affect my sex life? You ain't taking *that* out, if I can't get *this* up.' He's almost ninety, for Christ's sake, and he's worried about his sex life," recalls Maxwell House coffee heir Bob Neal, still shaking his head in awe years later at Connie's geriatric virility. "He sure liked to chase the girls pretty good."

In his eighties Connie still enjoyed flirting with young women, such as pretty and perky Gini Tangalakis, who worked as one of the Hilton Corp.'s lower-echelon secretaries. When she was at home sick with a cold, the most powerful hotelman in the world telephoned this twenty-one-year-old engaged-to-be-married office worker. "'Oh, I understand that you're not well. Is there anything I can do for you? Anything at all?' I told him I just had the flu and that I appreciated his concern. 'Well, Gini, do you have a nurse? If there's anything I can do, feel free to call me.'" The next day he called her again. "'When you get back to the office, why don't you come up. I'd like to see you.'" When Gini got a small paper cut and was asking one of the other ladies in the office for a Band-Aid, Connie suddenly was hovering over her with concern—and romance— in his eyes. "He took my hand in his—'Are you okay? Can I help? Here, let me see your little finger.'" She feared he was going to kiss it.

Connie had come on to another office girl who had occasionally visited him at his Bel-Air estate on weekends, where they would have lunch at poolside and he would watch her swim. "She would just spend the day enjoying his compound more than actually, I think, being with him," says Tangalakis years later. "She took it for what it was—just an old man who wanted a little female companionship. That was kind of how he flirted. He'd say, 'Why don't you come to my house for brunch and a swim?'"

As Bob Neal notes with delight, "The old man was a *real* cocksman."

**CONRAD NICHOLSON HILTON** came from the most humble of beginnings. He was born on Christmas Day 1887, in a primitive adobe dwelling in San Antonio, Socorro County, in what would become Texas but was then the rugged and barren New Mexico territory.

He was the first of four brothers (one of whom died at the age of two) and he had four sisters, brought into the world by slight, prematurely gray Mary Laufersweiler Hilton, a domineering, staunchly religious Roman Catholic of German heritage. Like clockwork, at sunup and sundown every day she dropped to her knees with her children gathered around her to pray, and on Sundays she traveled for miles through the wilderness to attend mass.

Connie was named for his maternal grandfather, Conrad Laufersweiler, and his middle name, Nicholson, was in honor of the longtime family doctor who delivered him. Connie was the fair-haired one whom his mother most loved and coddled. He would later describe her as "the loveliest lady I have ever known and the most gallant." She would have an enormous psychological impact on his bizarre relationships with women later in life, and two of the three women he chose to marry, the first and third of his wives, were named Mary, like his mother. In his eyes, "Mary was a lady."

While Connie inherited his strong religious beliefs from his mother, it was from his brawny, robust Norwegian father, Augustus Holver Hilton, a man who cared little about religion or prayer, that he got his mind for business. He had his father's big hands, big feet, big voice, and big ambition. Connie would even sport a mustache like him, too.

The Hilton-Laufersweiler union took place on Lincoln's birthday in 1885. Called Gus, or "the Colonel," the Hilton patriarch had built "a tidy little empire," A. H. Hilton, in San Antonio, that included a general store. Along with selling and trading, he was a loan shark of sorts—called "grubstakers" in those days—who supplied provisions and money to prospectors in return for a share of their profits.

San Antonio was a trading center, and A. H. Hilton sold and bartered everything from groceries to coffins, and when things were slow, the strapping Norwegian went into the wilderness buying and trading beaver pelts and furs and dealing tobacco and groceries to trappers. He liked to boast about his adventures and once even sold an article about them to the newspaper in Albuquerque, often reading it aloud to whoever would listen.

Connie remembered Gus Hilton as a "Viking of a man with energy to burn," who considered seven o'clock in the morning the middle of the day. A jovial backslapper, Gus loved nothing more than to bargain with his customers when they claimed his prices were too high; it was from his type-A father that Connie learned the "art of the deal."

The older Hilton instilled the values of working hard and making money in Connie, who earned five dollars a month during two summers laboring in the family store. Once, when he overslept, he heard the disappointment in his father's booming voice. "Mary, I do *not* know what will become of Connie. I'm afraid he'll never amount to anything. He'll sleep his *life* away."

Like many in the Hilton dynasty—all the way up through and including Paris—Connie would have limited schooling, bouncing from one institution of learning to another, though he dreamed in his youth of going to Dartmouth, a fantasy dashed by hard times. As he later acknowledged, "My so-called formal education was pretty informal."

He received his basic reading, writing, and arithmetic in a one-room adobe grammar school. He attended some classes at the Goss Military Institute in Albuquerque but found the discipline too rigorous, and he was pleased when the school burned down, a fire he later claimed he "took no active hand in." For a time he studied at the School of Mines at Socorro and at St. Michael's College, run by strict Christian Brothers, in

Santa Fe, mainly because his mother made him attend. For a time he was also a cadet at the New Mexico Military Institute.

**THROUGH THE 1890S** and early 1900s A. H. Hilton went through boom times, so much so that the money rolling in permitted the family to move in 1905 to sunny Long Beach, California, and rent a beautiful home a block from the ocean, while Gus Hilton stayed in San Antonio running the business. The Hiltons' high life, however, was short-lived. Everything went bust in 1907 when there was a run on a New York bank, touching off a currency panic that spread across the land. The Hiltons were left holding the bag, their warehouses filled with merchandise that no one had the money to buy.

One of their salable assets, Connie quickly realized, was the rooms in their sprawling adobe home that had been added on over the years as each new Hilton arrived into the world. Connie, then twenty years old, and his father envisioned their hacienda as a stop on the road for traveling salesmen, miners, and railroad people who needed a comfortable bed and a warm meal.

Thus, the first informal Hilton Hotel was born, with Connie running things as day manager, night manager, room service clerk, and concierge. When the midnight, morning, and noon trains arrived in town with weary, hungry travelers, Connie was at the station to hustle them to the Hilton. As he later stated, "I can't honestly say I fell in love with the hotel business as it was practiced by the Hilton family in 1907 or began to dream of the Waldorf or the Plaza." The business then was more "a case of urgent necessity."

But, like everything else Hilton through the years, it was a great success. The guests and the money rolled in. In less than a year the Hiltons had to hire outside help. Because the jerry-rigged hotel was a hit, Connie rated himself a "boy genius."

When Hilton was twenty-one, his father gave him control of the family store in San Antonio and a share of the profits in the family business, now called A. H. Hilton & Son.

In 1912, when New Mexico became the forty-seventh state, Connie, at twenty-five, thought politics would look good on his résumé. He decided to run as a Republican candidate for the new state legislature. Like Paris Hilton's maternal great-grandfather, her paternal great-grandfather also would become a politico.

The elections were "ruthless" and "only the fit" were able to survive. There were allegations that one side voted a herd of sheep, while the other the entire populace of the local cemetery. The dead and the sheep had spoken, and Connie Hilton beat his Democratic opponent by 243 votes, becoming the youngest representative to New Mexico's first state legislature.

Connie utilized his two-year term by conducting a self-improvement program. Despite his supreme self-confidence, he dreaded speaking publicly, which he realized was a fatal flaw for a politician. When he was asked to make his first big political speech, he looked at the crowd and froze. His ultrareligious mother, however, heard one of his practice speeches, told him to forget about the teachings of Grenville Kleiser's "Course in Public Speaking," and intoned, "All those trimmings are sinful.... You'd do better to pray about it than practice *this*."

He followed Mary Hilton's advice, prayed on the opening day of the legislature, and made an acceptable speech. His stage fright never returned.

Connie's womanizing days had started in earnest, too. He courted all sorts, including the vivacious debutante daughter of a judge and a hottie from Chicago who taught him ragtime "animal dances" like the grizzly-bear and the kangaroo-dip.

Politics, meanwhile, frustrated him. Once he witnessed the corruption, the graft, the self-interest, and the red tape, he never sought reelection. Instead, he envisioned himself as a wealthy banker. With almost $3,000 of his own money, plus some $27,000 more he raised from investors, he actually was able to open the New Mexico State Bank of San Antonio in September 1913, when he was just twenty-six. But the shareholders—"the smart-money boys," as he called them—soon took control and Connie was named the bank's cashier, unpaid no less. He fought back and collected enough proxies by the time of the first stockholders' meeting to win back control, but by then the bank had gone bust. But Connie, never one to give up, booted the old guard, became vice president, and in two years the bank grew with assets of $135,000. He considered himself a success.

His banking career, however, ended when America entered the First World War.

Connie enlisted in the army in 1917, went to officers' candidate school, and served in France, where, though he never saw a day of combat, he did manage to enjoy the painted ladies and the cheap champagne. The only personal tragedy he suffered was the death of his father, who was killed in a car accident back home.

At the time of the armistice with Germany, Connie was serving in the cushy Paris office of the army's chief purchasing agent, with headquarters in the posh Hotel Élysée Palace, on the Champs Élysées. Connie himself was comfortably billeted in a nice little apartment on Rue de Bassano, with a cook to serve him, no less. "This," he later acknowledged, "is going to war in style."

When he returned home in mid-February 1919, he had $5,000 and change in savings—and a big dream of becoming wealthy and powerful. The dream would be fulfilled in the dusty, raucous Texas town of Cisco.

# CHAPTER 17

In 1893, a tornado swept through Cisco, some fifty miles east of Abilene. The twister cut a devastating swath, killing more than two dozen and flattening most of the businesses and homes.

The next big wind to hit Cisco was Connie Hilton, his arrival coming just as the Roaring Twenties were about to begin. "I thought, dreamed, schemed of nothing but how to get a toehold in this amazing pageant that was Texas," he stated years later. "It was waiting for me in Cisco."

Once known as Red Gap, Cisco had been renamed in the early 1880s in honor of a New York financier, John A. Cisco, who built the Houston and Texas Central Railway, which intersected with the Texas and Pacific line. The railroad turned the town into the heavily touted "Gate City of the West," a bustling commercial center that attracted immigrant workers and entrepreneurs alike. Connie saw it as a "cow town gone crazy." He also saw his destiny there.

Initially, he thought of establishing another bank; there was one for sale, and three others in town. He was prepared to buy, but when the seller saw how anxious Connie was, he raised the price by five thousand dollars and told him "no haggling." A born haggler, Connie passed.

Then he took a look at the two-story, red brick Mobley Hotel down the dusty street. When he saw the jammed lobby and heard the desk clerk yell "Full up!" he sought out the owner, who considered the place nothing more than a fleabag, a "glorified boarding house," and was willing to unload "the whole shooting match" for $50,000 in cash. With his five thousand dollars in savings burning a hole, Connie anxiously telephoned friends and family for the remaining $45,000. Even his mother, looking for a tidy profit that she knew her little boy could make, chipped in five big ones.

When the deal was consummated, he sent her a telegram: "Frontier found. Water deep down here. Launched first ship in Cisco."

"The Mobley," Connie later told *Time* magazine, when he made the cover some years later, "wasn't exactly a hotel—it was sort of a flophouse. We considered it a bad day when we didn't have a three-time turnover on the beds. It was a bad night when I had a bed of my own."

The hotel generated three thousand dollars the first month. Practically overnight, he had renovated the Mobley's lobby, shuttered the little greasy spoon attached to the hotel, and put in more beds; he had the front desk cut in half, installed a newsstand that sold tobacco, and trashed the potted palm in favor of a stand that sold novelties.

With the Mobley, Connie set in stone some of the Hilton Hotel management philosophy that continued into the twenty-first century, which was to replace wasted space with moneymaking space. He also gave pep talks to his Mobley employees, giving them a sense of pride, with a promise of better wages.

In return, he asked them for complete and utter loyalty to him and his guests. He demanded that his employees offer service with a smile and provide clean rooms, spotless halls, fresh soap and linen. Connie also was credited with a ten-point "Code for Success" that would appear in "This Week," a Sunday magazine newspaper supplement, which boasted the "world's largest circulation" of more than fourteen million readers:

1. Find your own particular talent.
2. Be big.
3. Be honest.
4. Live with enthusiasm.
5. Don't let your possessions possess you.
6. Don't worry about your problems.
7. Look up to people when you can—down to no one.
8. Don't cling to the past.
9. Assume your full share of responsibility in the world.
10. Pray consistently and confidently.

**CONNIE'S NEXT HOTEL,** The Melba, was in Fort Worth and was a grim and grimy sixty-eight-room place. However, he got another good deal, and within ninety days he had the place spick and span and minting money.

Then came the Waldorf—not the biggie in New York that he one day would own, but the six-story frumpy-dumpy Waldorf in Dallas. Other small and medium hotels became part of the growing Hilton chain. He had savvy partners who helped him along the way with financing and business acumen, but they didn't always see eye to eye.

That was underscored tragically in the lobby of the Dallas Waldorf in April 1922, when one partner shot and killed another. When the shooter was released from prison, Connie feared he'd come gunning for him. There are two accounts of what happened next. In one, Connie convinced the prison chaplain to have the paroled gunman go to the West Coast and out of his range of fire; in the other Connie invited the man to his office and had his army automatic at the ready, but the man never showed, and the danger passed.

As Connie sped toward making his first million, his siblings also were doing well. One brother had gone to the Naval Academy in Annapolis and became an officer; another was studying at Dartmouth; a sister had married wealthy and was a young matron residing in a Massachusetts mansion; another was an actress in the road company of *The Gold-diggers*; and the youngest was valedictorian of her high school class. A cousin had won election to the U.S. Senate. The Hiltons were quite a successful, driven clan.

In the five years since he bought the Mobley, Connie had developed the expertise, put together the team, and had access to the kind of financing that allowed him to break ground on July 26, 1924, for the first full-fledged Hilton Hotel. It would be the Dallas Hilton, erected on land leased for ninety-nine years, rather than land he had to pay for out of pocket.

Connie used the leased land as collateral for a half-million-dollar bank loan, put up $100,000 of his own money, and raised another $200,000 from chums. He even convinced the building contractor to toss $150,000 in the pot. And when he ran out of money, Connie urged George Loudermilk, the former undertaker from whom he had leased the land, to put the finishing touches on the hotel and even furnish it. Connie was a natural-born businessman, a shrewd operator and manipulator who didn't need a Harvard MBA to succeed.

With his growing riches, he joined a fancy golf club, started playing tennis, danced with beautiful young women, and even leased a theater, the Circle, in Dallas, where he started producing plays with a stranded stock company.

Connie Hilton was going on forty and still a bachelor. But not for long.

**IN HIS 1957 AUTOBIOGRAPHY,** *Be My Guest,* Connie painted a saintly portrait of the young woman he married, who became the matriarch of the contemporary Hilton clan—Paris Hilton's paternal great-grandmother. Her name was Mary Adelaide Barron, of Owensboro, Kentucky. Despite Connie's glowing account of her in his book, she displayed, in fact, some of the same uninhibited traits as Paris's maternal grandmother, big Kathy.

Connie and his ghostwriter, Elaine St. Johns, described Mary Barron as a churchgoing gal—"pretty, vivacious, alert, with laughing eyes . . . and the soft Kentucky voice." He claimed he first spotted her in a red hat several pews in front of him at one glorious morning mass when she was visiting a cousin, Beauregard Evans, in Dallas, but lost her in the crowd when he tried to follow her out, and then spent "a month of Sundays" at mass in hopes of running into her again. They eventually were introduced; he wined and dined her; and they fell in love. Once his Dallas Hilton was completed, she promised she'd come back to marry him.

Before she bade him adieu, the love-struck bachelor asked her to leave her red hat with him. In her absence he contented himself "with flying the red hat from my bedpost."

What *Be My Guest* didn't reveal was that Mary Barron Hilton, for whom Barron Hilton was named, was a happy-go-lucky, curvy and buxom brunette with Mary Astor looks who hailed from the Kentucky backwoods. A barely educated eighteen-year-old who liked her moonshine, loved to gamble, cursed like a sailor, and savored telling dirty jokes, she had a raucous whiskey laugh and came from what today might be described as trailer park trash. What's more, *Be My Guest* quickly skipped over the fact that Connie was twice his teen bride's age.

But it's no surprise that Mary Barron pledged before she returned to her old Kentucky home that she'd be back to be the innkeeper's wife. After all, what pretty gal in her right mind who lived the real-life simple life in the country without indoor plumbing and six brothers wouldn't hitch her star to a sugar daddy who owned the beginnings of an international hotel chain?

On paper, though, Mary Adelaide Barron's lineage looked just fine. Her father, Thomas Mason Barron II, was a descendant of George Mason, a patriot, statesman, and liberal delegate from Virginia to the U.S. Constitutional Convention. He has been called the "father of the Bill of Rights," which makes Paris Hilton a distant descendant by marriage of one of the drafters.

But Tommy Barron, Mary's father, was no patrician politician. He was blue collar and a good ol' boy through and through—a tobacco-chewing, moonshine-swilling native of Owensboro who was known in those parts of Kentucky as a tobacco "pinhooker," a speculator who bought poorly prepared tobacco at auction, took out the bad parts, and resold it. "He made a modest living at that," according to Jarred Barron, Mary's first cousin.

"Mary's family didn't have much," says Jarred, who at eighty-seven (in 2005) was one of the last remaining Barrons who had a clear recollection of his late cousin and her world when she became involved with Connie. "Back then her family moved to different places. For a while they lived with my grandfather, on the farm right close to where I'm sittin' right now in Owensboro. They raised tobacco and corn pigs. Mary's house didn't have running water, and her father, who had seven kids to support, drank a little too much."

If Mary Barron graduated in the 1924 class of Owensboro High School, as Jarred Barron recollects, school officials had no record of her attendance.

"Mary was young, around sixteen or eighteen years old, awfully good-looking and had a terrific personality, and was visiting a relative who lived in Dallas and met Conrad Hilton down there," recalls Barron, who was a dozen years younger than his pretty cousin. "The family wasn't too happy about it because Mr. Hilton was so much older."

Mayme Mulligan Barron, Mary's mother, was like Connie's, a staunch Catholic who attended every mass at St. Stephen's Catholic Church in Owensboro. That fact alone helped smooth things over with the deeply religious Mary Hilton, who had her doubts about whether this unsophisticated teenage looker was the one with whom her prized son should spend the rest of his life. "Mayme was a strong—*strong*—Catholic," says Jarred Barron.

The grand opening of the Dallas Hilton occurred on August 4, 1925. The place was an instant moneymaker and was Connie's first "mini-max," as he later termed it—minimum cost, maximum hospitality.

"I had climbed Mount Everest," Connie boasted, and now he was raring to get hitched.

Keeping her promise, Mary Barron returned to Dallas to marry Connie just one month after the opening. In a simple ceremony at six o'clock mass on September 7, 1925, Connie Hilton, thirty-eight, and Mary Barron, nineteen, were married by the Reverend Thomas Powers at Holy Trinity Church in Dallas. Mary's hometown newspaper, the Owensboro *Messenger*, described the bride as "a popular member of the younger social circle of Owensboro. The groom is president of a chain of hotels and is a prominent businessman of Dallas." The newspaper noted that the newlyweds "left for a two months' tour of Canada and the Eastern states before returning to Dallas to reside."

One of their stops on the honeymoon was Chicago, where the newlyweds checked into the bustling LaSalle Hotel, which was fully booked. To impress his young bride, Connie whipped out his new business card—Conrad N. Hilton, President, Hilton Hotels—and the couple were quickly ushered to a room. Connie came away telling Mary, "Someday I'm going to come back and find a vacant lot. I'd like to build me a hotel here." It was that kind of talk that would make him so successful, and would eventually wreak havoc on their marriage.

Ten months after their nuptials their first son, Conrad Nicholson "Nick" Hilton Jr., future darling of the gossip columns, was born on July 6, 1926. Nick, who looked like his mother, had "big eyes, curly hair, and was quite a howler," said the proud father, who felt having a son as his firstborn was "the main event."

At the time, the Hiltons were living in Dallas's chicest residence, the eleven-story beaux arts–style Stoneleigh Court, an elegant apartment-hotel, which was the first luxury building of its kind in Dallas and the tallest hotel west of the Mississippi at the time. The Hiltons' suite boasted a telephone, a wireless connection to the hotel's own high-powered radio station, and circulating ice water in the kitchenette's mechanical refrigerator, and each bedroom had a Murphy "California" wall-bed. The Stoneleigh was heralded as "the ideal home where all housekeeping problems have been solved for you."

And what's more, hotelier Connie got a steep trade discount on the rent. He liked to make money, not spend it, and through the years he'd earn a reputation as a tightwad.

With the new baby in tow, Connie bought an elegant four-bedroom home at 4800 St. John's Drive, one of the most prestigious streets in fashionable Highland Park, an exclusive residential little city designed by a Beverly Hills landscape architect.

With wife and baby settled in, he returned to what he most loved—building the Hilton Hotel chain. His immediate plans were for more Texas Hiltons—Abilene, Waco, Marlin, Lubbock, El Paso, and way stops in between. He planned to open, as he vowed to Mary, "a hotel a year."

However, he did take time from his to-do list to make another baby, William Barron Hilton, who came into the world on October 23, 1927, fifteen months after Nick. Barron was born just two months before his father's fortieth birthday on Christmas Day 1927. By then, Connie had more than the holiday to celebrate. He now had hotels in Dallas, Abilene, Waco, Plainview, San Angelo, and Lubbock—and was close to renting two thousand rooms a night, all with the help of friendly bankers and venture capitalists. Outside of Texas, he planned for Hiltons in Oklahoma City; Wichita, Kansas; and Mobile, Alabama.

His biggest venture to date, however, was the Hilton in El Paso, to be built at a cost of $1,750,000 under the umbrella of his newly organized Hilton Hotels, Inc., a consolidation of all his properties in one fat, money-making group.

Connie, however, didn't see the approaching storm. Less than three weeks after he announced the El Paso venture, investors and speculators were jumping out of windows as they watched their stocks fall like dead ducks shot out of the sky.

"Wall Street Lays an Egg," the entertainment trade paper *Variety* famously declared, marking the devastating stock market crash of October 1929. The nation, the rest of the world, and Connie Hilton were about to sink into the Great Depression.

# CHAPTER 18

**D**espite the horrific economic climate, Connie managed to open his nineteen-story, three-hundred-room El Paso Hilton on November 5, 1930, a year after the Wall Street crash. Thousands had turned out, not for rooms, but rather to gawk at his new palace with its luxuriant penthouses. The way Connie saw it, the crowds were there seeking "reassurance" that the times weren't as bad as they seemed, and that the new Hilton edifice represented hope in the face of hardship.

Along with the financial doom and gloom—and Connie knew he was in for some rough times business-wise—he also now faced the prospect of a failed marriage.

Mary Hilton was at the opening in El Paso, but after all the congratulatory speeches were concluded, her husband looked over and she was nowhere to be seen. One of Connie's sisters, who also noted her hasty departure, asked whether he thought his hotel obsession bored her. He couldn't conceive of such a notion. Even more troublesome was his sister's perception that Mary Hilton viewed Connie's love affair with hotels as a "rival." His sister warned, "Mary's young and used to a lot of attention."

Connie argued that he paid his pretty wife lots of notice, that he lavished her with gifts, that he gave her two sons. But he realized he was rationalizing what was a deteriorating domestic situation, a situation that would only grow worse as he worked day and night to keep his hotels afloat in those bad economic times, while Mary was up to who knows what in his absence.

"And so it went," he stated in *Be My Guest.* "With me dashing all over Texas—and Mary alone at home . . . what happened to Mary and me didn't come all at once. But, as I floundered . . . fighting desperately . . . little by little the laughter went out of Mary's eyes."

Oddly, in the midst of their deteriorating marriage, twenty-six-year-old Mary became pregnant in early October 1932, and on July 1, 1933, gave birth to a third son, who was named Eric Michael Hilton.

The only mention of Eric's birth in *Be My Guest* is a reference to two brief notations Connie had made at the time in his diary, which was otherwise filled with his main interest—the Depression-era business affairs of his hotels. One was "Mary is expecting a baby." The other was "July 1, Eric Michael Hilton born at St. Paul's at ten A.M."

Later, there were other references in his diary regarding his marriage: "trouble at home . . . another quarrel, worse than before . . . Mary tense and tearful . . ."

Like his mother and his mother-in-law, Connie was a staunch Catholic who believed in all of the church's teachings, including the ban on divorce. With the Depression wreaking havoc on his business and the country at large, he noted in *Be My Guest* that he had become even more pious. "In over forty years I had never, without good reason, missed a Sunday Mass," he declared. "Now I started every single day on my knees in church."

One would have expected, then, that a divorce would be entirely out of the question for the devout hotelman. It was, as he himself stated, "a bitter pill to swallow." Nevertheless, he claimed, "all semblance of harmony had gone from our relationship. The breach was too wide to heal."

The way he described the marital situation, it was his wife and the mother of his children who wanted the divorce. As Connie put it, "I couldn't blame Mary. What kind of life had she led over the past three years? I couldn't honestly blame myself. What else could I have done but what I did?"

He said he intensely "resisted" a divorce because it meant "long, lonely years" ahead for him, and just thinking about his sons coming from a "broken home" made him feel "leaden." In the end, though, he rationalized the marriage's demise as a "casualty" of the Depression.

This is what actually happened.

Not long after Eric Hilton was born, Connie and Mary separated, and she moved with the baby to El Paso. Moreover, it was Connie, not Mary, who filed for divorce—strange, since she appeared to be the injured party in the marriage, according to the scenario laid out in *Be My Guest.*

On June 11, 1934, the divorce decree was issued, ending the Hilton union of nine years—eleven months after Eric's birth. Nick was about to turn eight, and Barron seven years old. While Connie showed up in court with his attorney, the court record shows that Mary Barron Hilton had oddly waived her right to appear.

Regarding the issue of child custody, Judge Royall B. Watkins ruled in favor of Connie. Such decisions are rare, with the mother usually being granted custody, unless there are circumstances regarding her moral character. But the court found that Connie was "able and capable of caring for and educating the minor children . . . and that he is a proper person to have the care, maintenance, and control of said children." Mary gained only visitation rights "at all reasonable times and places that may be agreeable" to Connie.

Judge Watkins also approved a property settlement between Connie and Mary that was far more punitive than generous. Though she was given all the household goods, furniture, and effects, all other property, including their home, was granted to Connie. In addition, the millionaire hotelman had only to give his wife a sum total of thirty-six hundred dollars, paid in installments of three hundred dollars a month, with the first such payment due on July 15, 1934.

The question remains: why was the wife of America's up-and-coming hotel czar treated so harshly? What never was revealed in *Be My Guest,* and has been a long-held Hilton family secret—one of many—

was that Mary, who felt abandoned by Connie, had had a torrid affair with a charismatic, renowned Texas football coach by the name of Mack Saxon. As Mary's cousin Jarred Barron states, "Connie was working so hard he wasn't giving Mary her proper attention and it ended up she strayed away."

One of the El Paso College of Mines' legendary players, Ken Heineman, who played under Coach Saxon, clearly remembers Mary "being around as Mack's girlfriend" while she was still married to Connie.

"She would come to El Paso and Connie wouldn't be with her and everybody knew that they were having an affair," says Heineman. "Mary was very good-looking—a real cutie—and Mack was a good-looking guy, and he was very attractive to women, and he had a reputation as a drinker and a rounder. We knew that he caroused. That's the way he came to the attention of Hilton's wife. Mack was a handsome celebrity in town, and she just got tired of Conrad."

The son of a Methodist minister, Saxon had lettered at the University of Texas in 1925 and was captain of the Longhorn squad and All-Conference quarterback in 1926. He was considered the team's greatest ground-gaining star at the time.

"Mack was a real intelligent, bright, energetic man, but he drank too much," says his nephew Milton Saxon. "He started drinking when he became a coach, and as head coach he was part of El Paso society, and that's how his meeting Conrad Hilton's wife all came about."

Although Connie had been given custody of little Eric, he would have no role in bringing up the boy. Instead, Eric was raised by Saxon and Mary, who were married in the Fort Worth, Texas, courthouse on Saturday evening, June 1, 1935—right after she had collected the last of Connie's monthly divorce installments. Their marriage made the "Dallas Social Affairs" column of the *Dallas Morning News,* mainly because of Saxon's celebrity.

Connie also would have only a minor role in raising his other two sons, Nick and Barron. Curiously, even though he and Mary had a horrific marriage and hellish divorce, it was Mary's mother, Mayme Barron, who left her home in Owensboro to move to Dallas and help care for the boys. As Mary's cousin Jarred Barron observes, "Mary's mother was a jewel and she went down and raised those two boys. She was just that kind of person."

Connie needed her help because his sons were a handful. In *Be My Guest,* he described young Nick as "mercurial, outgoing, spontaneous," while Barron was a problem eater and was "careful, quiet, single-minded . . . Nick got into more mischief, but Barron was harder to handle." Connie's mother, Mary Hilton, had rightly perceived, "Nick has charm. Barron has determination."

For example, when Barron was a young teenager away at school, he penned a letter to his father negotiating for a higher allowance. While it was poorly spelled, he detailed, accountant-like, each one of his expenses, such as "Tellephone . . . 50c per week." He determined he was losing seven cents out of each two dollars of allowance and demanded five dollars a week, leaving him two dollars and fifty cents for "weekend pleasures." He ended the letter by writing, "Sorry this is all business," and signed it, "Your loving son, Barron Hilton." During World War II, Barron would raise chickens in the backyard of his father's Bel-Air mansion, *Beverly Hillbillies* style, and sell them to the home kitchen, unloading the rest to his father's hotel in Los Angeles.

But the boys rarely saw their father, who was often away on business—his hotels took precedence—and, having watched their parents' marriage fall apart, the Hilton lads were out of control. At one point, the boys infuriated neighbors by painting the front steps of their elegant home a bright orange. In *Be My Guest,* Connie contended that Barron had suffered a severe eye injury when he fell out of a tree house. But years later, Nick told friends that he had actually thrown a toy train engine at Barron during one of their many fights, a sibling rivalry that would only get worse through the years.

**A DARK CLOUD** appeared to hang over the union of Mack and Mary Barron Hilton Saxon. Along with the loss of twins at birth (she'd been pregnant when they were married), she was almost responsible for the deaths of herself, Nick, who had just turned fourteen, and Barron, two months away from his thirteenth birthday.

Around 2:45 on the morning of August 13, 1940, a bellboy at the El

Paso Hilton was returning to the hotel after delivering mail to the post office when he saw smoke pouring from the ninth floor. Apparently inebriated, Mary had fallen asleep while smoking a cigarette. Her bed was in flames, and smoke had filled the room when firemen reached her ninth-floor suite.

Saxon had been awakened by heavy smoke and rushed across the hall, where the coach found Mary standing bewildered and choking. Saxon ushered her and Barron to safety at the end of the hall and then raced back to the smoke-filled suite where he found Nick at the living room window and brought him out without injury.

The front page of the *El Paso Herald Post* that day had the blaring headline:

## MINES COACH RESCUES FAMILY FROM FIRE
### *Mrs. Mack Saxon And Two Sons Taken From Smoke Filled Suite At Hilton Hotel*

Saxon's life started falling apart in the early 1940s when he was fired from his coaching job after the team had a string of losses. Privately, his drinking was blamed for his demise, and the word was out that he had been fired. Years later, his nephew, Milton Saxon, says he was told by a football coach that Mack could have coached more important teams "if he hadn't been such a heavy drinker."

After the Japanese attack on Pearl Harbor, Saxon joined the navy and headed the athletic training program at the Banana River, Florida, Naval Air Station, with the rank of lieutenant commander in the Naval Reserve. After the war, he was named civilian assistant to the head of the navy's aviation physical training program headquartered at the Pentagon.

The Saxons and their son, Eric, lived in circumstances far different from those of his Hilton siblings.

The Saxon family set up housekeeping in a rented two-bedroom, two-story red brick row house in Fairlington Village, modest housing in northern Virginia built for some three thousand defense workers during the war and located near Saxon's Pentagon job.

While Nick and Barron were sent by their father to private Catholic and military schools—they both spent some time at the same military school where Connie had gone—Eric was enrolled in the Arlington County, Virginia, public schools, attending Dolley Madison Jr. High School and Washington-Lee High School. Unlike Connie, Mack and Mary Saxon couldn't afford fancy schools for Eric.

Eric's friends from his school days in Virginia remember never being invited into the Saxon home or ever meeting the Saxons, possibly due to their drinking. However, they have fond memories of Eric as a scrappy, fun-loving regular guy who liked girls and basketball, not necessarily in that order.

Though the kids in his circle heard talk that he was the son of the famous hotelman, "I don't think he was close to him in those days at all," says a pal, Larry Linderer. "Eric's mother looked after him. We were pretty poor in those days, and our housing in Fairlington was very transient—people coming into the government, leaving the government. I wouldn't call them projects, but . . . it was nothing like you would think of for the son of Conrad Hilton."

Eric and Linderer were part of a street gang. "We were from North Fairlington and ran around the neighborhood and terrorized the guys from South Fairlington," recalls Linderer. "When we caught 'em, we'd give 'em pink bellies. We weren't vicious, just kind of, 'You guys stay on your side of the highway, and we'll stay on our side.'"

Eric was a bit of a junior Casanova and would later earn a reputation as a full-fledged womanizer. "Every Valentine's Day he used to leave a box of candy on my doorstep and run away," says one of his early pursuits, Carol Furman Kane, who went to junior recreation club dances with him and has never forgotten his "very, *very* bright blue eyes, black hair, great big grin, and lots of freckles. He'd always leave the candy when Lent had begun, and I'd given up candy, but my mother just absolutely adored him, so she got to eat all the candy."

By the time Eric was in his young teens, Connie, who had recovered from the Depression without too much damage and was on a hotel-buying spree, had purchased his fourteenth: the one-thousand-room Mayflower, rich with political legend, in the nation's capital, located just across the Potomac River from Arlington. Eric gleefully announced one day that he had been given permission by Connie to throw a party in one of the Mayflower's posh suites. "Eric was given the suite for a weekend," recalls Carol Furman Kane, "and he invited a group of boys and girls to dinner at his private suite, and, of course, all the mothers of the girls said, 'Oh, no you don't!' But I understand the boys all had a great time."

On Sunday morning, May 8, 1949, Mary Saxon awakened to find the love of her life lying lifeless beside her. At the age of forty-seven, after years of hard drinking, Mack Saxon had died in his sleep. The cause of death was listed as a heart attack, though friends of Eric heard he had taken his own life. Saxon was buried with military honors at Arlington National Cemetery.

At forty-three, with a teenage son to raise, Mary Barron Hilton Saxon, a serious alcoholic, was suddenly a widow. She soon moved back to El Paso where her drinking and carousing often left young Eric to fend for himself, sometimes "begging neighbors for food" because his mother had forgotten to shop for groceries. As a close Hilton relative observes, "Eric had a tough life growing up."

# CHAPTER 19

*T*hrough the Depression and his divorce, Connie Hilton remained an optimist. While other hotelmen were watching their properties sink like the *Titanic,* he planned for the future. Traveling across Texas doing everything he could to salvage his business, he read a magazine article about a grand new hotel that had recently opened in New York City. It was called the Waldorf-Astoria. He cut out the article, folded it neatly, and placed it in his wallet. One day, he envisioned, it would be his.

As the Depression wore on, Connie was able to buy back hotels he had lost in El Paso and Abilene, and soon he was buying new ones again, such as the Paso del Norte in El Paso, which he quickly flipped for a profit. The next was the Gregg Hotel in Longview, which became the Longview Hilton. The owner, a doctor, made Connie an offer he couldn't refuse—he could buy the place on time, could borrow against it, and the doctor would, if needed, even lend him money to expand it. Connie saw the Longview as a gift from heaven, and he went in a new direction; he started scooping up Depression-era white elephants at fire-sale prices.

Back in business, the hotel shopaholic began a nonstop spending spree. Forming a buying group, he snapped up some beauties. One was the elegant 22-story, 450-room Sir Francis Drake, in the heart of San Francisco, which even came with a new, thriving nightclub. The hotel alone had cost more than $4 million to build; Connie picked it up for chump change—$275,000 in cash. Comparing it again to a woman, he stated, "While I had loved my dowagers, gotten tremendous satisfaction from building my own dream girls, this was like marrying into the social register. This lady had a family tree."

Hilton also bought a place he could call home and hang his Stetson, a house befitting a bachelor and business visionary of growing stature and fame. It was in Los Angeles, midway between his Lone Star State dowagers and his City on the Bay queen. The new Hilton hacienda was a one-story Spanish stucco-and-red-tile affair adjoining the fancy Bel-Air Country Club golf course where the stars played; next to buying hotels, dancing, and praying, golf was Connie's thing. With the house he hired help, including his first chauffeur.

Next to the Waldorf, Connie dreamed of owning what was then the world's largest hotel, the Stevens, in Chicago. The three-thousand-room colossus could hold the equivalent of the entire population of a small Texas city and even had its own hospital, with five private rooms, two wards, and an operating room. Using some shrewd and complex maneuvers and good old-fashioned bargaining, it became Connie's, for $7,500,000.

Soon he'd break into the platinum club as the owner of two fine New York hotels, the famed Plaza, which he'd redo, and the Roosevelt. In Los Angeles, he'd buy the Town House, which he turned into one of the City of Angels' swankiest and most profitable getaways, with fancy bars and elaborate floor shows. Connie established his first West Coast headquarters there, and under the glass on his desk in his plain, modest office he put that clipping about the Waldorf that had been burning a hole in his wallet. He knew he'd get her someday.

**NOW IN HIS MIDFIFTIES,** the only thing seemingly missing in Connie Hilton's gilt-edge world, other than getting his hands on the Waldorf, was another sexy spitfire to have and to hold at the end of a hectic day.

She came in the voluptuous form of a Hungarian émigré by the name of Zsa Zsa Gabor, a shrewd little gal—once again, half his age like his first wife—who wanted nothing more than a sugar daddy.

Long before there was an entity known as Paris Hilton, there was Zsa Zsa, a glamorous and outrageous creature of convoluted background who had told so many stories about herself through the years that one just had to take them for what they were worth. Zsa Zsa was Zsa Zsa's favorite subject.

Before she arrived in America in 1941 (she came to be with her sister Eva, who was under contract to Paramount), Zsa Zsa had won and lost the title of Miss Hungary—won because she was hot, lost because the judges discovered she wasn't quite sixteen, a requirement for entrance. Instead she was given the title "Maid of Honor." Her mother, Jolie, had pushed her into the pageant and was furious when the title was taken away, while Zsa Zsa's father, Vilmos, twenty years Jolie's senior, compared what Mama Gabor was doing to "white slavery."

Like big Kathy Dugan Avanzino Richards Catain Fenton, Jolie Gabor was a stage mother from hell. A fashionista extraordinaire, Jolie was among the first Hungarian women to get her hair bobbed in the Roaring Twenties and among the first women to drive a car—a Mercedes, of course.

If Paris Hilton's maternal grandmother, big Kathy, had a clone on this planet Earth, it was Jolie Gabor. Like big Kathy, she gave up her own show business ambitions to make her daughters stars, and she also had three of them. Jolie taught Eva, Magda, and Zsa Zsa how to get attention and win men. As Zsa Zsa later remarked, "She was determined that we would make our mark. We would be no ordinary girls. We must be taught every accomplishment befitting young ladies. . . . She regimented our day to [the point of] exhaustion." And that included ballet, piano, tennis, riding, fencing, swimming—virtually the same lessons big Kathy made her daughter Kathy Hilton take when she was developing her to become a star and marry rich.

By the age of eleven, Zsa Zsa already had curves and knew how to use them. She would earn quite a reputation at a young age and, like

Paris Hilton, would become famous for being famous. Like Paris, Zsa Zsa "loved reading about myself"—she got her first boldface notice in Louella Parsons's column. The famed gossip declared Zsa Zsa "even prettier than Eva told us!"

Back in Budapest, young men were leaning out of windows yelling, "Zsa Zsa! Look at me! Please, Zsa Zsa!" She was already known for her wildness, and when the boys shouted she "imagined all sorts of delicious adventures happening to me, although I was not quite sure what they would be." At night under the covers, she read sexually explicit books where she became "the heroine—wicked, helpless, outrageously kissing my master's hands—books I dared let no one see," Zsa Zsa once wrote. She would fall asleep thinking, "Oh, to be wicked and glamorous, beyond good or evil, a great woman with countless distinguished lovers."

Her romance with Connie began one fabulous evening in December 1941, just three months after Zsa Zsa arrived in America. (She'd already been married to and was getting divorced from another much older man, a Turkish government official.) The setting was Ciro's on the Sunset Strip, a precursor to the kind of nightclubs in which Paris would play many decades later—a hangout for the louche Hollywood crowd, the beautiful celebrities, the wise guys, the chorus girls, and the wannabes, from Frankie and Marilyn to Bogie and Bacall. Ciro's was a glitzy joint with famous dance bands, lots of booze and brawls, and leggy cigarette girls in short skirts and high heels.

Zsa Zsa and Eva were partying that night at Ciro's with two of Hollywood's most handsome and prominent lawyers, Zsa Zsa with Gregson Bautzer, and Eva with his law partner, Bentley Ryan, a Hilton lawyer. The champagne hadn't yet gone to her head when she spotted the "tall, erect, sun-tanned man with gray hair showing white at the temples."

Connie, who had arrived with a Hollywood starlet, sat at their table. He sported a hand-painted necktie advertising three of his hotels, and cowboy boots. And he was immediately intrigued by Zsa Zsa, whom he called "Georgia," because he had trouble pronouncing "Zsa Zsa." He saw her as a "Hungarian siren . . . witty, vivacious, and just off the boat." She saw him as "a real American, rough, rugged, dominating." Connie asked

Zsa Zsa to dance, and sparks flew. "He held me so close that I could hardly breathe," she recalled. "I looked up into his eyes and knew that I was going to marry this man."

She later claimed in her memoir, *One Lifetime Is Not Enough,* that Connie offered her a whopping twenty thousand dollars that night to accompany him to Florida. Zsa Zsa, known to exaggerate, said she was "insulted" by the windfall and "refused" the big guy's generosity. But she told him that night, "I *theenk* I am going to marry you." Connie figured she was putting him on, especially since he was a confirmed bachelor and "marriage from a religious standpoint," according to *Be My Guest,* was "a forbidden fruit" because of his divorce.

Nevertheless, Connie began his courtship, taking Zsa Zsa and Eva to El Paso, where he "blushed like a little boy" when he introduced her to his very Catholic eighty-one-year-old mother. Mary Hilton, still dismayed over the fact that he had thumbed his nose at the Church by getting a divorce, gave her favorite son a disapproving look. What struck Zsa Zsa the most about the octogenarian matriarch was that she slept with a small pearl-handled revolver under her pillow, just as her grandson Barron would years later.

Though they met at Ciro's, Connie asked Zsa Zsa to be his wife at another Hollywood hot spot, the Mocambo. Shrewdly, Zsa Zsa chose the smaller of the two engagement rings he had offered her in order to dispel chatter among Connie's friends that she was marrying him for his money. She also suspected Connie was testing her with the two rings.

Four months after they met, on April 10, 1942, Sari "Zsa Zsa" Gabor became the second Mrs. Conrad Hilton, in a civil ceremony not recognized by the Catholic Church at the Santa Fe Hotel.

Zsa Zsa got her first hint of what life would be like with the hotel impresario on their wedding night. Connie was "strong, virile, possessive." After making love, she whispered into his ear, "Oh, my darling, I love you." His response? "By golly! I'm thinking of that Blackstone deal!"

That would be one of the last times they slept together in the same bed, let alone the same room. There were four bedrooms in the Bellagio Road house—one was for Connie, and one for Zsa Zsa because he was "a man who could never share a room with a woman," she stated much later. There was a guest bedroom, and in another wing Nick and Barron shared a room.

Nick, the handsome roué of the two, was particularly attracted to his glamour girl stepmother. Once, when he saw Zsa Zsa give Connie a little peck on the cheek, he asked his father "what does a man have to do" to get Mama to kiss him. According to Zsa Zsa, Connie "whacked him so hard I thought Nick might suffer a concussion." Later in the marriage it would be more than a kiss that Nick—and Zsa Zsa—would desire together.

On their first morning as man and wife, Zsa Zsa naturally wanted to have breakfast with her husband. She found him in his room seated at a table wearing a regal red velvet robe, and instantly she knew she'd made a mistake. "I thought, this is a high priest sitting opposite me eating soft-boiled eggs. I could have been his handmaiden . . . not his wife."

It's not that Connie wasn't a man who couldn't appreciate Zsa Zsa and sex, especially if a bit of kinkiness was thrown into the mix. One day they received a party invitation, but even though Zsa Zsa didn't recognize the hostess's name, Connie thought it might be fun to attend. The Hiltons were greeted by a beautiful, nude blonde floating in her enormous indoor swimming pool, around which were gathered other frolicking couples also wearing nothing.

"Sex and steaminess were in the air," Zsa Zsa wrote, "and I was overtaken by a kind of languor and after dinner became light-headed." Meanwhile, Connie had hightailed it. Zsa Zsa found him behind a red-velvet-curtained door. On the bed was a beautiful girl with Connie standing above her zipping up his fly. The pious innkeeper had taken his bride to what she later called "a whorehouse."

Conrad's main complaint about his bride was that she was a spendthrift. He felt women were childlike when it came to handling money. As a consequence, he put her on a strict household budget, banned her from using his credit, and declared she had to buy everything for the household and herself on two hundred and fifty dollars a month, which Zsa Zsa usually ignored, infuriating the multimillionare hotelier; they fought constantly about her spending. When she went over budget, he deducted the amount from the next month's check.

Zsa Zsa began to see her husband as a dictator, literally, figuratively, and quite shockingly. "Money," she later asserted in her book, "was Conrad's God, and white supremacy, not only Catholicism, appeared to be his religion." She suggested that Connie, who had German blood on his mother's side, might also have had "Nazi tendencies." One of his trusted employees, she claimed, was a former "Gauleiter"—a low-level Nazi Party politician. She also noted that Connie "laughed uproariously" when she accidentally introduced him to visitors as "my husband, Conrad Hitler." (Years later, Connie's great-granddaughter Paris reportedly had a propensity for making racial, ethnic, and religious slurs. In one instance she was accused of branding a Los Angeles event promoter "a lazy Mexican," and she was said to be fond of using the "N" word, all of which she has denied.)

Despite Zsa Zsa's claims about Connie's fascistic leanings, she also acknowledged that he helped Jolie Gabor when she fled Hitler's Europe during the war by putting her up in the Plaza when she arrived in America, and by buying from her the silver she had smuggled out of Hungary. The money helped her to open a little Manhattan shop that she eventually turned into a costume jewelry empire, in the process becoming a millionaire.

Meanwhile, there was little if any marital bliss in the Hilton household. Connie had started locking his bedroom door to keep Zsa Zsa out, and she had started thinking about sleeping with other men. She'd spend most nights cuddling with "Harvey Hilton," her French poodle, who used to nip Connie on the ankles when he made the rare appearance in her boudoir. On one occasion she wandered into Connie's room, unlocked by chance, wearing a sheer black nightgown with hopes of seducing him. She sashayed in at a most inopportune moment—he was on his knees praying. Glancing up at his tarted-up mate, he bellowed, "Dammit, go to your room and wait for me."

Zsa Zsa felt frightened and alone, became severely depressed, began acting strangely, developed paranoid feelings about her jewelry, began popping pills, had a couple of emotional outbursts, and wound up in a straitjacket in a psychiatric hospital for almost two months, where she was being given insulin shock treatments, according to her own memoir and a biography. Connie, who she said had committed her, never came to visit. *Confidential,* the scandal magazine, blared: "Hubby Conrad Hilton thought Zsa Zsa Gabor had lost her buttons. . . . It took a stretch in a swank sanitarium for the Hungarian playgirl to prove she wasn't nutty as a fruitcake . . . or was she?"

Zsa Zsa "desperately needed someone's arms around me." Enter handsome, young Nick Hilton. With her marriage on the rocks, Zsa Zsa had rented a house in Bay Shore, Long Island, and Nick came to visit. Before long they were sleeping together, Zsa Zsa later claimed in her book. As she put it, "I had always loved Nicky Hilton, my stepson; now I began to love Nicky, the man. He was sexy and exciting, but not quite as dazzling as Conrad was. . . . When Nicky and I made love . . . I was convinced my marriage was totally finished and that we'd [Connie] never sleep together again."

However, Zsa Zsa and Connie had one more go at it after they were split. She claimed he raped her in his suite at the Plaza Hotel and that the spawn of that assault was a daughter, Constance Francesca, the only child of all three Gabor sisters' many marriages and unions. Francesca grew up a Hilton and contends she's a Hilton, though Connie claimed to the journalist Lloyd Shearer of *Parade* magazine that she wasn't his daughter.

On November 13, 1944, just thirty-one months after they tied the knot, Connie got a formal separation from Zsa Zsa. Not long after, on the same day as their third wedding anniversary, Zsa Zsa announced that she planned to sue him for a whopping $10 million, claiming, "I don't want that money for myself. I wouldn't take it. I would give it for relief of European refugees—particularly Jewish refugees who have suffered so much." Three months later Connie took up the gauntlet and sued Zsa Zsa in Los Angeles Superior Court, charging "cruelty," but he made no specific allegations.

The last thing in the world Connie wanted or needed was the kind of tabloid press his separation and divorce was generating, which he had escaped with his first divorce. Now, though, Connie and Zsa Zsa's split was the big gossip story of the day—not quite on a par with Paris Hilton's cataclysmic temporary loss of her Chihuahua, Tinkerbell, in August 2004, but still headline-making. "Mr. and Mrs. America and all the ships at sea," as Walter Winchell introduced his gossip on the radio, were talking about how Zsa Zsa was taking the big hotel guy for millions.

Zsa Zsa told the divorce court that Connie chose his butler over her during the marriage, which certainly pricked up ears in Superior Judge Warren Steel's courtroom on September 17, 1946—testimony that appeared in the court record, but not in Zsa Zsa's two autobiographies, or even in Connie's *Be My Guest.*

"He hired the butler five weeks before we married," Zsa Zsa stated. "The butler was very fresh. He wouldn't take my orders. I complained to my husband and asked that the man be dismissed, but he said, 'If you don't like it, you can go.'" In the summer of 1944, Connie's swank Bel-Air home was destroyed by fire. She testified, "When the house was rebuilt, he returned with the butler. I did not go back." Zsa Zsa's sister Eva testified that shortly after the two were hitched, Connie told her he did not want to be married.

In the end, Zsa Zsa got a property settlement that Connie had convinced her to sign in 1944. Once again, it was a pittance—not quite as bad as the one the first Mrs. Hilton had received, but still very little. The multimillionaire gave Zsa Zsa $35,000 in cash and $250,000 in alimony, to be paid at the rate of $2,083 monthly for ten years. But if she remarried—which she would do, tying the knot with the British actor George Sanders—the payments were to be reduced to $1,041 for three years. He also gave her some stock in the Hollywood Roosevelt and Plaza hotels. (He gave lots of girls Hilton stock as gifts over the years.)

Jolie Gabor, in her autobiography, written with the help of New York gossip columnist Cindy Adams, said that Zsa Zsa had hired a lawyer recommended by the actress Claudette Colbert. "He was so nice he was stupid. A jerk. She [Zsa Zsa] made a stupid divorce. Not even a permanent suite for life at the Plaza. Not even 10 percent discount on any suite anywhere in the world. Wherever Zsa Zsa goes, in a Hilton Hotel she must pay herself. Ridiculous."

Years later Zsa Zsa famously quipped, "Conrad Hilton was very generous to me in the divorce settlement. He gave me five thousand Gideon Bibles."

While the actual settlement was small, Zsa Zsa wasn't destined for skid row.

About a year later she was the victim of what the press billed as "the biggest individual haul in New York criminal history" when a pimply faced, tan-gloved gunman wearing dark glasses robbed her of twenty-five pieces of jewelry worth more than a half-million dollars.

On April Fool's Day, 1949, she became Sanders wife, in a quickie ceremony before a judge in Las Vegas. He was the third of her nine husbands. Zsa Zsa went on to make a series of mediocre films, did the TV talk-show circuit, and in 1989 famously slapped a Beverly Hills cop who had stopped her for a traffic violation and spent three days in the slammer. Along the way she had an affair with Porfirio Rubirosa—"machismo incarnate," as she called him—the internationally infamous Dominican playboy, who during a couple of heated lovers' spats gave her a bloody nose and a much-publicized black eye.

# CHAPTER 20

The ringing telephone in midmorning awakened the pretty young actress from a sleeping-pill-and-liquor-induced sleep. Groggy, she fumbled for the jangling receiver and put it to her ear. She'd been out at a party until who knows when, and all she wanted to do was sleep. Wiping away the cobwebs, she heard the lazy Texas drawl telling her how sorry he was about what had happened the night before.

Her fiancé was apologizing profusely, but she couldn't imagine why. "I'm so sorry, honey. I truly am . . . I'm just so sorry," the Texan repeated, and when she asked for a third time, "What are you so sorry for?" he suggested, "Oh, you better go look in the mirror, honey."

Stumbling to the bathroom in her bachelorette flat on Doheny Road, off the Sunset Strip, she tried to focus on her reflection in the mirror. As her vision improved, nineteen-year-old Countess Elizabeth Caroline von Furstenberg-Hedringen, better known on the MGM lot as Betsy von Furstenberg and to the gossip press as "Madcap Betsy," suddenly saw the reason her fiancé was being so apologetic. Sometime during another wild night out there had been a tiff, and he had ended it by drunkenly throwing a punch. Staring into the mirror, Betsy saw she had a big black eye.

Giving shiners to gorgeous young gals seemed to be the prerogative of handsome young playboys like Rubirosa, and Conrad Nicholson "Nick" Hilton Jr., the country's best-known playboy back in 1951, was no exception.

Having taken a Seconal or two—Nick and Betsy's prescription sleeping drug of choice as a chaser to the alcohol they drank—she hadn't remembered feeling, let alone receiving, Nick's punch.

Recalling that incident more than a half-century later, von Furstenberg—retired Broadway and TV soap opera leading lady, New York socialite, novelist, children's book author, and grandmother—says, "I was feeling no pain, obviously. I don't know what party we were at, but there wasn't a commotion. It was just between he and I and then the next morning he called to apologize. I took it very lightly because, obviously, it was just a moment. If you aim right, it doesn't take much of a blow to give you a black eye. I've had several black eyes since then because I used to have a very bad temper of my own.

"Actually, I think I laughed when I looked in the mirror," she continues. "It wasn't anything like, I'll never see you again, I'll never speak to you again, or how could you do such a thing? We did a lot of wild things in those days."

When they became serious in 1951, Betsy and Nick, who was still in the process of divorcing Elizabeth Taylor, had decided to "go on the wagon," realizing their drinking had gotten out of control. While Nick would become known through the 1950s in the gossip columns as a boozer and brawler, Betsy possessed a respectable public image, having been on the covers of *Life* and *Look* and given an MGM contract after a critically acclaimed stint on Broadway.

But privately she liked her liquor so much that a businessman friend had started calling her "Betsy von *Thirsty*berg." Betsy had started drinking at fourteen, and fancy restaurants, knowing she was underage, served her alcohol out of a demitasse cup.

"*Everybody* in those days drank a lot," she points out. "I didn't think I had a problem, but to make it easier for Nick to stop I stopped drinking, too. But it didn't last long and before you knew it we were off and running again."

Years later she saw that she had been "an enabler" for his alcoholism "with my own jolly drinking."

It wasn't just what drinking did to their physical well-being that was of concern. In Nick's case, drinking turned him from a "sweet" young man into a monster. "It was worse for him because when he drank he became very abusive," notes von Furstenberg. "He'd get physically violent."

This became apparent at a lively party at his brother Barron's house, a fun occasion that suddenly turned into an ugly Hilton family scene. Nick, who von Furstenberg saw as the "black sheep," had been knocking down shots of Johnnie Walker Black, his drink of choice, when he had words with Barron and hauled off and slugged him. "I never saw him do anything like that when he was sober," she states. "But when he drank too much he'd get into a fistfight, or something like that."

The scene at Barron's became maudlin. "Nick cried, 'I hit my brother. I hit my brother,'" recalls von Furstenberg as if it were yesterday. "Nick was very, very upset about it. He was mortified and was terribly ashamed of himself. He stopped drinking for a time after he hit his brother, but to keep him on the wagon was beyond me. Then he'd get drunk and do something like that again. He was just destined to have this terrible, tragic life."

**NICK HILTON'S PROPENSITY** for violent behavior when he was drunk exploded during his 205-day marriage to Elizabeth Rosemond Taylor— the "marriage and love match of the century," as the world press ordained it, at least in the beginning.

Many years later "La Liz," after eight marriages to seven husbands (Richard Burton and Elizabeth were married twice), appeared on CNN's *Larry King Live,* and divulged, "Nick kind of got a kick out of beating the [shit] out of me." (The producers bleeped the "S" word.) When she made the charge, Nick had been dead for more than three decades, and she had not accused him of beatings when she divorced him. But his abuse of her was well known.

It started out like a fairy tale, or so it seemed at the time with the Hollywood spin machine at full throttle. In fact, it wasn't a fairy tale at all. Most of the story of their "love affair" was spun by studio publicists,

Hollywood gossip columnists, and movie magazine hacks and handed down as fact through the years.

Nick was twenty-three when he first laid eyes on seventeen-year-old Elizabeth. It was at the Mocambo, the same Sunset Boulevard hot spot where his father gave Zsa Zsa her engagement ring. Elizabeth was there for the wedding party of her friend the actress Jane Powell. Nick was there to get loaded. Like practically every hot-blooded American man at the time, Nick was knocked out by the gorgeous brunette's hypnotic violet eyes, and those spectacular glamour girl breasts.

Elizabeth was nearly finished shooting *A Place in the Sun* with the boyish and closeted Montgomery Clift, the man with whom Elizabeth had developed a close friendship and on whom she had a big crush, though she knew he was gay. By coincidence, the film, based on Theodore Dreiser's novel *An American Tragedy,* was about a man entangled with two women—the leitmotif of Nick's notorious womanizing.

Ellis Amburn, one of Taylor's biographers, says, "It seems to me she was so aroused from working with Monty who was gay and really couldn't consummate anything with her that Nicky—dark eyes flashing mischief and desire—just picked up from there. He gave her jewelry and that was always a good way to Liz's heart. Ironically, for someone so pretty she was desperate to get married."

Turned on by Elizabeth's looks, Nick called a friend, Pete Freeman, whose father ran Paramount Pictures, her film's distributor, and asked him to set up a date. The two had lunch at a Mexican restaurant across Melrose Avenue from her studio; Liz found Nick attractive, Nick was smitten, and by the time she arrived back at her dressing room, three dozen yellow roses were waiting for her along with a note, "To bring back the Sun—Nick."

By the time she met and fell for Nick, Elizabeth already had two well-publicized romances and had earned a gossip columnist's sobriquet, "Liz the Jilt." Elizabeth's mother, Sara Taylor, a former actress and a driven and ambitious stage mother in the same league as big Kathy and Jolie Gabor, was one of those forces behind the new relationship.

Sara Taylor was suitably impressed when Connie invited her and her husband to dinner at his new abode, a 64-room, 35,000-square-foot

behemoth, Casa Encantada—the House of Enchantment—on ten glorious Bel-Air acres, which he'd bought for a song fully furnished, including the Ming vases.

Like William Randolph Hearst, the newspaper king, Connie Hilton,
the hotel king, now possessed his own Xanadu. The two-story Georgian
mansion with an ocean view cost $2,500,000 alone to build during the
Depression by a frumpy nurse, Hilda Olsen Boldt Weber, who had inherited her millionaire patient-husband's fortune and wanted to shine in
Los Angeles high society. When she was going broke and needed money,
Connie picked up the place for $250,000. It was a deal he boasted about
for the rest of his life. (Not long after he bought the place, the seller gambled away the proceeds on the ponies, and committed suicide.)

The estate, at 10644 Bellagio Road, was more like a Hilton hotel in
terms of size, only far ritzier—Hilton hotels didn't come equipped with
fourteen-karat-gold fixtures in their bathrooms, and Connie's Casa had
twenty-six such johns, and much more: walk-in silver, fur, and wine
vaults; massage rooms; rare paintings; garage space for twenty-four cars.
Sara Taylor was transfixed and came away dreaming of a Hilton marriage for her daughter, just as big Kathy would for little Kathy years later.

Nick and Elizabeth began spending private weekends at the Hilton
estate, at the Hilton lodge at Lake Arrowhead, or at the home of brother
Barron. The first time they went out publicly to a charity benefit at the
Biltmore Hotel in Los Angeles, they were besieged by photographers. "Is
it always like this?" Nick asked as flashbulbs blinded him. She responded
briskly, "You'll get used to it."

But were they really in love? Passionate, yes. In love, no. If anything,
Nick was in love with the idea of being in love. Moreover, as Hilton family friend Hank Moonjean observes, "Nick was like a cat in heat. Every gal
he took out he screwed, and all were great beauties."

As for marriage to Elizabeth, Nick viewed it as a way to play catch-
up with Barron, who had already gotten hitched and had two children.
Nick also saw marriage as a way to show his father, whose respect he
would never win no matter how hard he tried, that he was ready to settle
down and be responsible like his younger brother. Besides all of that,
Elizabeth was *the* trophy wife.

**CONRAD HILTON** surrounded by his three sons. From left, the first-born, **NICK**, whose life of broads, booze, and brawling made him a favorite of the gossip columns and tabloids in the fifties. **ERIC HILTON** was raised by his mother and her second husband, Mack Saxon. Eric later became a Hilton executive. **BARRON**, Conrad's second-born and Paris's paternal grandfather, went on to run the Hilton empire.

**MACK SAXON** was a champion on the gridiron and a renowned womanizer who had an adulterous affair with Connie Hilton's first wife, **MARY BARRON HILTON**. Connie and Mary were divorced in 1934 after she took off with the football great.

**"THE MOBLEY** wasn't exactly a hotel," Paris Hilton's great-grandfather once said, "it was sort of a flophouse." But **CONRAD HILTON** had the golden touch and rightly predicted the Cisco, Texas, way stop would be the first link in his worldwide chain.

Dancing the light fantastic was one of **CONRAD HILTON**'s favorite pastimes when he wasn't buying hotels. Here he does his favorite two-step with his daughter-in-law, **PATRICIA SKIPWORTH HILTON**, to celebrate the opening of yet another Hilton Hotel.

**CONRAD HILTON** was a staunch Catholic who had two divorces and was a known womanizer who once took his second wife, Zsa Zsa Gabor, to a brothel. So he wasn't concerned about downing the bubbly in the presence of a religious leader—at least when he was looking the other way.

**MARY BARRON HILTON SAXON**, the matriarch of the contemporary Hilton dynasty, kept up a semblance of friendship with her hotel mogul first husband. Often left alone because of Connie's love affair with hotels, the mother of his three sons had an affair of her own that ended their marriage.

Playboy **NICK HILTON** had some of the most glamorous women in Hollywood at his feet, and one of them was teenage beauty **NATALIE WOOD**. The lovebirds infuriated Nick's father, Conrad, when they holed up together in bed during the opening ceremonies of the Mexico City Hilton.

The May 1950 Beverly Hills nuptials of **NICK HILTON** and a teenage **ELIZABETH TAYLOR** was billed by the press as the wedding and love match of the century. Two hundred five days later they were divorced. As Taylor revealed years later, "Nick kind of got a kick out of beating the shit out of me."

Eight years after **NICK HILTON** and Elizabeth Taylor split, he fell for another teenage beauty, Oklahoma oil heiress **PATRICIA McCLINTOCK**. Less than two years before Nick Hilton died, he and Trish and their two sons, Michael and Conrad III, vacationing at the Hilton in Rome, celebrated Trish's twenty-seventh birthday, one of the happy times in their dysfunctional marriage. Their life was darkened by Nick's drinking and addiction to sleeping pills. He was found dead on February 5, 1969, at the age of forty-two.

**KATHLEEN DUGAN AVANZINO RICHARDS CATAIN FENTON**, Paris Hilton's maternal grandmother, surrounded by her famous brood: from left, child actresses **KYLE** and **KIM RICHARDS**; their father and her second husband, **KEN RICHARDS**; and the future **KATHY HILTON**, the spawn of big Kathy's first marriage to a Long Island bad boy, Larry Avanzino. Big Kathy's mantra to her daughters, and later to her granddaughters, Paris and Nicky, was to marry rich. Her own dream to become a singing star ended when she became pregnant and had a shotgun wedding.

Paris Hilton's maternal grandmother, known as "**BIG KATHY**," celebrating with hubby number three, **JACK CATAIN**, who was identified by federal prosecutors as a member of the Mafia. He died after their divorce and shortly before he was to begin serving a prison term.

At her wedding into the Hilton dynasty, the future mother of Paris has a rare get-together with her estranged father, **LARRY AVANZINO**. His shotgun marriage to Paris's maternal grandmother ended in divorce, and he had no role in raising his daughter.

Paris's mother was cute as a button when she was discovered as a toddler by famed baby photographer Constance Bannister. These and many other photos led to the future **KATHY HILTON**'s career as a child model and actress, pushed by her "stage mother from hell," big Kathy.

PHOTOGRAPHS BY CONSTANCE BANNISTER

At a "Welcome Home Party" for the Reagans on January 4, 1989, held at the Beverly Hilton Hotel, Los Angeles, Paris Hilton's parents **RICK** and **KATHY**, staunch Republicans like all Hiltons, pose with **NANCY** and **RONNIE**, who have just turned over the White House to George H. W. Bush.

Baby **PARIS HILTON** and her joyous parents. Her mother, **KATHY**, called her "Star" from day one.

With an angelic schoolgirl face that any mother would love, who would have guessed pre-adolescent **PARIS HILTON** would one day be the boldface name in gossip columns and websites for her exhibitionistic behavior.

**KATHY HILTON** and her first-born share much in common: the fashionable crucifixes around their necks and their ambition and drive for celebrity. Mother was also an actress and wannabe singer.

**PARIS**, the infamous "celebutante" who became a household name and money-making "brand" by displaying her X-rated wares, pictured here at the Playboy Mansion for Hugh Hefner's Midsummer Night's Dream Party.

# PARIS HILTON
## A Night in Paris

## COLLECTOR'S EDITION
## NEVER BEFORE SEEN FOOTAGE

## Don't Wait!
## Be the first to own
## Paris' Hardcore Footage!

## Get yours today!

**PARIS HILTON**'s fame—and infamy—skyrocketed after the homemade porn video in which she co-starred with a boyfriend hit the Internet. Overnight, four minutes of the grainy film were seen by millions, and soon all twenty-seven minutes were marketed, outselling the video of Gone With the Wind. Even the Hilton Hotel chain showed a spike in guests after the video was distributed.

As for Elizabeth, marriage was an escape hatch from the clutches of her controlling and domineering mother, plus the Hilton money didn't hurt. She also was envious that her actress pals like Jane Powell were getting married. "Liz would have had a nervous breakdown," said a friend, "if she hadn't become a married woman."

If any marriage was arranged, the Hilton-Taylor merger was—engineered and stage-managed behind the scenes by Connie, working hand in hand with Sara Taylor, and with the stamp of approval of MGM, Elizabeth's studio. Except for the two stars of this production—in essence, two very mixed-up kids—everyone else had an agenda, and much to gain.

Bedazzled by Elizabeth's fame, her beauty, and particularly her paycheck, Connie telephoned ex-wife Zsa Zsa to boast, "By golly, my son is marrying a young actress called Elizabeth Taylor who earns five thousand dollars for a radio show." When Zsa Zsa emphasized that Elizabeth was, in fact, America's most popular starlet and made tons more money as an actress in films, his response once again was, "Hell, she makes five thousand dollars a radio show!"

Connie had only one demand before he gave his blessing, and that was that Elizabeth, who wasn't a Catholic, agree in writing to raise her children with Nick in the faith. Elizabeth thought his requirement was preposterous and on a par with some of the clauses in her studio contract. To keep peace, she agreed; in her heart she knew no children would come of the union, and she never converted to Catholicism (though she would convert to Judaism when she was married later to crooner Eddie Fisher). As part of the quid pro quo, Connie had put aside $100,000 for Nick's firstborn, and as a wedding gift Connie gave Elizabeth a block of Hilton stock—one hundred shares—and told her to think of the Waldorf-Astoria (which he had finally got his hands on in October 1949 for $3,000,000) as her New York home away from home.

Meanwhile, the suits at MGM were floating on air; they saw a publicity bonanza because Elizabeth's next big film, *Father of the Bride*—a comedy about a wedding—was scheduled for release in conjunction with the Hilton-Taylor nuptials. MGM publicists also were hoping for what they called Nick and Elizabeth's "little dividend." The studio was planning a sequel to *Father of the Bride,* called *Father's Little Dividend,* starring Elizabeth, and was hoping for a real baby tie-in.

The Hilton-Taylor "love affair" was the "Brangelina" of its day. When word leaked that a marriage was impending—Connie broke the embargo by telling a New York reporter the precise date—Louella Parsons, who had a line into Elizabeth, asked her about the future. Elizabeth's glib response was "Nothing comes off until the ring goes on."

When Nick went to buy the sparkler at George Headley's, the fashionable Beverly Hills jeweler, and demanded to see "something nice," Headley, who knew Nick's playboy reputation, quipped, "Blonde or brunette?" Nick responded, "Platinum and diamonds." The result was a ten-thousand-dollar, four-carat affair.

Nick took Elizabeth to El Paso to meet his mother who had been widowed just nine months earlier. Excited by the prospect of the world's most beautiful movie star paying a visit to Mary Barron Hilton Saxon's modest house, Eric Hilton invited his El Paso High School pals to the meet and greet.

"Eric called me all excited and said, 'Come out to the house to see Elizabeth Taylor. She's gonna be here!'" recalls Bob Keller, a classmate and football teammate of Eric's. "We're all seniors in high school and drooling over Liz, so we go out there and she wouldn't even give us the time of day. We were like little punks to her. Here she was going with Nick Hilton and she wasn't going to have anything to do with a bunch of high school kids. I never thought much of Elizabeth Taylor after that."

Bob Suddarth, one of Eric's closest friends back then, says Nick spent most of his time during the short stay away from Elizabeth "shooting dice with the boys in the private room reserved for men at the El Paso Country Club. One time Elizabeth came in looking for Nicky and it caused quite a stir because women weren't allowed, but she just came bustin' into the room where he was gamblin' with the boys.

"After Elizabeth's visit Eric always had a saying. He'd put out his hand and he'd say, 'Shake the hand that shook the hand [Nick's] that's been inside Elizabeth Taylor.'"

ick and Elizabeth's engagement was official as of February 20, 1950, even though she had been warned by a number of people, including Doris Lilly, a syndicated gossip columnist and author of *How to Marry a Millionaire,* that Nick was trouble and that she should walk away before it was too late. Lilly told her that Nick had beaten up a model friend of hers after a bout of heavy drinking, according to Taylor biographer C. David Heymann. Monty Clift also tried to steer her away from marrying the Hilton boy. When she called him and asked Monty whether he would hang out with her and Nick after they were man and wife, he answered, "I don't think dear Nicky is my kind of guy."

All wasn't negative and ominous, however. Connie's girl Friday, Olive Wakeman, sent Elizabeth a pile of cookbooks with the note, "The way to a man's heart is through his stomach." She also warned, "Don't forget his ego," advice that along with the cooking went in one pretty Elizabeth Taylor ear and out the other.

The setting was Church of the Good Shepherd, the Hilton family church, in Beverly Hills, on May 6, 1950, when Elizabeth and Nick tied the knot. It was Elizabeth's first of eight marriages, and Nick's first of two.

Every Hilton Hotel manager in the world had been invited, along with every big name in Hollywood. Special seating had been arranged by MGM for Spencer Tracy and Joan Bennett, Elizabeth's parents in the about-to-be released *Father of the Bride.* The organ player was even on MGM's payroll.

The ceremony started five minutes late after a few close calls—Elizabeth's gown almost got ripped when it got stuck in the car door on her arrival, and the organ needed to be hastily repaired before the "Wedding March" could be played. As Nick and Elizabeth took their vows, Connie whispered to his ex-wife and the groom's mother, "They have everything, haven't they?" Her response was, "Maybe they have too much. I don't think it's going to be easy for them." The ceremony took all of twenty minutes, and then Nick passionately kissed the bride.

When the newlyweds emerged from the church they faced a wall of paparazzi so thick that the twenty-five hundred frenzied fans, restrained by a phalanx of more than two dozen policemen, could hardly see the couple.

In the almost full-page photo that *Life* magazine—the celeb weekly of its day—used in its May 22 issue, eighteen-year-old Elizabeth was the epitome of Hollywood glamour, smiling dazzlingly. She wore the veil and white satin gown that MGM had had made especially for her. Embroidered with beads and seed pearls and cinched at the waist, the wedding dress emphasized her pinup girl bosom. *Life* called her "one of the loveliest ever seen on the screen—charming, sparkling and starry-eyed." A caption below one of the photos, however, noted pointedly that the wedding "was stage-managed" by the studio.

In the *Life* photo, boyish, dimple-cheeked Nick had an expression of shock on his twenty-three-year-old face, his eyebrows lifted skyward as if he was surprised by the whole event.

At the Bel-Air Country Club, near Connie's home, a wedding reception of Cecil B. DeMille proportions was thrown by the father-in-law of the bride and MGM: seven hundred guests were forced to walk a reception line, a trip that took as long as six hours. The guests washed down slices from a five-tier vanilla-frosted wedding cake with Dom Perignon—one hundred cases' worth. One of the guests, the gossip columnist Sheilah Graham, introduced Elizabeth to another reveler as "Mrs. Hilton," and Elizabeth "beamed, 'Isn't that a wonderful name?'"

The honeymoon began with a drive up the treacherous Pacific Coast Highway in Nick's Mercedes-Benz roadster, he with half a load on from all the champagne he'd consumed at the reception, to the Carmel Country Club where they had a cozy villa overlooking the ocean. Nick's drinking continued on their wedding night. While the setting was romantic, no lovemaking occurred. Nick spent the first three nights at the bar, according to another hotel guest, the humorist Art Buchwald.

"It amazed me," Heymann quoted Buchwald. "Any other man would have been in bed with his wife, particularly when the wife's initials were 'E.T.' Hilton spent an entire night at the bar, drinking himself into an absolute stupor."

According to a Hilton family insider years later, "Nick's impotency was linked to his feelings of inadequacy next to a star like Elizabeth. He just couldn't perform."

About two weeks after the wedding, the newlyweds boarded the *Queen Mary* and embarked on the European leg of their extended honeymoon, paid for by Connie—and destined to be the trans-Atlantic *Love Boat* cruise from hell.

By the time they boarded, Nick was sick of the whole staged event, and especially of how he was being treated. Everywhere they went together, the press's focus was on Elizabeth; Mr. Machismo was made to feel more like "Mr. Taylor" than Mr. Hilton, the husband. At one point he led photographers on a chase all over Los Angeles after he failed to show up at a studio-arranged press conference. As the gossip columnist Jimmy Fidler pointed out, "I'm afraid that Nicky, as the spouse of Hollywood's most celebrated young star, [would] be wise to accept the situation and quit dodging." Later, Connie said, "Nick was resentful, hot-tempered, and handled himself accordingly."

Nick saw himself as Elizabeth's baggage, literally and figuratively. That was underscored when it was loaded aboard the ocean liner; Elizabeth had fourteen suitcases and two steamer trunks filled with clothing, furs, jewelry, and cosmetics, and each bag had been carefully labeled for its contents by Sara Taylor, who had literally packed her daughter's belongings. Nick, who brought four puny bags, sarcastically told a reporter as he was about to walk the gangplank that he was "traveling with a film star." Their shipmates included the Duke and Duchess of Windsor, who promised to throw the newlyweds a party one night in Paris.

The entire crossing was one big brawl. Elizabeth was usually left on her own while Nick drank and gambled until long after midnight, losing as much as $100,000 in the ship's casino. One night Nick angrily tossed a stack of chips at Elizabeth when she begged him to stop playing. When he demanded she accompany him to a ship's movie, or to make a call to his father, she stormed off, which enraged him. On one very public occasion on deck he shoved her up against a bulkhead and warned her, "Don't you ever do that to me—I'm *talking* to you!"

It only got worse. At night he returned drunk to their stateroom and physically attacked Elizabeth, punching her in the stomach, knocking her to her knees, leaving her gasping for breath.

For Elizabeth, the honeymoon sex, infrequent as it was, was what made the trip exciting, if not dangerous to her physical well-being. Not only was Nick far more sexually experienced than Elizabeth, but he was well endowed. On that trip Elizabeth discovered that size does matter. (One of Nick's many companions in the post-Elizabeth era of the fifties, Terry Moore, later claimed, "He had absolutely the largest penis—wider than a beer can and much longer—I have ever seen. To make love to him was akin to fornicating with a horse." Another, the British temptress Joan Collins, was more explicit, stating that her onetime lover was a "sexual athlete" and that along with his brother Barron and their father, the Hilton men "possessed a yard of cock.")

Sex aside, Nick played the role of the ugly American to the hilt. At the Paris party thrown by the Duke and Duchess of Windsor, he embarrassed himself at the dinner table when he spat a wad of chewing gum into a napkin, which he popped back in his mouth after the fancy dessert. Like a number of Hiltons past and present, Nick had had a scattered education, which probably accounted for his lack of social graces and sophistication. (Despite their money and power, the Hiltons were in many ways socially unsophisticated. When drinking and angry, Nick was prone to use racial and anti-Semitic slurs like "kike" and "nigger."

Although Connie was a popular party-giver—mainly for business reasons—he was known to fart and belch freely at the dinner table.)

In Cannes, in the south of France, Nick spent his evenings at the casino and was spotted late one night with one of the high-priced, beautiful prostitutes who picked up their clients near the casino. He took her back to the hotel knowing Elizabeth had already gone to bed.

When they traveled to London, Nick didn't like the way the drinks were mixed at the posh Savoy Grill, so he demanded that a variety of bottles be delivered to his table, where he mixed them himself. Upstairs in the newlyweds' suite, he had practically an entire liquor store at his disposal.

When the honeymooners got to Berlin, Elizabeth fled from Nick. She reportedly asked the director Mervyn LeRoy, who was shooting MGM's *Quo Vadis,* to hide her on the set where she dressed in a toga and was part of a Colosseum scene. Another account stated that both she and Nick had appeared in the scene as a prank. At some point, Nick trashed a room in the villa they were renting, destroying costly antiques. Nick's drinking and gambling continued unabated. He and Elizabeth argued incessantly over her spending and his inebriation and violent tantrums, and when the booze kicked in, he slapped her around. On their return to New York aboard the *Queen Mary,* she feared his wrath and bunked one night with a teenage girl from New York with whom she had become friends.

The Hiltons' hellish honeymoon lasted three months, which is equal to almost half of their entire marriage.

The gossip columnist Sheilah Graham, writing in *Modern Screen,* charged that the pair were "behaving like spoiled children" who had "everything done for them all their lives . . . what [Nick] didn't smooch from his father, he smiled out of his mother. They gave him everything . . . except . . . consideration for others, emotional happiness for himself."

Nick returned immediately to California, telling his father that being with Elizabeth was like "life in a fishbowl," and he berated the press for making up stories. Nick was quoted in *Modern Screen,* which also did a positive piece by writer Kirtley Baskette, as saying, "I knew when I married a movie star what I was in for, although I didn't expect this much made of everything I do. . . . It's not very pleasant to be made out a louse." As Connie said later in *Be My Guest,* "He was angry, hurt, bewildered and defiant." His father told him, "It's the price you pay for marrying a famous woman." And Connie was a veteran, having had Zsa Zsa as a mate.

Elizabeth Taylor Hilton stayed in New York for a few weeks with the family of the girl who had harbored her aboard ship.

Zsa Zsa Gabor later claimed that she and Nick had one last sexual fling during his marriage to Elizabeth and that he complained bitterly about her.

One of his complaints was about her dog. In Paris, Nick had bought Elizabeth a French poodle, because her dog Butch had died while they were away. Back home, Nick had wanted to move into the Bel-Air Hotel, but the suite he wanted wasn't available, so he and Elizabeth had temporary use of his brother Barron's home. But Elizabeth never bothered to housebreak the pooch, who continually did his business all over the floor, infuriating Nick. It was one of the few things he vehemently complained about to Betsy von Furstenberg when they started dating. "He'd go out in the morning and come back that night and there were messes all over the floor," she says Nick told her. "He was disgusted by the fact that she never cleaned up after the dog. The same poop was still lying there. Why they didn't have a servant cleaning up after the dog, God only knows."

It might be because the servants had already taken enough "shit" from the imperious actress. During their stay at Barron's, Elizabeth hired, fired, and was walked out on by six servants, according to Sheilah Graham, who observed, "Servants don't usually leave considerate employers."

By September, four months after the wedding, the gossip columnists who had been calling it a love affair were now predicting a divorce. Dorothy Kilgallen, who penned the nationally syndicated "Voice of Broadway" column, reported it was all but over. "Before the wedding," she wrote, "he was said to have promised Elizabeth's parents he would give up gambling and drinking, but he broke both promises early in the honeymoon." Meanwhile, Elizabeth denied that her marriage was on the rocks and fibbed to Hedda Hopper, "I am especially happy now." When Hopper asked Elizabeth about Nick's "misbehaving" on their honeymoon, Elizabeth declared, "Doesn't everyone?"

**ON DECEMBER 1, 1950,** Nick and Elizabeth formally separated. MGM, on Elizabeth's behalf, issued a statement that said, "Nick and I . . . have come to a parting of the ways . . . there is no possibility of a reconciliation."

On December 22, Elizabeth Taylor Hilton filed for divorce. In a page and a half complaint, she charged Nick with extreme mental cruelty, alleging that he had "wrongfully and without provocation" treated her "in a cruel and inhuman manner," and "inflicted . . . great and grievous mental cruelty and . . . mental pain, suffering and anguish, thus destroying the legitimate objects of matrimony . . . making it impossible" for her "to continue to live with [Nick] as his wife." She asked for the return of her maiden name, Taylor. But there was no mention of alimony; the fact is, they hadn't lived together long enough to acquire much communal property.

Nick's attorney filed an answer categorically denying Elizabeth's charges of cruelty. Meantime, Nick took off on a hunting trip to Mexico. The "inside word," according to one gossip columnist, was that Connie was "showing more grief over the bust-up than the principals themselves."

Writer C. David Heymann observes, "She didn't realize it at the time she married Nick Hilton that he was a dangerous soul, that he was physically abusive. He masked from her his drinking, his gambling, and all of his nasty habits. Obviously, he represented to her America's foremost hotel chain and that was appealing to Elizabeth."

**SHE LOOKED DRAWN** and nervous. She could barely speak in a voice above a whisper. At one point she dropped her face into her gloved hands, and when she looked up, tears were streaming down her cheeks. That was eighteen-year-old Elizabeth Taylor's demeanor on the witness stand on January 29, 1951, when she told her dramatic story of neglect and abuse at the hands of Nick Hilton.

One press account said she had ended her marriage "with a broken heart and incipient ulcers." Of almost seven months of marriage, the Hiltons had had three months of honeymoon hell and two months of separation—leaving eight weeks of fighting over the poodle's doo-doo on the floor.

The courtroom of superior court judge Thurmond Clarke was standing room only—attorneys, the press, photographers, and spectators, all gathered for the best show in Tinseltown that day.

"He was indifferent to me and used abusive language," Elizabeth stated, her voice dropping so teeny-tiny that the shorthand reporter, C. W. Lyman, just two feet away, complained to the judge, who ordered her to "keep your voice up. Just pretend my reporter is a little hard of hearing."

Elizabeth's attorney, William Berger, was permitted by the judge to pick up the narrative—an unusual move, just to speed things along—with Elizabeth consenting to his statements, among which were that "almost from the beginning of the marriage" Nick was indifferent to Elizabeth and picked arguments "for no apparent reason. In addition," the lawyer continued, "Mr. Hilton spent night after night at the casino when they were in France . . . and remained away until five and six in the morning and forced her to take a cab back alone. This also was true after they returned to Los Angeles."

Looking prim in a navy-blue suit, white blouse, navy pumps, and a flowered straw hat, Elizabeth recalled one not very shocking incident that occurred just after the newlyweds arrived home from their honeymoon. "I had unpacked my clothes and my mother was there and [a friend] Mrs. [Marshall] Thompson. Mr. Hilton came in and said, 'What the hell is going on here?' I tried to keep him from saying more. It was embarrassing." She acknowledged that that was a sample of Nick's rudeness. Barbara Thompson, whose husband was an actor, took the stand and told the court that since the marriage Elizabeth no longer was her "gay and usual self" and that she had lost "a tremendous amount of weight" as a result of the stress of being married to Nick. The tabloid *New York Daily Mirror* headlined the trial: "Liz, Sobbing Of Nicky's 'Cruelty,' Wins Divorce."

# CHAPTER 22

**N**ick Hilton was still in the process of tying up loose ends with Elizabeth Taylor in the summer of 1951 when he spotted eighteen-year-old Betsy von Furstenberg lolling in the Bel-Air Hotel swimming pool. The five-foot-four blonde eyed him, too, attracted by his "cute, sort of boyish, lost boy quality," and before long they had become an item. "It was just chemistry, just one of those crazy things as the song goes," she says many years later.

Nick immediately telephoned her for a date, but she told him she required a chaperone. Instead, he planned a dinner party at his father's spectacular home where Nick had been bunking since his divorce. It was a posh party with guests like the actor Joseph Cotten and the actress Patricia Medina at the table being served dinner on solid gold plates. Betsy was impressed.

However, she would soon come to realize that the party was "a great smoke screen." As she notes, "Nick made a tremendous effort for me *not* to see the rather sordid side of his life in the beginning."

Not long after they began what would be a tempestuous relationship and engagement of sorts, Nick took Betsy to his home state of Texas to meet his alcoholic mother, the widowed Hilton matriarch, Mary Barron Hilton Saxon, who was hospitalized. They also took in a football game and went bird-shooting, and Betsy was sworn in as an honorary citizen of the Lone Star State, a cute ceremony arranged for by the well-connected Hilton scion.

"At first it was very romantic and we never left each other's side," she says. "He was terribly sweet with me. We would have dinner alone and I never saw that other side of things, and then slowly, little by little, I realized what his day was like, what his night was like. There was no pretense of him going to an office, or doing *anything.*"

Unlike most of the girls Nick had been with, including Elizabeth Taylor, Betsy came from far different roots. Born in Westphalia, Germany, she was the daughter of a chic southern belle, Elizabeth Johnson, from Union Springs, Alabama, who, while on a yacht in the south of France, met and soon married handsome and wealthy Count Franz Egon von Furstenberg. Their fairy-tale union lasted just four years.

Brought up as a Park Avenue princess, Betsy was partly educated at the prim and proper Miss Hewitt's Finishing School. At the age of fourteen she was a cover girl in chic French fashion magazines and made her first film in Italy at seventeen. She was photographed for her first of three *Look* covers by Stanley Kubrick. MGM summoned her after she dazzled critics in her first Broadway play, launching her on to the cover of *Life* (circulation 5,200,000) as "Betsy von Furstenberg, Society Girl on Broadway." Betsy's friend S. J. Perelman used her as a character in one of. his short stories, describing her as "Bitsy von Auchincloss, whose eyes and bathing suit were the same size and color." (Before she met Nick, she dated Peter Howard, grandson of Charles Howard, owner of the famed racehorse Seabiscuit.)

With all of Betsy's sophistication and glamour, however, Nick Hilton's world was still one giant eye-opener. She called it "primitive, very wild, and uncultivated. A friend was shocked that I was with Nick because she knew I was completely out of my depth."

This was underscored during that trip to Texas when Nick spent most of his time drinking and playing high-stakes poker with his cronies, relegating Betsy to another room where she discovered herself among a small coterie of rather glamorous, startlingly beautiful young women.

"They had these women around who I thought were quite nice, and the men would sort of separate themselves from the women and they would be playing cards and I would be talking to these women," she recalls. "I just assumed they were actresses. After their card game Nick came out and said, 'Don't you dare talk to those women!' I said, 'What am I supposed to do, sit in a corner and read magazines while you're playing cards?' And he said, "I told you—*do not* talk to those women.' When I asked why, he said, 'They're prostitutes!' Afterwards we all went out to dinner together."

Nick's chums were all older—he mostly sought out father-figure types because his relationship with his own father was so difficult. There was the Maxwell House Coffee heir Bob Neal, who had a reputation for tossing diamond trinkets at Hollywood cuties he was pursuing (like Debbie Reynolds). There was Nick's close confidante, the darkly handsome actor John Carroll, who played Zorro on the silver screen, and who had an affair with a young Marilyn Monroe while she was living with him and his wife, Lucy Ryman, Marilyn's protégé at MGM. And there was a Texas legend, the flamboyant hotelman Glenn McCarthy—known as "Diamond Glenn" and the "King of the Wildcatters"—who was the inspiration for Jett Rink as played by James Dean in the film *Giant,* which also starred Nick's ex-wife.

Nick's divorce from Elizabeth Taylor was still news—the papers had photos of them working out a settlement and having meetings in New York that sparked published reports of a reconciliation—when word broke about his engagement to Betsy, and this too received worldwide attention in mid-September 1951. Headlines screamed, "Ex-Countess Reveals Betrothal To Nicky Hilton, Hotel King Heir."

For the young actress now trying to make it in movies, the engagement to Elizabeth Taylor's ex-husband was a publicity bonanza. Reporters had caught the two of them together and under a barrage of questions about whether theirs was true love, whether marriage was in the future, they spontaneously said they were engaged.

"I've never been happier," she told reporters. "Nicky's a wonderful guy."

For Nick, who had had it with Elizabeth's fame and publicity, it was simply more of the same. Sharp-eyed gossip columnist Dorothy Kilgallen noted that Nick's fiancée wasn't sporting an engagement ring and asked, "Why hasn't the rich young man given her a diamond?" Years later Betsy explains that she and Nick "went to look for one, but we couldn't decide. And then I said, 'Let's forget about the ring.' I wasn't the type to settle down that easily."

Bob Neal, who describes him and Nick as "the Gold Dust Twins" because of how close they were, was extremely fond of Betsy. "She was the genuine article, very cute and had a lot of class, and Nick liked her." But more than five decades later at the age of eighty-four, he notes, "When she arrived in Hollywood, Nick was the biggest catch on the market. If a girl went out with him it was instant publicity. Betsy knew that. Besides, Nick was very attractive and Betsy was cute as anything he *ever* showed up with."

Their announced engagement, on a par decades later with the blast of press about Paris Hilton and Paris Latsis's so-called marriage plans, even pricked up Elizabeth's ears. Betsy explains: "Just after all that news about the engagement hit, Nick and I went to the opening of a movie and we were sitting somewhere towards the front and Elizabeth was sitting somewhere towards the back. When the film was over Nick said, 'Let's wait. Let's not go out. I don't want to run into her.' But *she* waited *us* out. The theater was empty and she waited for us to come up the aisle so she could look me over. I thought it was funny that she would wait just to see me. We said hello and that was it."

However, Elizabeth remained on Nick's mind. When he and Betsy had quarrels, he called her "Elizabeth," as in Taylor. "Somewhere inside of himself," Betsy notes, "he was appalled that this new affair with me was turning out to be just like the old marriage in the fact that we couldn't get along and that Elizabeth obviously also wanted him to live a different kind of life."

Betsy soon discovered that Nick was a hooked on downers, along with being an alcoholic. "He was taking all these pills that a doctor friend of his was supplying him with, so he had no motivation to do anything that would make him feel better about himself," says Betsy, still horrified years later. "I think Nick was terribly, terribly disappointed in his own lack of motivation and that he just couldn't get with it. The terrible thing was he had no enthusiasm for anything except that dreadful life he led, no real interest in anything, in what the rest of the world was like. He slept 'til God knows what time. He got up and he started drinking and playing cards. He didn't go to work.

"I couldn't deal with it. In the daytime I was at the studio and when we went out at night we danced and we flirted and I didn't deal with it. I was eighteen. There was nothing I could do."

Bob Neal says Nick was "doing the death wish, which is what I called it. The death wish is a combination of pills and booze. You can't beat it. He kept that very, very secret. He was on pills big-time. Down in Palm Springs where the Hiltons had a place, I once watched Nick go from the bed to the bathroom and it took him three hours. He was paralyzed."

Neal, who was practically a part of the Hilton family, believed Nick's descent into pill hell had a lot to do with how his father and brother Barron regarded him, and how he was never given a chance in the family business in those days. "Nick got squashed all the time and he blamed it on Barron, I'm afraid," observes Neal. "But the old man was behind everything like that. It wasn't Barron who instituted things. Everything had to have the clearance of the old man because he held the purse strings, and the old man was an asshole."

When Betsy found the long days at the studio exhausting, Nick put her together with his doctor friend. "He used to play cards with Nick and hang out with him and run errands for him," she says. "He was like a father to Nick. He supplied Nick and his friends with what they needed. He might have also been a pimp. He was a *very* evil person."

When Betsy complained to the doctor that she was having trouble sleeping, he whipped out his pad and prescribed the little red pill Nick was hooked on until his death, the very addictive downer Seconal. "I guess I had taken Nick's Seconal and found out how nicely it worked," says Betsy. Mixed with the alcohol it made for a very potent cocktail.

Seconal was *the* recreational drug in Hollywood back then—Judy

Garland, for one, gobbled them like M&Ms and eventually fatally over-dosed; Cary Grant and Carole Landis and Marilyn Monroe were among the untold number of star users.

With the downers doing their job, Betsy needed something to get her up and going, because she had to be at the studio early in the morning even though she wasn't making a film, so Nick's friendly phy-sician wrote prescriptions for Betsy's "uppers," which were the most addictive for her. "I had a very hard time getting off amphetamines," she acknowledges.

While the gambling, the drinking, the pill-popping, and the occa-sional violent outburst were a way of life for Nick, Betsy still found him "awfully cute, extremely endearing, gentle, and sweet—except on those occasions when he was terribly drunk."

At the same time, she was "dumbstruck" by his lack of interest in anything outside his own parochial circle. "I thought I could introduce him to things that are very enjoyable—traveling and seeing things, but he wasn't interested in expanding at all. He was only interested in play-ing cards and drinking—drinking and playing cards. It was an unbeliev-ably boring existence. It was really amazing that our relationship continued as long as it did, because we really had very little to talk about to each other after a while."

Betsy felt the same about some of the other Hiltons she met: "I was so amazed that they were so uneducated—all of them. I just remember bringing up something about the Second World War and they just didn't have the slightest clue. I was talking about Pétain, or DeGaulle, or some-thing like that, and they just knew nothing."

If there was any great suspicion that Betsy was after the Hilton money, it was mainly attributable to Connie's paranoia. To see if the new girl in Nick's life was up to something, he dispatched, of all people, his ex-wife, Zsa Zsa, under contract at MGM along with Betsy, to investigate. If anybody had the radar to spot a gold digger, it surely was the former Mrs. Hilton, with whom Connie had remained on speaking terms.

"I'm certain she had been put up to having lunch with me to find out what my motives were, because the Hiltons didn't know me well at all," says Betsy. "And, of course, what Zsa Zsa said to me was, *'Dahlink,* you *must* get and keep the ring. That's the important thing. Just *get* the ring.' It was *so* funny. I thought she was joking at first, and then I looked at her face and I realized she was *totally* serious. I felt like I was talking to a creature from a different planet."

As Betsy saw it, Nick was clearly "intimidated" and fearful of his powerful father. When she moved into her apartment on Doheny Road, for instance, she noticed that Nick never parked his black Cadillac any-where near her building. "He didn't want his father to know that we spent all our time together."

Some six or eight months into their relationship, an event occurred that infuriated Betsy, who was just about fed up with Nick's way of life. They had planned to fly to Mexico, and she had packed accordingly. But when the plane landed they were in snow-covered, frigid northern Cali-fornia. Instead of a sun-drenched, sensuous villa overlooking the Pacific, they moved into an isolated cabin in the snow.

"The plans were suddenly changed because of weather, and Nick thought, 'Oh, well, since we're on the plane, let's go someplace else,' so we wound up in Tahoe, or Arrowhead, and of course, I didn't have the right clothes and it was freezing cold. We were literally snowed in with absolutely no servants, nobody to wait on us, no restaurants to go to. I objected to being the one to make the bed, cook the food, to wait on him. And he was drunk and boring and played cards and I had *nothing* to do."

Betsy returned to Los Angeles and moved out of her apartment and in with a close friend, the actress Esperanza Bauer Diaz "Chata" Wayne, the Mexican actress and estranged second wife of the Duke himself, who was in Hawaii.

While Betsy was at the Waynes' mansion in the San Fernando Valley, preparing to return to New York to be in a play after having been let out of her MGM contract, she received an emergency telephone call from Nick's doctor. "Nick's in very bad trouble," he told her. He had been in an accident while driving drunk, suffered a broken arm, the police were looking for him, and he needed a place to hide out.

"He asked me if I could just keep him at Chata's for a while," she re-calls. "I don't even know how they knew I was there." Nevertheless, Betsy and Chata agreed to harbor Nick. "He never told me any details about what happened in the accident and I didn't ask. I didn't want to know. I was just being sisterly, motherly, because he didn't want the police to find him, and he didn't want his father to know about what had happened."

Lying low in the Wayne residence, Nick bonded with the lady of the house, and the two spent hours together playing cards, drinking, and who knows what else. "I went out," says Betsy. "I wanted no part of it." The Hilton heir and the Duke's wife must have gotten real chummy, because Nick ended up being one of the central figures in the Waynes' eventual divorce trial. Their "dirty wash," as John Wayne called it, was being splashed across the front pages of America's newspapers day after day.

Wayne charged that his wife had "entertained" Nick during his absence. He said he learned that his wife had a man in the house during his absence, but he didn't know it was Nick until the butler handed him his wife's doodlings, which read, "Esperanza Hilton . . . Chata Hilton . . . Chata and Nick . . ."

"When I saw this," the big guy testified, "I vomited."

He told the court that, early in his relationship with his wife, she used to doodle with *his* name, so when he saw her doodling with Nick's name, "I knew how she felt about him."

Mrs. Wayne accused her husband of having had "an all-night tryst," as the press called it, with sultry actress Gail Russell, who had played Wayne's love interest in a western called *The Angel and the Badman.*

During the four-day trial, Chata Wayne also testified that her husband, revered at the box office as a brawny cowboy in westerns and a warrior in combat films, turned their home into an actual war zone— bombarding her with everything from the back of his beefy hand to upholstered pillows, and even throwing rubbing alcohol in her face during their six-year marriage. On one occasion he left her stranded at a party and took off with some chums to go "someplace where there were stripteasers, call girls, prostitutes or whatever you want to call them. He came home the next morning very drunk and with a big, black bite on his neck . . . a human being bite," she testified. In response, the Duke charged that Nick was "the other man" in his marriage, and that his wife was in love with him—an accusation she denied.

But before Nick had a chance to give his side of the story on the witness stand, the judge granted both sides a divorce after a reported $500,000 financial settlement was reached.

"I'm the loser in this fight," Nick told reporters outside the courtroom. He claimed any romantic relationship with John Wayne's wife was "ridiculous. . . . Everybody leaves out the fact that I was a guest of Betsy von Furstenberg, not Mrs. Wayne. Betsy was my only reason for being in the house, not Chata."

Some months later, Betsy, then back in New York, got a call out of the blue from Nick. "He was staying at the Plaza and he wanted to see me," she says. "I stopped by and went up to his suite, and he was immediately very affectionate and very sweet. I just said, 'Look, I have to leave.' I literally had like fifteen minutes. I kissed him good-bye and that was the end of it. I think he wanted to get back together again, but it was just hopeless, though I really adored him while I was with him."

As with Elizabeth Taylor, Betsy received a gift from Connie— a chunk of Hilton hotel shares that she immediately sold off.

Nick, who couldn't stay out of trouble, also became embroiled in a headline-making child custody case involving stunning actress Claire Kelly, who was being groomed as the next Rita Hayworth, and her ex-husband, George DeWitt, host of a popular TV game show, *Name That Tune.* In 1956, *Confidential* ran a story about Nick and Kelly's involvement that was headlined "Nicky Hilton—He Prefers Scotch On The Rocks To A Honey On The Divan!" Subsequently, during the DeWitt-Kelly child custody case, DeWitt filed court papers accusing Kelly of "adulterous, immoral, and scandalous conduct" with Nick and Frank Sinatra. Nick remained mum, but Old Blue Eyes was furious, denied the charge, and had DeWitt blacklisted from show business, according to DeWitt's brother. DeWitt later died virtually penniless, while Nick's reputation was further tarnished because of the latest scandal.

# CHAPTER 23

**B**y the start of the Eisenhower-Nixon decade of the 1950s, Connie Hilton had become the world's most famous innkeeper with fifteen hotels in the United States, Mexico, and Puerto Rico—properties valued at more than $125 million. And more—many more—were about to open.

*Time* magazine had devoted a cover to Hilton, calling him a "party-loving, party-giving host" who knew how to treat his VIP guests and make the likes of Howard Hughes, Tallulah Bankhead, Gertrude Lawrence, and Noel Coward, among many others, feel like they were at home in Beverly Hills or on Park Avenue.

Connie had more than eleven thousand employees and bragged to his friends and the media that it would take him forty years to sleep in every bed in his more than 12,000 hotel rooms.

*Fortune,* engorging his already swollen ego, called him "an acquisitive genius . . . a fast man in an appraisal . . . a smart negotiator . . . [a] dashing trader . . . an extremely resourceful financial strategist who knows every move in the book."

Connie saw his hotels as cities within cities, with guests living a full life without ever having to step outside. "They have nightclubs, banquet halls, and shopping centers," he proclaimed. "You can read a book in the library and use the safe deposit vault as a bank. If you get sick, there's a hospital, with a doctor and a nurse. You can park your car, eat your head off, and sleep till noon. Home was never like that!"

Still, the man wasn't all business.

Despite his empire rising, he quit work every day at 6 P.M. Never later. That was a rule of his he rarely ever broke. A businessman, he firmly believed, had to have fun.

In his sixties, but as energetic as when he first danced the dance with Zsa Zsa, Conrad escorted pretty ladies in droves, the younger, the better, café hopping until three in the morning. He bought a World War II PT boat, the kind Jack Kennedy commanded, and had it converted into a pleasure craft to cruise the Pacific near his spectacular estate. He had a getaway on Lake Arrowhead where he raced on the waters in his Chris Craft. He kept a number 2 iron in his office to practice his swing, scoring in the high 80s, and bragged that he won a close match with his friend President Eisenhower.

On the business side, he had formed a new division, Hilton International, starting with three hotels in Bermuda. Then came the Caribe Hilton, in San Juan. Connie saw the future and rightly perceived that the world was shrinking, that jet air travel would make it easier for people to leave the United States and arrive in Paris in time for breakfast.

With the cold war raging, Connie had wrapped himself in Old Glory as a true patriot and anti-Communist for ideological *and* business reasons. He gave serious, intense speeches and even conceived a poem called "America on Its Knees," all of which received wide press coverage and letters of public support.

Connie's strong anti-Communist stance was an asset as he expanded his chain abroad; his hotels were used as propaganda machines and unofficial listening posts and intelligence-gathering centers in Europe and the Middle East as the cold war grew hotter. As one longtime Hilton family member notes, "Anything Washington asked him to do, he'd jump."

Connie, in fact, later acknowledged that the U.S. government had asked him to begin putting up hotels in foreign countries that were getting Marshall Plan aid after the Second World War. Washington's concept, at least on the surface, was that the hotels would help the U.S. foreign aid program by stimulating American dollars into travel and trade. "The government gave me a list of European countries," Connie allowed, "and I had to have these countries request funds to help finance the hotels before we could go ahead."

The Hiltons were the tallest, most luxurious, first truly modern edifices in some of those foreign cities. Moreover, they brought with them American culture (cheeseburgers were served in the restaurants)— a shrewd political and business move to draw American tourists nervously venturing overseas for the first time, and to indoctrinate foreigners in the American way of life in the face of the "Red Menace."

When America finally landed a man on the moon in the "space race" with the Soviet Union, Hilton buoyantly celebrated. He proclaimed he'd open the first hotel on the moon. A national advertisement showed the gloved hand of an astronaut carrying a hotel room key, the fob of which carried the words "Lunar Hilton."

After astronaut Neil Armstrong made his historic moonwalk, Barron and Marilyn Hilton threw a spectacular space-age sit-down dinner for some two hundred celebrity guests at their estate. The tables were decorated with enormous white Sputniks sprinkled with silver stars and white orchids—all bathed in blue moon-glow lights. The pièce de résistance was the Lunar Hilton menu offering the diners "Tranquility Sea-Food Savoy," "Roast Celestial Sirloin," "Starspuds," and "Apollo Pois," topped off by "Galaxy Glace," "Saturn Fours," and "Café Orbit."

**WHILE CONNIE WAS ATTEMPTING** to capture the hearts and minds of those heathen Reds, his number one son, Nick, was trying to capture as many red*heads*—and blondes and brunettes—as a hedonist could handle.

Like wolves in the henhouse, Nick Hilton and Bob Neal had set up bachelor pads in the same building on palm tree-lined Horn Avenue near Havenhurst Drive in swinging West Hollywood—an area literally teeming with gorgeous young starlets, models, groupies, and rich-husband hunters.

"We called it the 'Pussy Belt' because there were more girls in apartments up and down Havenhurst than anywhere else in LA," Neal fondly recalls. "There's an old saying out there that between Nick Hilton and Bob Neal nothing got away. *Nothing* escaped. Nick had it all. There wasn't one girl who ever turned him down for a date. And by 'date' I mean jumping in bed.

"Nick was usually a second-date artist. He had to get laid by the second date. Most of the time he wasn't turned down. Most guys gotta string it out and beg and give candy and brandy and all that shit," continues Neal, "but not Nick. Most of them went for it. He was a high scorer. I never heard any complaints. If a girl made it with Nick she never forgot it!" Whenever Neal spotted a likely candidate for Nick, he'd make a duck-like sound, their code for "Pussy Alert."

On the rare occasion when Nick couldn't get a girl to be his arm candy and go partying with him, he had a real mallard duck accompany him for drinks. His partnership with the duck began when Nick had been partying at one of his usual haunts, the Luau, in Beverly Hills, a spot known for the beautiful babes at the bar. He had gotten so drunk that the bartender sent him home in a cab to sleep it off. Waiting on the corner for a taxi to return to the nightspot, Nick saw the duck waddling across the street. He picked up the bird, got into the cab, and brought it back to the Luau, where he set it on the bar and ordered a bourbon for himself and one for the duck, which he named Charley, in honor of Charley Morrison, who owned the Mocambo. A crowd had gathered to watch the fun, which consisted of Charley taking a drink and then pooping on the bar, and after a time the duck just sort of fell over. Nick said, "Oh, don't worry about him, he's just a little hungover."

Noreen Nash Siegel Whitmore, an actress who at the time was married to Dr. Lee Siegel, the "physician to the stars" who had become Nick's doctor and confidant after the first "Dr. Feel Good" left the inner circle, recalls, "Nick would come by our house with the duck, and for a while he took the duck everyplace. At parties he'd put the duck in someone's pool."

Then, suddenly, the duck was gone. When Al Mathis, the Luau's owner, asked Nick what happened to it, he responded, "He must have died of cirrhosis of the liver."

**FISTFIGHTS WERE A CONSTANT** in Nick's life because of his drinking. One night at the Mocambo, a fight broke out over him using profanity, and a beautiful blond model from Texas was knocked to the floor and suffered a sprained back when she got in the way as Nick traded blows with her boyfriend, an air force navigator.

Ever protective of the prestigious Hilton name, Connie was furious about Nick's increasingly bad press. As Dorothy Kilgallen reported, "Nicky Hilton's usually indulgent father has given him the off-to-Siberia treatment since his latest escapade on the front pages."

Nevertheless, the bloodshed, the alcohol, and the headlines continued to flow. There was the "slugfest" at a Sunset Strip nitery, and five broken bones and a few head stitches that Nick received after a spar with his chum Francis Warford "Joe" Drown, who owned the Bel-Air Hotel.

"Nick would get drunk to where he didn't know who he was," says Bob Neal. "We were down at his old man's house in Palm Springs, and he was out of his mind. We were outside and he couldn't find the key and it made him so fuckin' mad he pounded the door and stuck his arm through the glass and goddamn near bled to death.

"When the ambulance guys came, he was going to kill all of them. They were putting him on a stretcher and he was battling them."

The Hilton Hotel heir had mostly escaped any form of punishment for his alcohol-induced crimes and misdemeanors, but he couldn't get away scot-free forever with his bad behavior.

Newspaper readers were greeted with a shocking Weegee-style tabloid photograph with their morning coffee on May 15, 1954. Under the glaring headlines "Hotel Heir Gets Room With Bars" and "Nicky In Clink" was a film noirish shot of a ravaged-looking twenty-seven-year-old "Playboy Nicky Hilton, heir of the wealthy hotel family . . ." in a Los Angeles County Jail cell "crying bitterly" after being "arrested by a stationful" of Hollywood sheriff's deputies on a drunk charge.

He had been thrown into the slammer after his Beverly Hills neighbors at 882 North Doheny Drive—a low-slung apartment complex where

Marilyn Monroe lived on and off with her then-boyfriend, the New York Yankees slugger Joe DiMaggio—complained of loud cursing and fighting in progress that "could be heard for blocks."

Deputies said that when they arrived Nick shouted, "You want a fight? Here I am." Nick then bolted out of his second-story flat, threw punches, and was finally thrown to the ground on the sidewalk and handcuffed. When the officers finally got him into the backseat of their radio car, Nick started yelling, "I can buy and sell the lot of you, and I'm going to do it, too." He then solidly kicked a deputy in the back of the head, who had to struggle to keep control of the swerving patrol car.

Though "barely able to walk unassisted," Nick started throwing punches at the sheriff's substation while he was being booked. He gave his occupation, truthfully, as "loafer" and turned over his gold cufflinks and eleven dollars and sixteen cents in change. (As Bob Neal points out, Nick was "a very strong guy. I'm talking about *physically* strong. He could have twisted a guy's head off.")

Decades later Neal, who had an apartment below Nick's on Doheny, recalls the fight was with their actor pal John Carroll, who received a black eye when they began throwing punches after returning from a nightclub. "Carroll almost beat him up. They were both drunk. John Carroll was a pretty tough guy, too—a big, rangy guy."

Released from county jail the next day on twenty-five dollars' bail, Nick told a swarm of reporters that he had "a story that will blow the lid off Los Angeles," but he wouldn't reveal what it was. It was enough, though, to generate national headlines such as "Nicky Hilton, Freed From Jail, Threatens 'Exposé'."

Several days after his arrest, Nick was given two years' probation by Beverly Hills municipal-court judge Charles J. Griffen. He warned Nick he'd face a year in prison if he violated it. "Any more trouble with liquor and you'll be right back here again," the judge told him.

Despite Nick's subsequent stint of rehab at the Mayo Clinic, nothing could be done for him. Observes Neal, "Nick and booze—they just didn't mix."

# CHAPTER 24

**N**ick had a "secret formula" to deal with the hordes of women who wanted to be with him, and the ones he was obsessively chasing. It was quite simple: "Never take any of them seriously." He was especially wary of all those women he thought were "wanting to mother" him, especially after his divorce from Elizabeth Taylor. But his bad-boy quality was what brought out the maternal instinct in women of all ages, from an ingenue like Betsy von Furstenberg to Nick's doctor's wife, Noreen Siegel.

Decades later Noreen observes, "Nick was like this hurt child. There was something so engaging about that for a lot of women. He made you want to take care of him. A lot of women he went with"—and she knew a number of them, such as Natalie Wood and Kim Novak—"would kind of hold his head when he got drunk and kind of take care of him. Nick always put his head on your shoulder and he'd say, 'Oh, I don't feel good.' He seemed to want and need that sort of attention."

While Nick could be loud and obnoxious when inebriated, he was virtually a mute when sober. A man of few words, he especially despised the press. In rare instances Nick did communicate with journalists, including a brief interview with a wire service correspondent on the subject of women. "If you hear or read about me going head over heels in love with any girl," he told United Press's Jay Breen, "just mark it down as one hundred percent fiction. This new system [of not taking females seriously] is working too well to jinx it."

Asked what kind of girl he'd like to marry if he took the step again, Nick glibly responded, "There are only three types, the way I see it. They're blonde, brunette, and redhead. After that girls are all the same."

Nick's womanizing became legend through the 1950s. According to the gossip columns, it went something like this: "Nicky Hilton's latest heart-interest is a beauty named Ilsa Bey. . . . Nicky Hilton has been dating Gloria DeHaven. They choose the quiet little spots far away from Mocambo and Ciro's. . . . I saw Nicky Hilton drinking lemonade with Ruth Ann Binns. . . . Nicky Hilton whose pop owns those hotels, is more interested in Mona Knox than in Fort Knox. . . . Nicky Hilton is pursuing Pat Morrissey. . . . Nicky Hilton around with beautiful Conover model Kim Smith who denies she is just one of Nick's knacks. . . . Nicky Hilton's latest is the movie's Piper Laurie. . . .

"Nicky Hilton is dating beautiful Betsy Steiner of the Copacabana chorus. . . . Nicky Hilton and Laura Bartlett of the Riviera chorus line left some of his $5,000 card game winnings at Nino's Continental. . . . A beautiful young concert singer named Russell Lee—a strawberry blonde—is Nicolo's current big thrill. . . . Nicky Hilton has it bad for Paula Stewart, a New York showgirl. . . . Nicky Hilton's visits to Boston have been for the purpose of wooing Rusa Lee, the young concert pianist. . . . Nicky Hilton who dates in all directions, dating Mary Murphy, the film beaut. . . . Nicky Hilton appears to be deeply smitten over Melinda Markey. . . . Nicky Hilton and Lili St. Cyr have found each other. What fun! . . . Nicky Hilton was with a studio messenger girl, Arlene Soloff, at the Luau. . . . Nicky Hilton stripping his gears over striprootzy Lee Sharon. . . .

"Nicky Hilton sends bokays to Margaret O'Brien who's a big girl now. . . . Nicky Hilton and Andrea Petti playing petticake. . . . This week's Nicky Hilton item: Barbara Schmidt, the Rose Bowl Queen. . . . Joe Boulton & John Carroll, rich Nancy Metcalf & Nicky Hilton. . . . Joe Stalin has come back to life here in Denmark but a gal from Dallas and Hollywood who's been around with Nicky Hilton has caused more excitement. . . . Nicky Hilton fraternizing with Zabra Norbo at the Villa Maria. . . .

"Nicky Hilton is squiring an Oriental Princess around town, Shih Hsieh, attractive daughter of the Gov. of Formosa. . . . Surprising sights: Nicky Hilton stag at Blue Angel. . . . Nicky Hilton—seven weeks on the wagon—was at El Morocco with glamour gal Carey Latimer, a frequent date. . . . Nicky Hilton's latest coast dates are with model Kim Smith. . . . Happy days are here again. Dick Haymes' ex-wife, Nora, dating Elizabeth Taylor's ex-husband, Nicky Hilton. . . . Nicky Hilton and Barbara "Wiggles" Nichols have found each other. . . .

"Jean Smith is the latest beauty to catch Nicky Hilton's roving eye— and hold it a little longer than most girls. . . . Nicky Hilton took Jayne Mansfield to the Photog's Ball and, Jayne says, 'was a perfect gentleman'. . . . Conrad Hilton hosted a big party including his son, Nicky, and the Swedish beauty, Ingrid Goude. . . . Nicky Hilton spent an hour in the telephone booth at El Borracho the other night chatting with stripper Lee Sharon. . . . Today's Nicky Hilton Item: Elaine Conte, whoever she is— and who cares. . . . Today's Nicky Hilton item: Dorothy Johnson. . . .

"Nicky Hilton's been dating Marisa Allasio at the Plaza's romantic Rendezvous Room. . . . Nicky Hilton's pals say he vowed to follow Italo actress Marisa Allasio to Hellton. . . . The beauty with Nicky Hilton at Birdland the other night was cover girl Helene O'Connell. . . . Nicky Hilton took Carolyn Mitchell to Molly Bee's opening at the Club Largo but they had a quarrel and Nicky stalked out. . . ."

**DURING THAT NONSTOP** girl rush there were some special relationships that were mostly under the radar of the gossip columnists—relationships in which Nick didn't always live up to his public reputation as a playboy extraordinaire, or even that of the "perfect gentleman."

After Betsy von Furstenberg, Nick's next serious romance was with knockout Joan Lucille Olander, who hailed from a small town in South Dakota. Once she got to Hollywood and began winning beauty contests (as a fifteen-year-old), she found herself in that elite circle of starlets who caught the roving eye of eccentric Howard Hughes, and she was soon winning parts in RKO films (along with working as a Las Vegas showgirl and gracing the cover of *Esquire* as an Alberto Vargas pinup). In New York, she was in the Broadway show *Million Dollar Baby,* and every night the world champion prizefighter Jack Dempsey came to see her. They began a relationship before she decided "he was too old or I was too young."

Practically overnight, Joan Lucille Olander was transformed at Universal International into platinum blond bombshell Mamie Van Doren, a legend in her own time, and was in that class of sexpots that included Jayne Mansfield and Marilyn Monroe. Mamie was known for wearing what was called the "bullet bra," a look that drove male fans of all ages wild with desire; her trademark line was "Mamie likes 'em young."

To generate buzz for their new star, Universal's publicity department chief, Al Horowitz, arranged for Nick—America's most eligible bachelor of the decade—to take Mamie, wearing a white, strapless, slinky Ceil Chapman gown, to the 1953 Hollywood premiere of *The Glenn Miller Story* at the Pantages Theater. When they were given seats too close to the screen, Mamie was embarrassed and told him, "Maybe you said yes to the wrong starlet," but Nick squeezed her hand and responded, "Hell, Mamie! You're with a Hilton!"

Their date that night made the columns. The snarky syndicated gossip*teuse* Edith Gwynn told inquiring minds, "People are still sniggling over Mamie Van Doren's theater-aisle march at the *Glenn Miller Story* prem. She was gowned and made up to look exactly like Marilyn Monroe was for M.M.'s *How to Marry a Millionaire* opening! Mamie didn't quite make it. Imitators seldom do! Anyway, she was dragging her white fox along the floor—with Nicky Hilton trailing behind."

A photo of the two, smiling and looking glamorous—Nick in tux and bow tie—ran in the scandal rag *Confidential* and got bigger placement on the page than one of Academy Award winner Humphrey Bogart and beautiful actress Cyd Charisse "in a huddle at Mocambo."

"It was my first big outing as Mamie Van Doren," she recalls years later. "Except for Rock Hudson, Nick was my second date. He was sexy-looking, handsome. He had it all—he had money, he had popularity, he was a celebrity, and all those things together turned me on."

Nick was infatuated, and why not? Mamie was industrial-strength arm candy—platinum blond hair and a body to die for. Nick squired her to the best restaurants—Romanoff's, Chasen's—to A-list parties, to the racetracks where he won and lost bundles.

But just like Betsy von Furstenberg, Mamie nailed Nick's modus operandi early on. "He was on his best behavior in the beginning and then he started getting really bad," she maintains. "I took him to the Golden Globe Awards. I was the hostess that year and Nick sat at the bar and he got loaded while I was onstage."

Once again Nick was playing second fiddle to a glamorous movie star who was getting all the attention; it was a rerun of his relationships with Taylor and von Furstenberg.

Despite her sexpot image—and Nick's reputation as a horndog—Mamie was not about to jump in bed with him right away. "I didn't sleep with him for quite a while," she asserts. "We dated for a couple of months before I went to bed with him. He got very upset over that. It was pre-Pill America, and I didn't want to get pregnant." But when their relationship finally turned intimate Mamie was surprised to discover that the real-life Nick Hilton in the sack didn't live up to his publicity as a stud. "All he wanted to do," states a very candid Mamie years later, "was drink and then *maybe* fuck. But he really wanted to drink before he wanted to go to bed. Unlike what the newspapers had to say about him, he wasn't a real sensuous Romeo, or a Casanova, but Nicky was *really* well-hung. He had a large cock, but was curiously unskilled at using it. He was not that great of a lovemaker. He wasn't kinky at all, but quite conservative. Lovemaking was straight on, the old-fashioned way, and that was it—there wasn't much foreplay. When we were in bed, all he wanted to do was watch *Dragnet* or some other stupid show on television. I can't say Nick was bad in bed, but when a man's drinking a lot, he can't always perform. We fucked often—as often as Nicky's drinking would allow. He drank—that was the most he did."

Nick wasted no time asking Mamie to marry him, but she had qualms, which she kept to herself. For one, she didn't like his drinking, and, second, her career was starting to boom and she didn't feel marriage would be conducive to her goal of becoming a major star. The Hilton wealth, though, was an attraction. Mamie quipped to Hedda Hopper, "Nicky's selling a new kind of fountain pen — one that writes with oil."

Nick sensed Mamie's hesitation about marriage and took her to a party where his actor pal John Carroll lobbied for him. The bash was at his brother Barron's, where Mamie and Marilyn Hilton did an ass-wiggling hula-hula dance together. Afterward, Carroll sidled up to Mamie and told her, "Nicky wants to marry you. Baby, you can have it all. Play your cards right. Marry him. He wants you."

Nick soon took Mamie to Casa Encantada for dinner, hoping for his father's approval. The dinner was a "bizarre" affair, says Mamie. Connie sat at the head of an immense table, which was set with solid gold plates and silverware and with almost as many servants to wait on the three of them as there was help in a Hilton hotel dining room. While Connie eyed Mamie — and she certainly was an eyeful — he never spoke a word to her but directed all of his conversation to his son. "Conrad talked to Nicky, Nicky talked to Conrad, and Nicky talked to me. When I spoke to Conrad, he answered through Nicky. It was though we were speaking different languages and Nicky was our interpreter," says Mamie. "Conrad wanted to meet me to make sure Nicky wasn't getting into another bad scene. He was an imposing man, and he made Nicky look small and weak. Nicky and his father were completely different types. Nick adored him, but he knew he couldn't come up to what his father was. Nicky didn't give a rat's ass about hotels.

"Conrad had a pool house on the estate and he wanted Nicky to live there, and Nicky wanted to get his own place because he wanted me to move in with him," continues Mamie. "I knew there was going to be a problem. Conrad said to Nicky, 'I want you to move in here. I want you to stay here, and I'll do it any way you want to do it.' Conrad was *begging* Nicky to stay. Conrad really had him under his thumb. He dominated him like crazy."

At dinner Conrad smoked big Cuban cigars, blowing smoke everywhere and belching loudly. Beyond that, a noise that sounded like the staccato of a machine gun erupted on and off during the course of the meal.

"I heard rumblings under Conrad's elegant chair and I said, 'What the hell is that?' Between the smell of his cigars and his deep, rumbling farts at the table I felt sick. He was a real cowboy."

Nick never moved into the pool house but stayed in the apartment above Bob Neal's at 882 North Doheny.

"Nick wanted me to see it to make sure I liked the décor before I moved in," recalls Mamie. "He had hired a decorator and I went to visit the place and it was *the* worst I'd *ever* seen—so many colors, so wild. He'd put a lot of money into it, but it was awful. No taste."

Mamie never moved in, and they never lived together. "I'm the one who broke it off," she says. "We had a big scene where it was really a blowout—such a bad argument, and that was the end. He was about to give me a diamond engagement ring. He wanted to get married in Vegas. But I had a contract with Universal and I was just starting. I had a third movie coming up, and I thought, all I need to do is get married and then have problems with him getting drunk all the time. I never even thought of the Hilton money, or a big settlement if we split up. I was young. I was just so glad to get my studio contract and make two hundred and fifty dollars a week.

"And I don't think the old man approved of me. For one thing, I wasn't a Catholic."

According to Mamie, she and Nick double-dated one night with Bob Neal and a girlfriend of Mamie's, and at the end of the evening they all returned to Neal's apartment. She says Nick and Neal were inebriated.

Mamie didn't like Neal, who she felt "was very instrumental in leading Nick to a lot of things because Nicky was sort of weak in some ways. He had a lot to do with the way Nicky was. He had a lot to do with Nicky's behavior. Bob Neal was older, more secure and wiser, and he was jealous because Nick was better looking. I never liked Nicky running around with him, and the minute Nicky and I broke it off, guess who called me? Bob Neal."

Says Neal years later, "Mamie had the greatest fucking figure. We'd pull up to her house and I'd look over and she'd be naked in her car. She told me she didn't drink and she didn't smoke, because she didn't want a damn thing to interfere with her sexual pleasures and feelings."

Mamie soon met and married the popular bandleader Ray Anthony—

the first of her four husbands—and they had a baby, a son. When she was performing her singing act in the showroom where Liberace was featured at Las Vegas's Riviera Hotel and Casino, Nick, whom she hadn't heard from since their split, suddenly made an encore appearance.

"I was now married, and a mother, and I'm on my way to my dressing room and he's standing outside the door," she recalls vividly. "He said, 'Hi, I'm going to catch your show tonight,' and he asked me if we could get together. I got all nervous. He made it clear he was still interested in me. He never gave up."

The last time she saw Connie was in Manila in 1968 when she was returning from Vietnam, where she had entertained the troops. Connie had just opened the Manila Hilton. "I went down to the dining room, and there he was with about six beautiful, young Filipino girls. I was sitting at a table where I could watch him. He knew it was me but he never came over to say hello. And I thought, well, fuck you!"

But the Hiltons remained in her life. Hugh Hefner had invited Mamie to his bacchanalian Halloween party at the Playboy Mansion in 2005, and she ran into Connie's great-granddaughter face to-face for the first time.

"I'm pretty wild on the dance floor and here comes Paris Hilton as an angel wearing wings and trying to dance. I wanted to tell her I slept with her great-uncle, but I thought, oh, shit, she probably couldn't have cared less and didn't even know who he was.

"She's got the Hilton name, but she's not put together well. She's butt ugly and she's got stumps for legs. I don't understand what all the fuss is about. She's famous for being famous and it's just like Marilyn Monroe. What *really* made Marilyn pop out was when her nude calendar came out in the fifties. Back then something like that was unheard of.

"And today what made Paris famous is that X-rated video. But there's a lot of difference between a photograph and a pornographic video. We've come a long way. A pinup picture isn't going to do it these days. You have to be giving blow jobs on camera."

**FOR A TIME** Nick dated B-movie actress and stunt golfer Jeanne Carmen, another blond bombshell in the mode of Mamie. Carmen was a close friend of Marilyn Monroe's, and after Marilyn's death in August 1962, Carmen was one of the confidantes who claimed to have been a witness to Monroe's affair with Bobby Kennedy. Connie introduced Nick to Carmen, and soon the gossip columnists were reporting a hot romance.

But years later Carmen acknowledges that they actually were walkers for each other. "When Nick didn't have a date and he wanted to go somewhere and not be alone he called me, and if I didn't have a date and needed someone, I'd call him."

She believes he was simply a publicity hound who savored being seen with beautiful women. "We'd be out at a club and sometimes photographers would be lurking and when Nick saw the camera he'd reach over and kiss me," she recalls. "I was never a publicity hound, but *he* would do that, he'd call attention to us. And I'd say, 'Nicky, *please.*' And as soon as the photographer would go away that would be the end of that. He probably wanted everybody to think he was laying every girl in town—and he might not have been laying *anybody.*

"I honestly don't remember him making a sexual play for me, which is really strange. Maybe it was the booze. I never heard anything about him being gay, but who knows."

# CHAPTER 25

T hrough most of the 1980s, British actress Joan Collins's claim to fame was her starring role in what was then the world's most popular soap opera, *Dynasty,* in which she played Alexis Carrington Colby—one of the great bitchy, sexy, and conniving TV divas of all time. But back in the mid-1950s, after she arrived at 20th Century-Fox to pursue stardom after *La Dolce Vita* across the pond, she was hot prey for playboys like Nick Hilton.

By the time Joan hooked up with Nick, she was considered "one of the most dated girls in town." She'd been linked to actors Robert Wagner, Michael Rennie, conductor Buddy Bregman, and both of Charlie Chaplin's sons. At one high point, she'd set an unofficial Hollywood record by dating fourteen different bachelors in as many days and had just ended a brief live-in relationship with Arthur Loew Jr., grandson of MGM's founder, with Loew telling her, "You are a fucking bore," and Collins telling him, "And you are a boring fuck."

Nick was captivated by Joan's sultry looks and sexy, clipped accent. Early on he showered her with attention—a 24/7 chauffeur-driven car was a nice touch. And the twosome spent time in swinging Acapulco.

Collins's relationship with Nick was part of what had the potential of being a volatile triangle that involved another starlet, Natalie Wood. The celebrity exposé magazine *Uncensored* put the Collins-Wood competition for the heart and mind of the hotel scion on its cover: "Natalie Wood & Joan Collins: The Untold Story Of That Feud Over Nicky Hilton."

When asked by a gossip columnist about sharing Nick, twenty-three-year-old Joan said, "Oh, it doesn't bother me. Besides, Natalie is much younger than I am—she's only nineteen." In fact, Joan wasn't interested in a serious romance and neither was Nick.

Natalie, however, would see things a bit differently, and so would Nick.

Joan liked men with machismo, men who could dominate her but not push her around, so Nick was a mixed bag in her book from the start. She viewed him as "dissolute and rakish"—quite aware that he fancied himself a girl-chaser and "Hollywood's swingingest bachelor." Years later she observed, "He appeared as if he had seen and done everything. He had been everywhere, could get practically any girl he wanted, and was completely jaded."

But there were more serious issues that eventually turned her against him. For one, she claimed in her memoir *Past Imperfect* that he was "racially bigoted," noting that his ideas went with his "southern drawl," which was actually Texan but sounded Alabaman to her British ears. And while she viewed him as a "devout Catholic" who kept a rosary and a crucifix next to his bed, she was shocked to discover that his night table also featured "an amazing array of pill bottles in all shapes and sizes, girlie magazines, pornographic books, bottles of Coca-Cola, and a gun."

All of the Hiltons of Nick's generation were brought up with guns for hunting, but Nick, drunk or stoned, was dangerous with a weapon in his hand. Joan said Nick loaded the gun he had next to him in bed with blanks and frighteningly fired at the ceiling in the middle of the night "to the horror of his neighbors on Doheny Drive, who would call the police in a frenzy of fear."

Before long Joan Collins had had it with Nick Hilton and moved on, but Natalie Wood hung in.

• • •

**NATALIE WAS EXCITED** by the prospect of having an affair with a man who had slept with Elizabeth Taylor, one of her idols. As Dorothy Kilgallen reported, "Pals of reckless young Natalie Wood say her torch for Nicky Hilton is bright enough to light up all the territory west of the Mississippi."

"Nick *never* discussed that he even *knew* a girl," states Bob Neal. "He was *very* discreet and the girls knew this, and they liked it because they didn't like guys with big mouths, so it took me about twenty years to find out who was the love of Nick's life.

"It ended up it was Natalie Wood. Their relationship was based on something very simple—very fucking simple, and there's one in every house. It's called a bed."

Nick and Natalie had met just before the opening of the new Hilton Hotel in Mexico City; she was one of a number of starlets and other celebrities who, in typical Connie Hilton fashion, had been invited to add glitz to the ribbon-cutting ceremonies. Each was wined and dined, given first-class accommodations, and anything else they desired. Nick, for instance, got Natalie.

Within hours of their arrival below the border, they were sleeping together. (Connie was not to be outdone. The world's innkeeper divided his time between Barbara Rush, his first date on the trip; Ann Miller, his favorite dancing partner; and—on a quick hop over to Acapulco—Hillevi Rombin, the Swedish Miss Universe.)

At the big white-tie dinner, with all the dignitaries present, Connie noticed that two important chairs at the main table were unoccupied. "The people have come, the party is going, everything is functioning as it should, but Natalie and Nick are suddenly missing," says Bob Neal, who shared a suite with Nick. "The old man comes over to me and he says, 'Bob, I want you to go upstairs'—and he was talking between his teeth, he was very pissed—'and get *that* guy and *that* girl outta bed and get 'em down here to this table. They are starting to serve dinner and they are embarrassing me. Goddamn it, get 'em outta that bed!'

"So I go upstairs and knock on the door and I said, 'Nick, it's serious. The old man's ready to burn the fuckin' place down if you don't get downstairs with Natalie. *Now!'* I bore down on him pretty good—and he knew when I was serious. So they got all their clothes on and they came down and had their consommé, or whatever, and they got up and they danced.

"The next thing I knew the old man came over to me and he says, 'Now where the fuck are they?' I look around and I said, 'Well, sir, I'm not sure. I don't know. I delivered them to your table as you requested, but now I have no idea.' He said, 'Goddamn! Nick can't stay out of that fucking bed.' And, for goddamn sake, they were back up in the suite in bed."

Natalie was eighteen when she became involved with Nick, a dozen years her senior. Within a week of their get-together in Mexico City, the two were photographed dining at the Cocoanut Grove in the Ambassador Hotel in Los Angeles.

Nick gave Natalie a gold bracelet that she treasured, but no ring.

Meanwhile, Walter Winchell was reporting that Natalie had "transferred her affections again. From Nicky Hilton to Bob Wagner," but noted in a subsequent column, "Coasters now believe Natalie Wood and Nicky Hilton will make it official," and still later he wrote that when Natalie had trouble sleeping she "wakes Nicky Hilton by phone who chats with her until she dozes. That's a gooooood bwoi. Whutz his number?"

By the time Nick and Natalie were going steady, she was starting to film *Marjorie Morningstar,* a plum role, and had already starred in *Rebel Without a Cause* and was cast for *Splendor in the Grass.* (She won Oscar nominations for all three films.) Natalie, née Natalia Nikolaevna Zakharenko, whose parents were Russian Orthodox immigrants, was driven and ambitious—controlled and dominated by a stage mother on a par with big Kathy, Jolie Gabor, and Elizabeth Taylor's mom. But unlike Kathy Hilton and Zsa Zsa, Natalie had real acting talent.

Unfortunately, she was also constantly stressed and riddled with anxiety and hypochondria. She was considered rather promiscuous, or at least that's the impression she gave with so many men at her beck and call, much like Paris Hilton decades later. Besides Nick and Wagner, Natalie had been linked to Dennis Hopper, Robert Vaughn, Nick Adams, and the playboy Lance Reventlow. Curiously, Natalie also had a thing for gay and bisexual men, all of whom were closeted in those days. Among them were Sal Mineo, with whom she starred in *Rebel Without a Cause* and the handsome, sullen-appearing actor Scott Marlowe, whom she slept with on occasion; the gossip columnists hyped their relationship as Natalie's "great love."

Natalie's pal Troy Donahue firmly believed she was madly in love with Nick. But she felt safer with Robert Wagner, whom she considered gentle and better looking, and who didn't have alcohol and violence issues. Moreover, there was talk that during a visit to Casa Encantada Connie tried to coerce Natalie's mother into permitting her to marry Nick by offering a financial incentive. Many years later, Natalie's sister Olga maintains, "Nick's father, Conrad Hilton, *wanted* them to have a relationship, and he tried to talk my mother into encouraging that by promising her stuff, but she didn't go for it."

On the other hand, Natalie's British biographer, Gavin Lambert, asserts the mother "judged Natalie's boyfriends on whether they were famous and whether they were rich. That's what mattered to her."

Nick, observes Lambert, "was a lord if not a prince of darkness, endowed with equal parts charm, sexual expertise, and cruelty. He probably slapped her around." However, he found that Natalie was "excited" rather than put off by Nick's playboy persona and intrigued by his bad-boy glamour. "Nicky was the dark excitement."

Natalie's younger sister, Lana, contended that their mother gave "full cooperation" regarding Natalie and sex, including her affair with Nick. While only a child at the time, Lana Wood remembered Nick and Natalie "stealing kisses in the pool."

Nevertheless, Natalie chose to marry Wagner. But a decade later Nick and Natalie were still deeply attracted to each other. At a holiday party in London in December 1966, Nick, inebriated, came on to Natalie and she reciprocated—with Nick's second wife, Trish Hilton, and Natalie's second husband, Richard Gregson, at the same gathering, according to Lambert. (Trish Hilton denies it ever happened.)

Gregson said he "found Natalie and Nicky necking and dancing. . . .

We had a huge row. Natalie became very wound up, full of guilt, and appalled at the way she'd behaved. Then she said she wanted to kill herself and grabbed a bottle of pills."

Nick's and Natalie's lives would be forever entwined, and both would die tragically and young—Nick at the age of forty-two, Natalie at the age of forty-three.

# CHAPTER 26

**D**espite Nick's reputation as a rounder, much of it engorged by the columnists, he more often was interested in being *seen* with lovelies, such as Jeanne Carmen, rather than actually being *with* them, in the biblical sense. And to get turned on, he needed liquor or pills, and then was too stoned to perform, or he became physically abusive.

Many years later a number of women in Nick's life wondered about his sexual preference. Was he gay? Was he bisexual? Even Bob Neal, his closest surviving friend who still boasted of Nick's heterosexual exploits a half-century later, looked back and acknowledges he wasn't certain if Nick really liked women. "I don't know," he says plaintively.

Nick's Hollywood in the 1950s—not much different from Paris Hilton's Hollywood in the twenty-first century—was a hothouse for sexual experimentation. Girl-girl, boy-boy, and all other combinations were in vogue, and the drugs and the booze added to the orgy. The studios covered up the sex scandals, and gossip columnists kept the secrets. Rock Hudson's gay life, for instance, was an open secret in the industry, but didn't become public until decades later when it was revealed he was dying of AIDS.

Nick Hilton had a secret life, too. He was part of a small, private social circle that included John Cohan, who claimed psychic powers and
advised a number of Hollywood stars, such as Joan Crawford. Nick had
an interest in the psychic world, astrology, and the like and developed a
kinship with Cohan, who began doing readings for Nick about his future. On one occasion, Nick had planned to drive up the coast to San
Francisco with a friend, but Cohan foresaw danger and advised him not
to go. Nick took the advice, and the friend was involved in a serious auto
accident. Whatever it was that Cohan felt, Nick was forever grateful.

As friends, they'd sometimes have lunch or dinner, so Cohan didn't
think it odd when Nick asked to meet in a suite at the Knickerbocker
Hotel, in Hollywood. As it turned out, though, Nick and Cohan's meeting
would be far from routine.

"I go up and the door is open because he was expecting me and we
were going to do [psychic] readings, and he said from the other room,
'John, I'm in here. I'm just getting up.' I walked in and my jaw dropped
because who's in bed with him but Troy Donahue. They were both nude.
I sat on one of the chairs and then they both got up—stark naked."

Donahue was one of the blond, blue-eyed, pretty-boy heartthrobs in
1950s films who, along with Tab Hunter and Rock Hudson, were managed by the predatory homosexual agent Henry Willson—known as the
man behind Hollywood "beefcake." After Hudson appeared with Donahue in the film *Tarnished Angels,* Rock wanted to have sex with the six-
foot-three hunk. "He saw me as a score," Donahue later stated. When
friends asked Hudson about Donahue, Rock responded, "Great cock-
sucker, tiny dick." Donahue, however, consistently denied that he was
gay. He told *People* magazine in 1984, "Once in a while people get me
confused with another blond, blue-eyed actor who was around at the
same time, but it's no big deal . . . I love women. Sometimes, I guess, too
much." (For nine months in 1964 he was married to the actress Suzanne
Pleshette and had two other short-term marriages, fathering a daughter
and son.)

Like Nick, Donahue was an alcoholic. In addition, he was addicted
to painkillers, amphetamines, and cocaine, and at one point he reached

such a low that he lived on a park bench before he became sober and pulled his life together.

Cohan claims Nick confided to him that his relationship with Donahue was "an on and off kind of thing. Nick liked to have experiences with women *and* men, but he told me he wanted to settle down only with a woman."

**SEVENTEEN-YEAR-OLD** Tulsa, Oklahoma, oil heiress Patricia "Trish" McClintock was a five-foot-four, 103-pound brunette, an Elizabeth Taylor archetype in bobby sox. From a big-money Oklahoma banking and oil family, she had gone to a fancy Connecticut girls boarding school, traveled in Europe with her socialite mother, summered among the wealthy in La Jolla, and bet on the thoroughbreds at Del Mar. She grew up in an enormous home with maids and butlers and wings on the family homestead "where everyone spoke every once in a while." Her parents were divorced and her mother had recently married multimillionaire producer W. Horace Schmidlapp, onetime husband of beautiful blond 20th Century–Fox actress Carole Landis, who had committed suicide by drinking and overdosing on a handful of Seconal, Nick's favorite.

Trish was one pretty, prim, and sophisticated teenage package. As she says many years later, "I was privy to things a lot of girls aren't."

It was at the track one glorious Southern California Saturday afternoon in 1958 that Nick, then thirty-two, spotted teenage Trish, who was there with her grandfather, a member of the Federal Reserve Board; Nick was with another board member, a friend of Connie's. "They introduced us," she says. "That was how I met him."

Nick wasted no time asking her out—to a Gay Nineties party in Los Angeles being thrown by his friend, the head of the Hyatt Hotel chain. And Nick made a rather odd request of Trish: he wanted her to wear one of Natalie Wood's outfits—a costume from a film she had made. They were the same size and, well, he thought it would be kinky.

When Trish told her father, Frank Grant McClintock, that the infamous playboy was sending a plane for her, he practically locked her in her room; she had never dated a boy older than twenty. Moreover, she says, "I never thought there was anything between Nick and I. It was so ridiculous. I was so young, and he looked so much older to me. He looked like my father's age. I had never, ever had anyone that old pay attention to me, so that sort of amazed me. I looked like a child."

Trish saw Nick a few times, always at Del Mar, and she thought that was the end of their friendship. At summer's end, having just turned eighteen in August, she flew east to begin her freshman year at Briarcliff College, outside New York City. She was there just ten days when Nick tracked her down and aggressively began pursuing her. Academics were out, and love was in.

"His sense of humor, the way he kidded me, how very, very protective of me he was—that's what attracted me," she says. "He was good-looking—tall and handsome, and very athletic. He'd never had children, and I definitely think he saw me as a woman he wanted children with."

He asked her to marry him just before Halloween 1958, and their engagement made headlines across the nation. It was announced at a private party at the chic Colony restaurant in Manhattan in late October 1958. Just a few days after that momentous occasion, Trish saw Nick dead drunk for the first time in a scandalous incident that left her future brother-in-law Barron hospitalized. That same evening she also received a warning to "be careful of this guy" from Nick's ex-girlfriend, Natalie Wood, who had become Trish's friend.

On the evening of November 4, the newly engaged couple, along with Natalie, her beau, Robert Wagner, and one of her other former boyfriends, the actor Nick Adams, had gone out to dinner. Nick Hilton drank steadily, and by the time they got back to his suite at his father's Plaza Hotel he couldn't walk a straight line, but continued drinking. "It was the first time I had seen him drink—*ever*," recounts Trish, almost a half-century later. "He got really, really drunk, and I think it had to do with the whole thing about getting married to me."

At some point, Barron came into the suite, and he and Nick got into an argument. "I remember Nick was really drunk and saying something like, 'I don't believe that!' And then he pushed Barron, and Barron stepped back on a piece of newspaper and slipped, went straight up in the air, and fell on the floor. It was an accident that you would never dream could happen."

Barron was in severe pain. Whatever happened in that boozy instant, Nick's push had resulted in Barron suffering a fracture of his right leg, and he had to be rushed to Manhattan's Hospital for Joint Diseases. "Nick went to pieces and sobered up quickly over what happened," says Trish.

While Nick accompanied his brother to the hospital, Trish stayed in the suite with Natalie and Wagner, spending the night with them. Natalie, who had had long experience with Nick, and Trish, who had very little but was about to marry him, stayed up and discussed her future as the wife of America's most notorious playboy.

"We talked about Nick into the night," recalls Trish. "Natalie said, 'Have you ever seen him drunk before?' I told her no, and she said, 'If I were you, I'd go home and take a hard look about marrying him.' She was very sweet and was warning me about what I was getting into. She said, 'He's one of the brightest men I know, he's one of the most charming, but you'd better be careful.' So that day I went home to Mother, and Mother said, 'I don't think you should marry him.' And I said, 'Nope, I'm going ahead.'"

And so, against her father's and mother's wishes, and with Natalie Wood's warning ringing in her ears, Trish McClintock became the second Mrs. Nick Hilton the day before Thanksgiving, 1958, in a civil ceremony in the White and Gold Suite of the Hilton-owned Plaza Hotel. Nick's brother Barron, walking with a limp, was best man. Their mother, the widowed gambler and reformed alcoholic Mrs. Mary Barron Hilton Saxon, was present, as well as her ex-husband, the groom's father, Connie.

Forced by the Catholic Church to marry Zsa Zsa in a civil ceremony because of his divorce from Mary, the hotel czar was ashamed—and angry—that Nick had been put in the same situation because of his divorce from Elizabeth Taylor.

The *New York Times* reported that Trish wore a long-sleeved gown of reembroidered Alençon lace over white satin, made with a portrait neckline and an Empire sheath skirt terminating in a full court train, and carried a bouquet of white orchids. The "Gray Lady," however, noted slyly, "Mr. Hilton's marriage to Elizabeth Taylor, the actress, ended in divorce."

Trish's father felt his daughter's betrothal to the notorious playboy was so scandalous and embarrassing to his moneyed and ultraconservative oil family that he banned her from being wed in her hometown of Tulsa. "He didn't want me walking down the aisle with bridesmaids who were seventeen and eighteen years old, and Nick's friends who were in their forties," Trish says. Instead, Frank McClintock threw a country club party for seven hundred.

Trish's mother couldn't believe Nick would actually marry her teenage daughter; she predicted to Trish, "It'll be a great *first* marriage."

Trish acknowledges that she was "a virgin" when she was betrothed and believes that her lack of sexual experience was what appealed most to her groom. "Had I dated a lot and been to bed with other men," she observes, "Nick would never have married me."

Despite his playboy reputation, she states, "Nick was never terribly, overly romantic. He didn't go around kissing me. On top of everything else he was a *prude,* which is hard to believe about a man who supposedly slept with everyone. But when it got down to his wife and making babies he was *definitely* a prude.

"Looking back, Nick may not have really liked women," she acknowledges. "My feeling is that the reason he behaved like that with other women is that, on the whole, he did not respect women, but I don't think he disliked them."

And she added emphatically, "Nick was not anywhere near being a homosexual, I can promise that."

Moreover, she acknowledges sadly, "I do not think Nick loved me when he married me."

Aware of Nick's past transgressions with the ladies, Trish laid down two rules of behavior for her husband, who was fourteen years her senior. "I told him I'd leave him if he screwed around on me, or if he ever hit me."

However, still "starry-eyed" by the quickie marriage, she had no intimation that Nick had had a serious prescription drug problem, which he hid from her (as he did with many of the women in his life) during the honeymoon period.

Beyond that, Trish found herself living in the shadow of one of the world's great beauties. For years after they were married, Nick was dubbed "the first Mr. Elizabeth Taylor" by the press, which had him seeing red and made Trish feel insecure. Moreover, throughout their marriage, whenever Nick heard that Elizabeth was ill and in the hospital, which was often, he'd dispatch Trish to send her flowers in his name.

The thoughtlessness of people didn't help, either. For example, one night Trish was at the ritzy El Morocco nightclub in New York. The ladies' room attendant knew her and greeted her by name. "Suddenly," Trish recalls, "the woman standing next to me at the mirror turned and said, 'Are you married to Nicky Hilton?' I just wasn't used to things like that and I said, 'Yes, I'm Mrs. Hilton,' and she said, 'Tell me, darling, what's it like to go to bed with the man who's gone to bed with Elizabeth Taylor?' I didn't know how to answer. What I finally said was, 'It's fine!' and I went downstairs—we had Jack Kennedy's table—and I broke into tears and no one knew what the hell I was crying about.

"The things I had to live with when I married Nick were horrible," she continues, the bad memories still lingering. "People would ask me unbelievable things about my being married to Nick, about being a member of the Hilton family. I even changed my credit card from 'Mrs. Nick Hilton' to 'Trish Hilton.' I always said, if I didn't have seventeen years in Tulsa, I'd be completely nuts."

But it was hard to hide from the world back then if you were a Hilton. Early on, at a ball at the Waldorf, a photographer prodded Nick and Connie to kiss Trish on each cheek, and the next morning her picture between them was on the front page of the *New York Post.* "It was because the Hiltons were so famous," she observes. "We couldn't make a move without the press writing about us."

The first stop on their whirlwind honeymoon was West Berlin, where they attended the opening of the latest global Hilton, a seven-million-dollar, fourteen-story affair. The flight out of New York started on an ominous note and just may well have set the tone for the Hiltons' tumultuous marriage. The chartered four-engine airliner, carrying some sixty celebrity passengers including Connie and the newlyweds, developed engine trouble over Nova Scotia and had to turn back. It was a scary and bumpy ride.

In Berlin, at the fancy black-tie dinner celebration that included such dignitaries as West Berlin's mayor Willie Brandt, who was Trish's dinner partner, and German statesman Conrad Adenauer, among many others, the bride shockingly witnessed for the first time her groom getting plastered, at least in public.

"Nick was way down at the end of the table with Bob Neal, and he was absolutely smashed. I got up and walked over and accidentally on purpose spilled his parfait on him, and I got one of the waiters and we carried him out to make it look like we wanted to clean him up."

From Berlin they flew to the Middle East, followed of course by a pack of invited, freebie-loving gossip columnists who never reported Nick's German drinking episode.

Once several months after their honeymoon, and twice within the first year of marriage, Nick left Trish for short periods to carouse. The first time was devastating for the child bride because he chose their first Valentine's Day together to go to Miami Beach and hang out with Bob Neal. "It just killed me," she remembers. But because of a sudden cold snap in Florida, he returned after several days, tail between his legs. She rationalized that he needed his freedom because he was "terrified" from the start of getting married. "He just suddenly woke up and he was married and he hadn't been married since 1950."

The second time he took off for the Playboy Mansion to party with his friend Hugh Hefner. "I thought, he's off to his bachelor ways and I'm not going to put up with this. I'm not dumb and I'm not naive to think nothing happened there between him and one or more of those Bunnies. But I had to get over it very quickly."

**THE HILTONS BOUGHT** a charming three-bedroom, two-bath "starter home," as Trish calls it, in Beverly Hills, on Alpine Drive, where their neighbors were movie stars and titans of industry. As Trish observes, "The only thing Nick wanted to do was prove to his father that he could be a settled, married man."

As he had with Elizabeth Taylor, Nick, egged on by Connie, ordered Trish to convert to Catholicism. "I went to Good Shepherd in Beverly Hills for about three sessions," she says, "and I came home and told him

I couldn't be a Catholic, but that I would raise our children as Catholics up until seventh grade, and he agreed."

A few months after they were wed, Trish became pregnant. Nick, as she recalls, was "speechless, overjoyed, and unnerved." He found the best obstetrician money could buy; it was to be the same doctor who had handled the pregnancy of the Shah of Iran's wife and delivered Lucille Ball's babies. As far as Trish can remember, it was the only time Nick was willing to give up his play dates with his crooner pal Dean Martin—golf and gin rummy every day at the Bel-Air Country Club. "That's when I knew he *liked* me," she says.

At nineteen, Trish gave birth to a son, whom they named Conrad Nicholson Hilton III, in honor of his grandfather. Fourteen months later, Trish had a second son, Michael, who was named in honor of Nick's friend Miguel Aleman, the president of Mexico. Nick would have liked four or five little Hiltons to compete with Barron.

While Nick and Trish had many acquaintances from their separate lives—her teenage schoolgirl and young Tulsa socialite pals, and his carousing buddies—between them they shared a very small circle of close and loyal friends who stood by them through their turbulent marriage. Besides Bob Neal and his B-movie beauty and future wife, Dolores Faith, their circle included Carole and Lawrence Doheny IV, he the scion of the fabulously wealthy Southern California oil- and property-rich Doheny family, and she the gorgeous actress Carole Wells, who starred in a number of TV series through the mid-1950s and 1960s; and Nick's doctor, Lee Siegel, and his actress wife, Noreen Nash.

"Nick and Larry and Bob Neal were wicked, rich, bad boys," observes Carole Doheny years later. "Nick and Larry really liked each other—Larry looked up to Nick, and Nick was kind to him, and they were the guys who played gin rummy together—Nick and Larry and Bob Neal and Dean Martin—they were all the same skin. The Katzenjammer guys."

As a father, Nick was like his own dad; that is, he wasn't much of one. But every year he took his boys on a two-week trip—hunting, perhaps, or to Europe, but as Trish points out, "Nick wasn't a day-to-day husband-type daddy."

But Carole Doheny, Trish's closest friend, remembers being at the

Hiltons' one evening and thinking how happy Nick seemed having a family. "I saw him as a loving father. He adored Trish. He adored those two babies," she says. "Trish was lying on the floor and she had one of the boys near her and she was wearing black jeans and a big silver belt and she had that gorgeous little body and those beautiful boobs, and we were sitting there quietly talking and having a drink, and Nick was just staring at her. Just entranced. And he suddenly said, 'She's the best-looking girl I've ever known.' And because I knew his history with women, I said, 'Wow! With all the girls you knew, that's quite a compliment.' And he said, 'And she's even better-looking naked.'"

# CHAPTER 27

**H**aving proved he had settled down by becoming a family man, or at least that's how it appeared, Nick was finally brought into the Hilton business fold by the old man, and even *Newsweek* magazine took note of the move in March 1960, observing that the "onetime full-time man-about-town . . . has been looking more and more like his man-about-the-world father . . . plugging away" on a new chain of Hilton hotel-motels called Hilton Inns, "with Nick running the show as vice president in charge."

The article, however, misjudged Nick's standing with his father by stating that he had been "singled out as heir apparent," noted that he had "mastered executive syntax," and quoted him (or more likely a Hilton press release) as saying, "The division has unlimited expansion potential. Its future is parallel to transportation factors, new modes of living, and the healthy complexion of a growing America."

According to Trish, Nick for the first time seemed to feel good about himself, because his father was giving him a modicum of respect and responsibility. "Nick was thrilled," observes Trish. "He wanted his father's attention. That's all he *ever* wanted."

The Hiltons' home life, however, was something else altogether. Trish learned that Nick was hooked on Seconal—just as he had been in the early 1950s when he was involved with Betsy von Furstenberg. He had never kicked that addiction, though he was drinking a bit less.

"Seconal was the drug of choice of whatever anyone was doing back then," says Trish, scornfully.

On one horrific occasion, about two or three years into their marriage, Nick and Trish were vacationing in Acapulco when she caught him stoned and flushed his beloved downers down the toilet. It almost killed him, literally.

"I had to learn quickly about addiction," she says. "I called a Mexican doctor and he told me I almost killed Nick by throwing away his pills. He was withdrawing and you can't withdraw off those pills. He was three days in withdrawal. He carried on frighteningly, and then he had a convulsion. I thought he was going to die. The Mexican doctor gave me more Seconal to start Nick back on them in low doses. I didn't know what to do, but throwing away the pills was a no-no."

Trish claims that their close friend and Nick's physician, Dr. Lee Siegel, was obligingly writing Seconal prescriptions for him. "Nick always had a friendly doctor in his back pocket," she asserts. "The downers, that was Nick's big love, and Lee was getting them for him. I thought what he was doing was awful, and that I had to get this man out of Nick's life. He was in our lives for *years*."

Noreen Nash Siegel, the doctor's widow, denies that her husband was a "Dr. Feel Good," though she acknowledges that he was like a "father figure" to Nick and that Nick confided in him. She was aware of Nick's use of Seconal, because, she says, Nick was "an insomniac."

"I know that my husband was very sympathetic to people who had insomnia. But he was also very cautious. It's very easy to say 'he supplied' Seconal to Nick, but sleep deprivation is a horrible thing, and he was sympathetic to people who had it. Lee would try to limit the pills, but these addictive personalities—and that's what Nick was—get hooked."

There are others besides Trish who viewed Siegel as a "Dr. Feel Good" in Nick's life. Pat Hilton, Eric's first wife and Nick's sister-in-law, was shocked when, on one of the overseas Hilton celebrity junkets, she says she saw the doctor "going up and down the aisle in the plane saying, 'Here, take this. It will make you feel *really* good.' He came up to me and said, 'Here, this will keep you awake so you can *really* enjoy everything,' and he said, 'If you need a pill to go to sleep, I've got those, too.' I said, 'I don't need anything to make me feel better than I do right now.'"

Siegel's widow, Noreen, acknowledges that her husband adored the Hilton Hotel opening freebies. "He always gave up everything to go on those junkets. We had a good time."

There are those who felt the doctor acted inappropriately. For example, not long after Eric Hilton married Patricia Skipworth in El Paso in August 1954—Nick was the best man—they were visiting Nick in Los Angeles and Siegel also was present. Says Pat, "He asked, 'How many times have you done it since you got married?' I was a new bride and blushing beet red, I'm sure. Then, he said, 'What you need to do is put a penny in a jar every time you do it, and after the first year start taking them out and you will never get to the bottom of the jar.'"

She thought the doctor's advice and philosophy on sex was "weird, in bad taste, and totally uncalled for. I told Eric it really bothered and embarrassed me, but he said, 'Don't worry about it. That's just the way he is.' But I thought he was a creep."

The doctor's widow acknowledges that Siegel "had plenty of advice about women and sex" to offer patients and friends. "He counseled a lot of people on those issues."

The end of Connie and Siegel's friendship came about in 1967, when the *Los Angeles Times,* reporting on the fifth marriage of seventy-five-year-old author Henry Miller in the living room of the Siegels' elegant English Tudor home, stated erroneously that the doctor was the brother of the notorious mobster Bugsy Siegel.

When Siegel saw the mention in the story's fourth paragraph he howled with laughter. Connie, however, fumed. He immediately called Siegel and demanded that he sue the paper for libel and defamation.

Noreen Siegel, who married the actor James Whitmore after the doctor's death in May 1990 at the age of eighty-one, recalls Connie telling her husband, "You've got to sue the *Times.* I want it made clear that I *don't* cavort with criminals! You've got to prove that's not true!"

As Noreen notes, laughing about the incident years later, "Lee didn't care what anybody said or thought about him. He told Connie, 'So what, it doesn't bother me. We just called the paper and they ran a little retraction.'"

She says Connie and Lee never spoke again.

**BECAUSE OF NICK'S** prescription drug abuse and alcoholism—"drinking was a thread through our entire marriage"—Trish left him several times, threatening divorce if he didn't straighten out. He tried, but it never worked. "There were many months of normalcy, but it [his addictions] sat like a little black cloud over our lives. It was never going to be a marriage made in heaven. I was just too young to deal with all of it. My lack of knowledge [about addiction], my fear that I wasn't doing right made me feel I was an enabler."

Nick and Trish had their first formal separation—at least one that became public—five years into the marriage. Some six months later, in February 1964, she sued for divorce for the first, but not the last, time. She charged that Nick had caused her "extreme mental and physical suffering." Trish sought custody of the boys, four-year-old Conrad and two-year-old Michael, and asked for community property and child support.

Years later Trish asserts that the split was over Nick's drinking. "He went on one of his binges and I kicked him out, and that's when he went into Hazelden [the alcohol and drug rehab center], and he came out looking like a god, and from that time on I had to always do something drastic to get him to do things, and the only drastic thing I knew to do was to leave him."

A few months later, their roller-coaster ride of a marriage appeared back on track. As Dorothy Kilgallen reported, "The Nicky Hiltons' reconciliation seems to have worked out nicely, and she's wearing a huge new ring—an emerald surrounded by diamonds—to prove it."

**BY THE TIME** Nick turned forty in 1966, Connie believed he had settled down enough to take on the biggest job he would ever hold in the worldwide hotel organization: chairman of the executive committee of the New York Stock Exchange–listed Hilton International Company. Nick would oversee Hilton's whole overseas operation, although it was vet-eran Hilton executives who would actually run the show. It was more of a figurehead position, but to Nick it showed he'd gained more of his father's respect.

The Hilton international empire was immense. Since the late 1950s, and by the time Nick took over, Connie had put together a mind-boggling thirty-nine hotels in twenty-five countries, employing forty thousand workers. Most of the hotels were leased from their owners—a far more lucrative deal for the Hiltons than actually owning them. One press wag declared that Connie had "an edifice complex."

The "empire builder," as the *Los Angeles Times* called Connie Hilton, had also become involved in domestic and international political affairs and was often invited to give patriotic speeches. Awards and honorary degrees were bestowed upon this living legend.

Celebrity friends celebrated his enormous international success. The actor Bob Cummings, one of the frequent Hilton junketeers, threw what Earl Wilson called "a smasher of a Beverly Hills party" for Connie, with guests wearing the native costumes of the countries where Hilton had its hotels. Nick showed up as a Turk, while Barron bedazzled as a French wine steward.

With Nick running the international division, thirty-eight-year-old Barron, by then the father of eight—one of them being Rick Hilton, Paris's father—was named president of the Hilton Hotels Corporation, the domestic division, of which he'd been vice president since 1954.

By the time Nick and Barron moved up the ladder, Connie, though still chairman of the board, had stepped down as president and chief executive officer of Hilton Hotels Corporation to devote all of his ener-gies to the international arm, which allowed him also to keep close tabs on Nick's behavior.

With his new position, Nick, with Trish, sold their first home and bought a palatial stone colonial in ritzy Holmby Hills for $450,000 and change—a *lot* of money in those days. Like his father who picked up Casa Encantada for a song, Nick had negotiated down the price of his new house by more than $200,000 and brought it up to speed with an-other hundred thousand or so in renovations.

Trish, meanwhile, got into the swing of Beverly Hills society, becoming one of the ladies, or, in her case, one of the very *young* ladies, who lunched at the chichi Bistro Garden. And she ran in a circle that included Dino's wife, Jeannie Martin, Janet Leigh, and Sammy Davis's bride, Altovise. Along with them she was part of the fund-raising, charity, and gala circuit, joining the organization SHARE.

While Nick lent his name to some charity events and organizations and contributed money, he rarely made an appearance at the functions and, after years of well-documented nightlife, had become something of a stay-at-home loner. "We didn't have friends together per se," says Trish. "Our life was really very, very separate in many ways because I had my own friends, he had his work and golf." Besides golf and cards (and drinking and popping pills), Nick liked to read—his favorite book, read over and over almost obsessively, was Ayn Rand's *Atlas Shrugged.* However, on Saturday mornings he could not be interrupted from his other favorite form of entertainment—watching children's cartoons on TV— and on Sunday evenings he was riveted by *Bonanza.*

Because the Hiltons were staunch Republicans, Trish joined an organization of prominent women—among them Shirley Temple Black and Mamie Eisenhower—who were backing the 1968 presidential ticket of Richard Nixon and Spiro Agnew. Trish was among a large group of rich, coiffed California women pictured in a full-page political advertisement in the *Los Angeles Times* that declared in big, bold words: "Women For Nixon Look To You For A Better America."

**LESS THAN A YEAR** after Nick took over the international division, Trish was finally able to wean him off of Lee Siegel's downers and replace Siegel with a new doctor. But she soon came to realize that the situation had gone from "bad to worse" because, she asserts, Nick was now getting "mayonnaise jars filled with Seconal" from him.

Nick, like other people who were insomniacs, had started taking the pills to sleep. But he had become so addicted over the years that they had the reverse effect on him. "Instead of going to sleep, he became absolutely crazed," Trish says, the memory still painful. "He'd stay up for forty-eight hours at a time, just absolutely loop-legged, and finally he'd crash.

But during those four or five days I'd have to have nurses with him. I didn't want him out of the house."

Beyond that, the sudden death of Nick's mother, Mary Barron Hilton Saxon, whom he worshipped, left him devastated.

Of Mary's three sons, Nick, Barron, and Eric, it was Nick who was most like her, and it was Nick who helped her financially after Connie gave her virtually nothing in their divorce. (Mack Saxon left her with little but a navy pension.) Concerned about her financial welfare, Nick had established a small venture for his mother selling ballpoint pens to the Hilton Hotel chain for guest rooms, but when a cheaper vendor was found, Connie dropped her company, and Mary lost the account.

"But she was never in want of anything," says Mary's friend, the producer Hank Moonjean. "She got in to all the Hilton hotels for free. Nick took care of her because Nick was her favorite."

For years, the first wife of one of the wealthiest and most influential businessmen in the world had been living quietly and alone in a simple second-floor walkup apartment in a nondescript stucco building wedged between high-rises in West Los Angeles. She kept to herself and had few friends. Her only real pleasures in life were playing cards, shooting dice, and betting on the ponies; she read the *Daily Racing Form* like the Bible and had her own personal bookie.

Despite their marriage scandal and divorce decades earlier, Mary and Connie kept a semblance of a friendship through the years. As Trish points out, "Connie just sort of forgot about everything that had happened between them, and he just wandered around and made business deals. He just didn't hold grudges. In business he would, but in his personal life he was like *la-la-la*. In many ways he was a very naive man. Mary used to say to me, 'I can't believe a man who's that smart gets lost coming home from the Dallas Country Club.'"

Trish was at home alone on Sunday morning, November 20, 1966, and Nick was at the golf course when his mother telephoned to say, "I'm in terrible pain."

"I went over to her apartment," recalls Trish, "and she was sitting on her little daybed in the second bedroom and she just looked very uncomfortable. I called for an ambulance and I went with her, and they took her to St. John's Hospital in Santa Monica. The doctor told me, 'I don't know how to tell you, but she may not make it.' It was her heart. So I called Marilyn who then called Barron, and I found Nick at Bel-Air, and they all met at the hospital. She died about eight o'clock that night with all of us standing around outside her cubicle. Nick and Barron went in and I let them be alone with her."

The true matriarch of the contemporary Hilton clan, a woman long lost to history, died just five months before her sixtieth birthday. A requiem mass was held three days after her death at St. Paul the Apostle Catholic Church, and Mary was the first to be interred in a new Hilton family plot at Holy Cross Cemetery, in Culver City, where stars like Rita Hayworth, Loretta Young, and Bela Lugosi were buried.

# CHAPTER 28

**B**ehind Nick's back, secret negotiations had started to sell off his baby, Hilton International. The eventual sale would destroy him.

It all began in 1966 when Trans World Airlines (TWA) jealously watched as its competitor, Pan American Airways, built a new and very profitable subsidiary, the Inter-Continental Hotels chain. By the late 1960s, the air-travel business was growing meteorically; the first jumbo jetliners that carried hundreds of passengers were being put into service, and the airlines realized they had to guarantee hotel space to all their new transoceanic customers. The Pan Am operation worked smoothly and flawlessly—passengers flying the friendly skies of Pan Am were directed to its thirty-six hotels on the ground around the world.

TWA had taken a hard look at the very successful Hilton International operation and saw nothing but dollar signs. The divisions' revenue had increased almost 200 percent in five years; the overseas chain grossed $143 million and earned more than $5 million in the first nine months of 1965. And 1966 boomed with $122 million in revenue from some 4.8 million guests.

By mid-January 1967, TWA's president and Connie—with Barron prodding him—had hammered out a preliminary merger agreement, a stock swap deal under which the household Hilton name would remain along with top management to operate its thirty-nine overseas hotels with more on the way (and two cruise ships that sailed the Nile River). But TWA would own the whole shebang—lock, stock, and bidet.

Nick and Trish were on a trip out of the country and returned to learn that the deal was in the works. No one in his own family had consulted with him.

"We came back to this dreadful news and it just broke his heart," Trish says, remembering sadly what became almost two years of living hell for the both of them.

Nick immediately lobbied Hilton board members to vote against the sale. Among those on his side was Hilton's second-biggest stockholder, Colonel Henry Crown, who had once been chairman and principal stockholder of the Empire State Building and was one of Connie's longtime friends and advisers. Like Nick, Crown thought the international division was too valuable to divest, and he and Nick told Connie it was a terrible deal. "I was there for the two weeks that Henry Crown stayed in Los Angeles, and every night they would meet with different board members," says Trish. "But when it came right down to it, the board voted with Conrad. I went to Connie and told him what a mistake he was making. He practically threw me out of the house."

At first, Nick didn't realize from whom he faced his biggest opposition, and when he learned his main adversary was his own brother Barron he felt as if he had been stabbed in the back. Their competitiveness and sibling rivalry had now reared itself in a major business deal, and Nick was the victim.

"Barron convinced Connie to make the deal, and Connie just listened to Barron," asserts Trish. As she put it years later, "Barron sold out his brother. There's no doubt about that. Nick absolutely was crushed. He couldn't imagine that Barron would do such a thing. Barron wanted all the power, and there's no doubt when they sold Hilton International, Nick was a goner."

On May 9, 1967, TWA's takeover of Hilton International went into effect with Connie continuing as president and a director, and with Barron overseeing the domestic end. Looking back to that time, Trish observes, "Nick really wanted to be successful in his father's eyes, and he really tried, and he did a very good job for many months at a time—and even for a year at a time, but he had this thing hanging over him. Nick could have had it all, but Nick couldn't live up to Connie's expectations because he'd go on these [drinking and pill-popping] sprees. Barron was the entrepreneur, but Nick had the brains and he had the charisma, and I think that Connie would have loved to have both of his sons working for him. But Nick definitely needed to be under care of some sort."

Devastated, Nick, who was named to the TWA board, a gesture he felt meaningless—and was meaningless—wrote a moving "Dear Dad" letter, probably the last communication between son and father. In the letter, Nick wrote that he felt "alone, disrespected, and unloved." In a heartrending synopsis of his life, he said he was "grateful" to his father for all he had done for him "financially" over the years, but declared, "There is still something missing which is vitally important to me, your respect. I remember you once told me that without respect, there can be no love."

He made mention of a shocking IOU missive that Connie had sent him, a letter he described as "the itemized debt which was kept in infinite detail for the past eighteen years." He noted that when he and Trish separated the last time, Connie would not even allow him to move into the Beverly Hilton. "Could it be I'm not wanted anywhere?" he asked.

Specifically regarding the sale of Hilton International, Nick wrote, "I ask myself, why did Dad inform the world that he had assigned me to a high and important position and then embarrass me by stripping me of my coveted job, by having my brother negotiate a sale without my knowledge, undermining me, and leaving me to fall flat on my face without explanation or warning? . . . What did I do wrong? What mistake had I made? . . . And if it was good business for the company to sell, why wasn't I allowed to negotiate?"

He concluded the letter by expressing his "love" for his father, brother, wife, and children and declaring, "I want you to love me. For without you there is very little."

As far as anyone knows, Connie never responded.

From that point on Nick descended into his own private hell—drinking more than ever, popping pills, acting violent at times.

In mid-August 1967, Walter Winchell reported, "Hollywood chums of Nick Hilton (son of the immensely popular Conrad Hilton) say Nicky is seriously ill."

Friends realized that he was falling apart. Dean Martin, Nick's golf and gin-rummy-playing pal, called Trish offering to help, but didn't know what to do.

Eventually, that summer Trish talked Nick into taking a vacation, and they took the boys to Marbella, in Spain, for two weeks. It didn't work. "He was just a nightmare, then he was great for a while, but when we came home he was a nightmare again," she says. "I could not get him to stop drinking."

In August 1967—almost nine years after their wedding day—twenty-six-year-old Trish filed for divorce for a second time in their marriage. This time she charged Nick with "repeated acts and threats of physical violence" and claimed he struck her in the face. She demanded $5,600 in monthly alimony and custody of the boys—Conrad, then seven, and Michael Otis, six.

But once again they came back together. A few days after the Hiltons' ninth wedding anniversary, the New York–based syndicated society and gossip column "Suzy Says," written by Trish's mother's friend, Aileen Mehle, reported, "Speaking of reconciliations, Trish and Nicky Hilton, who have stretched apart, have snapped back together again."

Trish says she kept the divorce papers "in place" but "went back" to Nick "with his promise of good behavior."

Despite the Hiltons' rapprochement, Trish was growing more concerned by the day about Nick's drinking and Seconal addiction and what it was doing to him. "He was not a happy man and he was just hanging on," she says.

Around that time, Nick was staying at one of the Hilton homes in Palm Springs. At two or three in the morning, Nick's sister-in-law, Pat Hilton, was awakened in Houston by a call from the emergency room of a Palm Springs hospital.

"They said, 'Is this Patricia Hilton?' I said, 'Yes, it is.' And the person said, 'We have Nick Hilton here and he asked us to call you because we need permission to sew up his wrists because he tried to kill himself.' I never was sure why Nick had them call me, but Nick and I got along great. I called my husband, Eric, who was in Dallas, and he immediately left and went to California to be with Nick. I never heard any more about what happened, and I never asked."

**BY THE NEW YEAR 1968,** Nick was nearing bottom. He "never sobered up" and had become physically threatening to Trish and the boys.

There were frightening incidents with Nick and his guns, which he kept in the house. Noreen Siegel says her doctor husband once rushed to the Hiltons' home after getting a telephone call that Nick had a gun and was shooting at the television. "My husband took the gun away from him," she says, "and he came home with it, and he was very shaken by what happened. Lee was really very fond of Nick, so it was scary. But he talked Nick out of it, and he was able to put the gun down and give it to him. Nick called him the next day and wanted the gun back and Lee said, 'No, you're never getting that gun back, Nick.' And my husband kept the gun and hid it in a closet, and I found it after my husband died."

On another occasion, according to Carole Doheny, "Nick got crazy one night. He was actually doing target practice shooting decanters of liquor at the bar from outside on the lawn."

Trish feared for her family's safety and demanded that Nick get treatment or she would divorce him once and for all. She says, "He really went off the deep end."

Trish says she received no assistance from members of the Hilton family who were aware of Nick's physical and emotional state. Still upset years later, she says, "They did *nothing*. Barron never talked to me, never asked me if I needed help." She called for a meeting at her house with Connie and several doctors who were aware of Nick's situation—Judd Marmor; Rex Kennamer, a Beverly Hills physician to stars such as Elizabeth Taylor and Frank Sinatra; and Robert Buckley, a psychiatrist who had been involved in treating Nick and who became one of the directors of the Conrad N. Hilton Foundation along with Barron Hilton.

"It was the first time I ever asked Connie to come to the house, and the last," Trish says. "The doctors started by telling my father-in-law that his son would die if he didn't go into treatment. And Connie looked at them, said nothing, and changed the subject. He didn't want to hear about it. They told him that Nick had a fifty-fifty chance if he went into treatment, and he had absolutely no chance if he didn't—that his situation was so serious.

"While they briefed him, Connie looked at me and suddenly said, 'Trish, have you noticed anything different about me?' I said no, but, of course I had. He had dyed his existing fringe of white hair a reddish brown and put a wig on top to cover the baldness. What was I going to say, 'What happened to your hair?' The doctors are sitting there and they can't fathom what's going on. So Connie said, 'I had a shot at the Mayo Clinic and it grew my hair.'" (The hotel magnate was said to be so excited about his new look that he bizarrely commissioned his longtime society portrait painter, C. J. Fox, to paint his new head of hair on a number of existing portraits of him that hung in Hilton hotels.)

As for Nick's situation, Connie had closed himself off. "That's the only time I ever discussed Nick's problems with anyone in the family," states Trish. "I kept it all secret because Nick would have killed me if I told any of it to the family. They never tried to help before or after. I don't know why. Connie ran from problems even though they involved his own flesh and blood. His thing was business and that's all."

The doctors advised Trish to go to court and have Nick committed if he continued to refuse treatment voluntarily. But Trish wouldn't do it. She was fearful of the publicity and the impact it would have on her sons. Nick wouldn't even consider Alcoholics Anonymous at that point. "There were so many doctors saying so many different things," she says. "At the time I was twenty-eight years old. I had to make a huge decision about committing him and as it turned out I didn't make the right decision."

**BECAUSE TRISH COULDN'T** handle Nick anymore, she hired private male nurses to watch over him around the clock. She also gave Nick an ultimatum: unless he went into rehab, or was institutionalized, she declared she would divorce him.

To prove she was "deadly serious," she put their house up for sale in early 1968 for $550,000, and a mention about the listing appeared in the *Los Angeles Times* in a story about the booming market in half-million-dollar homes. The article, which ran in March, said the house was for sale because Nick "was suddenly in the throes of a divorce." (Within months, the Hiltons' home was bought by the novelist Sidney Sheldon.)

The first time private duty nurse Elliott Mitchell, an African-American, arrived at the Hilton home, Nick was furious because Trish was hoping to have him admitted to the psychiatric ward at Cedars-Sinai Medical Center. He was refusing to leave the house, and Mitchell couldn't believe the scene he was witnessing.

"There was another nurse on duty, a little gay guy, and Nick realized he was gay and, man, that really upset him," recalls Mitchell. "Nick had a belt and he was chasing the little guy around the room, and the little guy was jumping over a couch to get away from Nick, who was cussing and telling him he didn't want to see him in the house anymore. He was calling him a 'faggot.'"

Mitchell convinced the nurse to leave and attempted to calm Nick, who was out of control. "God damn it," he told the nurse, "I'll knock the shit out of you, too," and came at him, fists flying. But Mitchell, a one-time boxer, ducked out of the way. Nick liked Mitchell's moves, and the nurse was finally able to calm him down and convince him that hospitalization was best. Nick said he'd go peacefully only if the nurse stayed with him, which he promised to do.

At Cedars, though, there were more problems, at least at first. Nick was kept in a room in the psychiatric ward with two beds, one of them for Mitchell, who stayed with him around the clock. "We were in the room together and I told him something he was going to have to do and he said, 'No goddamn nigger's telling me what to do!'" Mitchell didn't react, but said calmly, "'If you want to call me nigger, call me Mr. Nigger, okay?' And Nick just laughed so hard he cried, and after that the two of us got along."

During his stay of a couple of weeks, Nick was counseled and given medication and came out much calmer. Mitchell said it was clear to him from long, soul-searching conversations with Nick that his depression, anger, and belligerence had to do with the Hilton family and, in particular, his brother.

"Nick was upset because his dad had put Barron Hilton in charge of the organization and Nick felt he should have been there, and this was driving him crazy," states Mitchell. "His dad was always too busy all the time and never spent enough time with him. He felt they disrespected him in the family."

After Nick was discharged from the hospital, Mitchell took it upon himself to make contact with Barron, who invited the nurse to meet with him at Hilton headquarters. "I said, 'Barron, you should get together with Nick and fix up all these differences you two are having because Nick's not going to live too long.' And he told me he wouldn't do it. He said, 'No, I can't be around Nick because every time I see him he wants to fight with me.' I told him, 'There's no way I would want to die and not be close to my brothers. For the life of me, I can't see why you would let your brother die. He's a Hilton and you should make up with him.'"

When Mitchell got back to the house he found Nick on the sofa crying. "He was really sobbing. Barron had called him and Nick got upset after they talked."

For a time back at home Nick seemed stable. But then he went off the deep end again, and Trish, who had finally had it with him, ordered him out of the house. Nick moved to a split-level, hillside rental on Gloaming Way off of Coldwater Canyon. Trish sent a longtime trusted maid, Mary, to look after Nick and keep Trish informed of his condition. Meanwhile, she moved with her stepfather and mother temporarily into the home of Natalie Wood, who was away making a film. When Dean Martin heard that she had left Nick, he called and pleaded with her: "He can get better, but he needs you with him. Don't do this to him," she remembers him saying. But Trish had been advised by doctors that the only way to motivate Nick into getting help was by playing hardball. At one point Nick showed up to confront her into taking him back.

"He waved this piece of paper at me, which was his will leaving me one dollar, and he said, 'If you don't go back with me I'm going to put this into effect.' And I told him to shove it. I told him to put it in effect, that the money wasn't why I had married him, and I really meant that."

Nick's behavior grew worse, and the nurses were called back for around-the-clock duty. While giving Nick a bath, Elliott Mitchell felt the right side of Nick's stomach area at the liver and noticed it was hard. "I thought, 'Oh my God, he's got cirrhosis of the liver.'

"One time I came to work and he was waving a gun—and in his state of mind he was pretty dangerous," says Mitchell. "I went in the kitchen and said, 'Mary, Nick's in there with a gun. I don't want to go in there with him like that.' And she went in to his bedroom and said, 'Mr. Hilton, give me the gun.' And Nick said, 'No, I'm not going to give it up.' I couldn't believe it, but she threw him on the floor and took the gun from him. He told her, 'It ain't loaded anyway.'"

One afternoon Nick returned to the Gloaming Way house with two expensive new cars—a Cadillac Eldorado and a Buick Riviera. "He came in the house," Mitchell recalls, "and he says, 'Mary, I bought two new cars, which one do you want?' And Mary said, 'Nick, you ought to ask Mrs. Hilton about this.' And he said, 'No, I'm asking *you*.' Mary went out and looked at the cars and chose the Buick."

Meanwhile, Nick was having secret conversations with his longtime friend, actor John Carroll, and revealed that he was planning to sue his father and brother.

At the same time, Carroll was talking to members of the Hilton circle, such as Dr. Buckley and Eric Hilton, among others. In one such conversation Carroll asserted that Connie and Barron were "scared to death" of Nick. "The father won't send him away," Carroll observed, "because the father's scared he's going to come out and kill him, and so is Barron."

Upset at how Nick was acting, Carroll, in an apparent tough-love heart to heart, asked Nick what he stood for, what his principles were, and how he thought he got to be who he was.

When Nick responded glibly, Carroll lashed into him: "Everything you've got your father gave you and everything you are your father gave you, from your name all the way down to the four hundred thousand dollars you just stashed away and the money that you're getting ready to sue him for. You are nothing except what your father made you. And what did you do with what he made you? He handed you three hundred million dollars on a silver platter and you threw it back in his face." (Trish Hilton says the $400,000 mentioned by Carroll had been placed in a hotel safe by Nick, but the money disappeared and she believes it was stolen.)

Carroll told Nick that if he went ahead with his planned lawsuit, it would end their friendship. There was talk that if Nick sued, Connie would fight back. As a member of Carroll's little circle pointed out, "[Connie] didn't get to where he was playing hearts and gin rummy and shooting pool and playing golf like Nick."

In an effort to help Nick, Carroll invited his friend and prominent Los Angeles criminal and divorce attorney Arthur Crowley to consult with Nick. "John was very concerned and felt that Nick needed some kind of help from somebody he could trust," says Crowley.

Crowley had known Nick around town for years, usually seeing him at the Luau getting drunk back in the 1950s. The attorney thought of him as a "good-looking guy" who got the girls. But by the time Crowley went to meet with him at Carroll's request sometime in late 1968, the Nick he remembered was in a terrible state. "I was shocked at how he looked," says Crowley. "Nick was in bad shape. He didn't look like he was going to live very long the day I saw him. He had burns all over his hands from falling asleep while he was smoking, that sort of thing. He was in the bedroom passed out and it was an hour or so before Nicky really woke up and came out to talk to me.

"Nick needed help badly, but he didn't get adequate treatment," states Crowley. "It was my recommendation when I saw him that he be institutionalized to dry out. But he wouldn't go. The day I saw him I don't think he could put two and two together."

Crowley adds sadly, "Unfortunately, he left a lot of unpleasant memories for a lot of people."

# CHAPTER 29

**A**t 9:30 on the morning of Wednesday, February 5, 1969, the telephone rang in Natalie Wood's home. Trish, who was still living there, answered the phone and froze in horror. Nick's accountant, Richard Cohen, informed her "fairly brutally" that Nick was dead.

The onetime playboy of the Western world was just forty-two years old.

"I never forgave both of them for that—Nick for dying, and Dick for calling me like that."

Despite her threatened divorce, Trish had visited Nick the night before, still pleading with him to seek help. There was nothing that indicated an impending death—nothing had changed emotionally or physically; he didn't seem any better or any worse.

In a state of shock, Trish got into her car to pick up her now fatherless sons, nine-year-old Conrad and seven-year-old Michael, at their Catholic school in Beverly Hills.

Meanwhile, Nick's closest and dearest chum, Bob Neal, was testing his new Maserati on the winding roads outside of Rome with his fiancée,

Dolores Faith. Barron left a message for him at the Hilton Hotel, requesting Neal to return posthaste to be a pallbearer at his brother's funeral. Barron had already arranged to hold a TWA flight to Los Angeles for the couple.

Elliott Mitchell, the nurse, had just gotten home after a routine twelve-hour shift with Nick—everything had seemed as normal as normal could be with a patient like him—when he received a call from his relief nurse that "something was wrong." He got in his car and headed back and on the way spotted a policeman whom he convinced to escort him because of the emergency situation.

"When I got there Nick was on the floor in his bedroom and he was already dead."

Nick's death certificate was signed by one Dr. Webster Marxer, who listed the cause of death as "cardiac arrest" due to, or as a consequence of, "probably coronary artery disease" and stated he had been Nick's physician from September 1964 until the time of his death. He said he had last seen Nick two days before he died.

Trish Hilton, however, contends that everything on the death certificate was a pack of lies, part of a cover-up by Connie to hide the truth from the public about Nick's condition, that his consumption of pills and alcohol was what killed him. She said it all stemmed from the loss of his job when the international division was sold behind his back.

"Dr. Marxer was *not* Nick's physician," she maintains. "He was Connie's doctor. I met Dr. Marxer *once* at a party, but he was never in our home. He never treated Nick." (At the time of Nick's death, Marxer was a "physician to the stars" and was medical adviser to MGM. Marxer died in 1985.)

Trish also emphatically maintains that if Nick had been hospitalized for a heart condition, as Marxer claimed, she would have known about it from talking to Nick on the phone or visiting him almost daily after they split, or from the maid, Mary, who was regularly reporting back to her about Nick's condition. Moreover, she says, "I'd never even *heard* that Nick had a heart problem, *ever,* in his entire life. As his wife, I certainly would have known.

"It never got in the paper that Nick overdosed. His death was induced in the last three or four months of his life by drugs and drinking. I don't think he did it on purpose. I don't think he sat down at eight o'clock that morning and took twenty Seconals and alcohol, but who knows?"

As far as she can recall, there was never an autopsy. Newspapers across the country reported Nick's death, most stating that he died of a heart attack. However, there were reports that he had shot himself. United Press International, whose story appeared in hundreds of newspapers, also said Nick had been "ill about a month." It also quoted an unnamed Hilton family spokesman as saying that Nick had recently returned from the hospital because of "a heart condition" and that it had worsened in recent days. The *New York Daily News,* which displayed parts of the UPI story across the top of page three, ran almost a full page of photos, showing Nick with Elizabeth Taylor, along with headshots of three of the "many beauties" he courted—Betsy von Furstenberg, Mamie Van Doren, and Terry Moore, along with "Nicky's estranged wife," Trish.

Trish took over the funeral arrangements because, as she says, "none of the Hilton family came to my rescue. *None.* I will never know why Connie didn't, except after spending ten years with him I realized he couldn't deal with family issues. And so I was terribly angry at everyone— at Connie, at Barron, and I refused to talk to them, and they treated me like I had divorced Nick, like I was the divorced wife."

The night before the funeral, Trish, accompanied by Carole Doheny and Dolores Faith, went to church. "I spent an hour with Nick privately at eleven o'clock," Trish remembers.

A requiem mass was held the next day, a Saturday, when Nick usually was at home watching cartoons on TV. An estimated thousand people came to his funeral, a depressing scene with autograph hounds looking for celebrities. Elizabeth Taylor, whose looming presence was a part of Nick's short and troubled adult life, was not among the mourners. However, just prior to his death, she had finally agreed to give Nick the annulment that he had been seeking for years, one that the Catholic Church secretly granted, influenced by Marilyn Hilton, Barron's wife. "A contribution was also given to the church," says Trish.

Because of the rumors that her husband had committed suicide by gun, Trish wanted to show the world otherwise and arranged for an open casket, which required a special dispensation from the church that was arranged for by a friend.

Connie Hilton came to the funeral of his firstborn son, but an angry Trish made her eighty-two-year-old father-in-law sit in the second row, right behind her. After the service, Connie wandered around looking for a ride to the cemetery. He approached a Los Angeles policeman and said, "Is there a car for me?" When the cop asked him if there should be, Connie responded, "I think so. I'm the father of the deceased."

Nick was buried at Holy Cross Cemetery in the same family plot near his beloved mother, Connie's first wife. Afterward Connie threw a huge wake at Casa Encantada. "Not one member of the family came to my house, except for close friends," Trish recalls sadly. "People thought I had divorced Nick, or was divorcing him, so they blacklisted me. They had *no* idea what was going on in our household. So I sat with my twenty friends and had a glass of wine and a cigarette."

Pat Skipworth Hilton, Eric Hilton's wife before their divorce and his remarriage, had dinner with Barron shortly after Nick had passed away. "I was being very frank with Barron, and I said, 'You know what was wrong with Nick?' He said, 'What?' And I said, 'You saw to it that he never had a chance to become president of the international division.' He said, 'I had *nothing* to do with that.' I said, 'Well, that's what helped kill Nick, and he thought you did have something to do with it.' I remember the day Nick died, Barron called me to tell me he'd passed away, and Barron said, 'But he forgave me.' I'll never forget that because Barron never called me, and he called me to tell me that."

In his last will and testament, dated December 18, 1968, less than two months before his death, Nick, furious that Trish had separated from him and was threatening to divorce him, declared, "I have intentionally and with full knowledge omitted to provide for Patricia M. Hilton," stating that she had "filed for the dissolution" of their marriage.

Trish was shocked by the will. Years later she says, "Everything I did [the threatened divorce, the sale of their home] was really to get him to go and get help, and it turned around and bit me."

For no discernible reason, Elizabeth Taylor also got a mention. Nick noted in the first paragraph of his will that they had been formerly married and divorced, and no issues remained from their seven-month union. He left trusts for his two sons for their schooling, with monies to be divided when they reached the ages of twenty-five, thirty, and thirty-five. Eric Hilton was bequeathed fifty thousand dollars, and Nick appointed him guardian of his minor sons' estate.

Several years after Nick was dead and buried, Connie quietly acknowledged to Trish that the sale of the international division, which led to Nick's decline and fall, "was one of the worst business deals" he had ever made.

Ironically, in early 2006, Hilton Hotel Corporation's stock spiked upward when it made a deal for more than $6 billion to essentially reacquire its international hotels from a British group.

**ALMOST FOUR YEARS** to the day of Nick's death, his friend, thirty-year-old Larry Doheny, committed suicide on Valentine's Day, 1973. After suffering three heart attacks in one year, he had just come home from the hospital in an agitated state with prescriptions for Valium and sleeping pills. Carole Doheny, Trish's best friend, was visiting with Marilyn Hilton, Barron's wife, and called her home to see how her husband was feeling, but there was no answer. When she arrived home he was dead. "Larry just took all the sleeping pills, everything," she says years later.

About a week after her husband's funeral, Carole was sitting with her young son, Sean, in front of the fire in the library of her Brentwood home on a dark and rainy afternoon when she received an unexpected caller—Conrad Hilton.

"It was out of the blue," Doheny recalls. "I always saw Connie in a group of people, or at a party, so it was strange having him in the house like that. He came in and he just stood there and stared at me and at my little boy and then my one-year-old toddled in and Connie didn't say anything. I asked him to please sit down. I offered him a drink and he said no, and he just sat there. It was all very strange.

"Then, after a while, he started to talk, and he spoke in a very low voice. He told me how sorry he was that Larry died, how *horrible* it was that he had left me with two small children. He said how hard it was for a father to lose a child.

"And the more he talked I realized that he wasn't talking about Larry after all. He was talking about Nick. He said Nick was the brightest of his children, and that he had been too hard on him. He actually said that Zsa Zsa told him many times that he was in competition with his own son, and he said, 'I shouldn't have always tried to compete with Nick.' And that to me was one of the most telling things he could have ever said. It said it all because Nick was always trying to please him.

"And then Connie put his hands up to his face and started crying. He stopped for a moment, and he looked at my little boys, and he said he was sorry he never spent enough time with Nick, and then he started crying again, and my little boy went over to him and held his leg. He spent several hours there. We just sat there quietly. And then he left.

"A few weeks later Trish called me and said, 'Connie really likes you,' and we joked about whether I should marry him, and then I could be her mother-in-law. It was the first time both of us had laughed in a long time."

**THE MOST SUCCESSFUL**, flamboyant, and scandalous hotelman in history had outlived his firstborn son by a decade.

Barron had been running the company, but Connie still demanded respect from his son and received it. Tim Applegate, who had worked closely with both father and son from the early 1970s through the mid-1980s, recalls that after Applegate had private meetings with the old man, a concerned Barron would pull him aside and ask, "What did Dad want this morning? What's he saying?" More often than not, Applegate says, the senior Hilton "was worried that somebody was manipulating the market. He would say, 'The wolves are after us!'

"He got to be a handful in his last years. He would show up at stock-holders' meetings and tell people that he was really in charge, not Barron, so Barron had to be careful and make sure his father didn't jump up and start talking. He'd say, 'It's okay, Dad, everything's in control here.' A lot of people just kind of ignored Conrad at that point, but Barron showed respect, which wasn't reciprocated. Conrad acted like you would expect the chairman of a corporation to act toward the president, and the fact that he happened to be the father of the president didn't seem to matter."

A pioneering visionary and entrepreneur in business and an icon in public, an icy and eccentric man in private—but a true red, white, and blue American original—Connie Hilton died at 10 P.M. on Wednesday, January 3, 1979, three days after being admitted to St. John's Hospital in Santa Monica with pneumonia. Long before he died, the name Hilton had become synonymous with the word *hotel.* Travelers the world over had begun saying "Take me to the Hilton." At the time of his death, the Hilton banner flew over almost two hundred hotels and inns in the United States, and there were more than seventy in foreign lands.

Connie had celebrated his ninety-first birthday a little over a week earlier on Christmas Day and had been working right up until just before the holiday when he became ill. With him at his birthday celebration at Casa Encantada, with its nineteen servants, were some members of the Hilton tribe and his third wife, Mary Frances Kelly Hilton, whom he had married in December 1976, when she was sixty-one and he was eighty-eight. They had been good friends for years; Mary Frances was a chum of one of Connie's sisters, was a religious Catholic, had served with the Red Cross during World War II in the South Pacific, and had worked for an airline. When she and Connie tied the knot, there were fears she "might be a gold digger," says former Hilton Hotel Corporation vice president Tom Parris. "Certain members of the family were upset. But she was actually very good to Conrad."

A funeral mass was offered for the hotel czar at St. Paul's Church, where Nick's mass had been held. A memorial mass at St. Patrick's Cathedral in New York drew dignitaries from around the world. Connie's body was flown to Dallas, where he was buried in Calvary Hills Cemetery next to one of his brothers, August Harold Hilton. His death certificate was signed by Dr. Webster Marxer.

Connie's final will and testament, one of thirty-two such documents he had drafted over the years, left an estate worth hundreds of millions, but less than two million dollars was bequeathed to survivors, among them Barron, who received $750,000; Eric Hilton, $300,000; and Zsa Zsa's daughter, Constance Francesca Hilton, $100,000. The big prize, Connie's 27.4 percent controlling interest in the hotel chain he had started with a fleabag in Texas, went to the Conrad N. Hilton Foundation to be used for charity, which he called in his will "a supreme virtue, and the great channel through which the mercy of God is passed on to mankind."

Barron, who had become chairman and chief executive of the hotel and casino superpower, went to court in 1983 and sued the foundation. His lawyers claimed that there was a little-understood provision in the old man's will that permitted Barron to buy the stock for about $165 million—the market value when his father died. At the time he made his challenge, the value of the stock had soared to $490 million.

One of the key witnesses at the 1986 trial, which Barron subsequently won, was one of Connie's top advisers, James Bates, who testified that the innkeeper to the world didn't want to leave "unearned wealth to relatives and members of his family." Bates told the court that Connie believed in "a strong work ethic" and that his goal was to have all of his relatives and children "get out and go to work and earn their own living."

If that was the case, Connie isn't "rolling over in his grave," as a number of Hiltons contended years later, about his great-granddaughter Paris's moneymaking hustle, although he'd probably be offended at what she did to earn her millions. But no one could question the fact that Paris had certainly inherited her great-grandfather's work ethic, good or bad.

# EPILOGUE

I n the summer of 2006, Paris Hilton, then twenty-five, and having been in the public eye going on nearly a decade, was on a major promotional tour—hawking everything from her first single and her first record album, to her first music video and her first videogame (which she embarrassingly called by the wrong name at its highly publicized introduction), to her signature perfume line.

With the money rolling in from her numerous and sundry lucrative ventures, Paris ordered a 190-mile-per-hour Bentley convertible and considered buying a fancy Manhattan apartment and becoming truly bicoastal, not that she didn't already seem to be everywhere at once— partying in New York on a Friday night, boogying in a trendy Hollywood club on Saturday night, and exhibiting herself in a London hot spot on Sunday night, at least according to the gossip columns.

With her home base in Hollywood but playing often in New York, she pondered snapping up an almost $8 million, four bedroom, six-and-a-half-bath bachelorette pad in Hilton family friend Donald Trump's building on Park Avenue, a short walk from what had once been the jewel in the crown of Connie Hilton's empire, the Waldorf-Astoria. Paris's mother, Kathy, who had considerable influence over her firstborn's career choices and personal decisions just like her mother had over her, was said to have done a walk-through of the apartment and given the place two thumbs up.

No doubt Paris's great-grandfather would be extremely proud of the Hilton entrepreneurial spirit that Paris had inherited and was aggressively exhibiting. At the same time she rarely talked, or seemed to know much, about Conrad Hilton's history. Though she believed his ambition and drive "runs through my veins," she thought he "was a bellboy"—*a bellboy!*—"and had a dream to do a hotel chain. . . ." Her "hope" by the middle of the first decade of the new millennium was to become a bigger mogul than the great hotelman. However, she asserted, "I don't want to be known as the Hilton heiress," while, in fact, her fame came about only because she had the Hilton name attached to her. Paris had achieved the kind of stardom her late maternal grandmother, big Kathy, and her mother, little Kathy, had themselves always wanted. Of her daughter's madcap, moneymaking antics, Kathy Hilton once haughtily boasted, "My daughters are stars, and stars may do anything they please."

Other Hilton family members saw it differently.

"Yes, Kathy's very proud of Paris's ambition and drive and claim to fame," says a Hilton, rolling her eyes and fuming at Paris's publicity-seeking ways. "Kathy's okay with anything Paris does. *Any-thing.* I can't say that for the rest of the family. Paris is an embarrassment. In my opinion she's tarnished the Hilton name forever. She makes her great-uncle Nick seem like a saint."

Paris had become one of those celebrities many people loved to hate; her fame and infamy had provoked schadenfreude around the world. The more outrageous she acted, the more publicity she received, and the more money she made. If anyone understood the shallowness of celebrity culture in the early years of the twenty-first century, it was the Hilton gal. As the British social critic Taki pointed out, "Paris underlines our ongoing interest with celebrity-for-the-sake-of-celebrity today . . . our apparent interest in her and her ephemeral emptiness says more about us than it does about Paris."

But Paris had become inured to criticism and attacks—the *ka-ching* of the cash registers racking up sales of whatever she was peddling made up for the slings and arrows. She was able to cockily thumb her nose at all those naysayers who put her down, those who thought of her as everything from "spoiled brat," "stupid," "dead-eyed dope," "superficial," and "publicity whore," to a bimbo who fixed herself up to look like "a high-class escort." As one savvy marketing expert had noted about her, "You don't have to have stories saying nice things about you; you just have to have stories saying *something* about you." And as Paris declared, "I'm laughing all the way to the bank." She claimed her image—"the whole Paris thing . . . It's all a game."

With her TV appearances, record, books, and movies, Paris was being thought of in mid-2006 as the "dominatrix of all media." As a child, though, she wanted to be a veterinarian. (She was once quoted as saying that in every girl's life there should be four pets: a Jaguar in the garage, a mink in the closet, a bed with a tiger in it, and a jackass who pays the bills. It was much the same philosophy handed down by big Kathy.) As an adult, Paris saw herself as "a businesswoman, a brand. . . . There's nobody else like me." She modestly envisioned herself as an icon. "It's just something I always wanted to be," like Monroe and Madonna. "I love that timelessness."

The Paris blitzkrieg was amply demonstrated when hundreds of her fans descended on Macy's famed Herald Square department store in Manhattan. They were there to buy Paris's "fragrance": $49 a bottle, or $76 for the gift bag, which included a stuffed Tinkerbell dog and a Paris T-shirt. (Paris claimed $220 million of her perfume had been sold.) The purchase gave her followers the exclusive right to stand in a sweaty line on grubby Broadway for more than two hours to meet Paris face-to-face for about thirty seconds and get her personalized autograph on a glossy headshot. All were warned, "No personal memorabilia will be signed while Ms. Hilton is on-site." (On the other hand, Paris, unlike her own customers, liked to get *her* stuff for free if she could get away with it. One such incident occurred not long after the Macy's event, when she strode into a chic Melrose Avenue, Los Angeles, jewelry boutique seeking a pricey silver dog tag as a freebie. Her line to merchants on such occasions was "You get publicity, and I get whatever I want." The jeweler didn't buy it, but other shopkeepers in the past had; after all, Paris wearing their things meant enormous exposure and sales.)

The lineup of Paris's fans outside of Macy's included adolescent boys and girls with their mothers in tow; cosmetically enhanced suburban teenage Paris wannabees wearing fashionably low-slung jeans and strappy high-heel sandals; plain-Jane secretary-types on their lunch break; Upper East Side ladies who lunch; downtown club kids; some oddballs; and lots of gay boys. (The flamboyant celebutante had, indeed, developed a large gay following, much like a drag queen star. In 2005, Paris had been crowned a gay diva when she was named—along with her mother—as grand marshals of the Los Angeles Gay Pride parade. The getup Paris wore that day became part of an exhibit at the Hollywood Museum, along with outfits of such gay icons as Bette Davis, Judy Garland, and Paris's personal favorite, Marilyn Monroe. Paris even learned her red carpet wiggle from a popular black drag queen, the voguer Willi Ninja. Paris believed she was embraced by gays because "I'm free-spirited. I'm real. I like to have fun. I enjoy life and I think that's what the gay community's all about." She made no mention of the AIDS epidemic that was still killing off members of that community, like Ninja.)

A full-page Macy's ad in the *New York Post,* the daily tabloid that had first recognized Paris's outrageousness in its "Page Six" gossip column—she was known to personally call the column with items about herself—and the first to dub her a "celebutante," "celebutard," and "heirhead," had announced her appearance at the store. "Spending an afternoon with a hotel heiress and world-famous socialite," blared the ad. "That's hot!"

And so they came, packing Macy's first-floor fragrance arcade, tossing credit cards and cash at harried salesgirls in order to possess the outrageous entrepreneur's perfume, which offered "a feminine, flirtatious charm and classic sophistication," and in the process get to meet her and secure her autograph.

Paris seemed to represent different things to different people. As a whole, she felt that "people think of me as like an American princess fantasy, like Tinkerbell the fairy, the little blond pixie." A well-dressed mother of a ten-year-old boy carrying a homemade sign reading "I Love You Paris" said her *whole* brood actually loved Paris. "We all watch *The Simple Life* as a family. I'm obviously not thrilled about that X-rated video she was in, but we don't really focus on that. I think her talent is appealing to all people. We adore her." But she had difficulty defining whatever talent it was that Paris had. "Well, she's Paris Hilton. That's all. That's enough."

A man of indeterminable age with a shaved head, who was sporting a Spice Girls T-shirt and rose-colored boxing shorts engraved with the names of Naomi Campbell, Hillary Clinton, and Reese Witherspoon, and with the words "Fountain of Youth 1969" over the crotch area, said he had met other celebrities through the years with "better talent than Paris," but he loved her because "Paris is the *total* package. She shows that *anybody* can make it. She represents the American dream, whether you're born rich like her, or if you come from the projects. She has *determination*."

A gay Hispanic man announced he was a big fan because Paris "is, like, *very* different. She's *very* crazy. She's *very* flamboyant. People dislike her because she's rich and beautiful, but they're just jealous. Paris is smart. She knows how to promote herself, and she doesn't care what anyone thinks. I respect that."

Arriving fashionably late by twenty minutes to screams of "Paris! Paris! Paris!" she was showcased on a thronelike platform in front of a battalion of paparazzi, and every so often between signing autographs she struck sultry poses for the cameras. Although other celebrities try to avoid photographers, Paris learned early on to use them to her best advantage. Her rule: "It's better just to smile than give the middle finger, or [be] rude to them, because that's what they want you to do. They want to get a bad picture." (Paris sometimes affected a pose, and, when she felt it was perfect, she'd actually yell to the stunned photographers, "Shoot!") Kathy Hilton, keeping a critical eye on her daughters' performance, sat nearby on the Macy's podium, and later posed (along with Rick Hilton) for digital snapshots with some of their daughter's fans, who were rather disappointed because Paris herself skipped out in a sea of security.

However, Paris was extremely gracious throughout the tedious Macy's event—after all, the cash registers for her product didn't stop ringing up sales. She smiled sweetly and chatted briefly but amiably with each fan seeking her autograph—people who had eagerly shelled out hard-earned money for her fragrance package just to meet her. As one wag noted as he watched her sign hundreds of photos, "I'll bet she's never written so many words at one time in her life—but they're all the same words, 'Paris Hilton.'"

An enormous detail of plainclothes security guards, along with brawny uniformed members of New York's finest, one of whom acidly referred to himself as the "Paris Pussy Patrol," kept tight surveillance over her. As fans climbed a few steps to stand in front of their idol and get her autograph, their shopping bags and handbags had to be turned over to, and examined for weapons by, bodyguards, some with bulges in their jackets. *What the fuck!*" exclaimed one tailored, coiffed, and trash-talking twentysomething who refused to give up her $5,000 Birkin bag "for privacy reasons" and left the line after an hour's wait. "She's just Paris friggin' Hilton, not the friggin' Queen of England."

One of those waiting in line to secure Paris's autograph was a dapper, mustachioed businessman by the name of David Hans Schmidt. He was not a fan, but he had a vested interest in talking to her face-to-face.

Known in the tabloid world as a "celebrity porn peddler," Schmidt had earned a purple reputation after he arranged for Bill Clinton's gal-pal Paula Jones's *Penthouse* spread and brokered topless shots of convicted killer Scott Peterson's girlfriend, Amber Frey.

In Paris's case, Schmidt made worldwide headlines in early 2006 when he became the broker for all of the contents of her Los Angeles storage locker after she failed to pay the rent on it. The locker was said to contain a trove of Paris memorabilia, including raunchy photos, video-tapes, and sex toys, along with personal documents, letters, and more than a dozen diaries reportedly brimming with tales of X-rated dalliances, all of which Schmidt hoped to sell back to her, or someone else. One figure bandied about had been $20 million. Most of the weekly tabloids and celebrity glossies, who often pay for such mother lode, had passed on buying the material, considering it too risqué.

To prove he was genuine, Schmidt showed Paris a G-rated photo of herself as a child with her sister, Nicky, that was part of the locker's contents. When Paris asked him what she should write on her photo, he said, "Make it out to, 'The guy who has my storage locker stuff.'" Paris told Schmidt, who was looking to do a reality show called *The Sultan of Sleaze,* that she'd meet with him in Los Angeles, presumably to talk about buying back her belongings. Though she had been described as "incredibly upset and angry and victimized" by Schmidt after news broke of his involvement, Paris diplomatically signed her photo, "To David, Love Paris Hilton xoxo."

That night Paris made another appearance, this one at a trendy downtown Manhattan club called Butter, where she wasn't as diplomatic. She had a fiery confrontation there, one of several over a period of weeks, with one of her archenemies, the nineteen-year-old actress and playgirl Lindsay Lohan. (Paris tended to have schoolgirl-like feuds; members of her enemies list have included Lisa Marie Presley—who Paris claimed threw a drink at her "because she thinks I fucked Nic Cage!"—Mary-Kate and Ashley Olsen, Sophia Bush, Jessica Simpson, Hilary Duff, and Mischa Barton, who once accused Paris of "hating everyone around her age who is more successful," to which Paris responded, "I could care less . . . she seems to be spending a lot of time thinking about me." Paris also was accused of planting a false story in the *New York Post* about diamond heiress Zeta Graff, a onetime gal-pal of Paris Latsis. Graff brought a lawsuit claiming that Hilton had fabricated the story that Graff had attacked her in a London nightclub. Hilton admitted the incident never took place but denied planting the story, though her publicist at the time claimed she instructed him to give the story to the *Post.* During a deposition Paris went after Graff, declaring, "She is old and should stay home with her child, instead of being at night clubs with young people. . . . She is not cute at all.")

With Lohan, there appeared to be an extended history of bad blood. Some weeks before the Manhattan incident, Paris and Lohan had gotten into a brawl at the Los Angeles hot spot Hyde. Paris's party-pal Brandon Davis, who once squealed about Paris's alleged racial and religious slurs, made headline-making sexual innuendoes about Lohan to the paparazzi stationed outside the club. Paris, who was said to have been furious because Lohan was seeing her ex, Stavros Niarchos III, was at Davis's side, laughing and seemingly egging him on, all of which was caught on video and aired on the Internet. Later, Davis offered Lohan a semblance of an apology for referring to her as "fire crotch," among other lewd remarks. Not long after the verbal assault, Davis was admitted to Passages, a $75,000-a-month rehab center for cocaine and alcohol addiction, under orders from his wealthy family, but soon left.

In the bathroom of club Butter on the evening of Paris's perfume-touting personal appearance at Macy's, Paris and Lohan, who was with a party that included Prince, Sean (Diddy) Combs, and Beyoncé, were said to have had another "huge fight." Comparing the bout to a "high-school catfight," the *New York Daily News* gossip column asked, "Sometimes don't you wish there was a principal who could suspend Lindsay Lohan and Paris Hilton?"

**AS PART OF HER** mid-2006 promotional tour, Paris had made a heavily advertised guest appearance on the *Late Show with David Letterman* on CBS. Letterman had had her on his show a number of times because he enjoyed using her as a foil for his snarky humor, and he just plain enjoyed laughing at her. She'd often been the target of his wacky "Top Ten" lists. Following her appearance in *1 Night in Paris,* Letterman did the "Top Ten Paris Explanations" for her starring role, two of which were: "He told me we were making a workout video," and "It was a tender act of love between me and my then-boyfriend—Rick something."

After Paris's Sidekick 2 cell phone was famously burgled and hacked, and the private numbers of her celebrity pals in her phone book were posted all over the Internet (another headline-making incident that invariably helped push up sales of the device to the teen and young adult market because of her involvement), Letterman's Top Ten list included hilarious fictional voicemail messages such as "It's Bill Clinton. I've been meaning to call you for some time," and "Sorry I missed you. You must be at work. . . . Just kidding."

For Letterman, chatting with Paris was like pulling teeth; in interviews with him, and with other talk-show hosts, she never had much to say. Her only reason for sitting on Letterman's couch before millions of viewers across America that night was to talk about her singing career and get free plugs for her first-ever single, "Stars Are Blind," one of the tunes on her first CD, released in summer 2006.

The song was featured on her first music video that one critic described as looking like a Calvin Klein underwear commercial shot on a beach. It showed a skimpily clad Paris writhing around with a hunky boy-toy as her lyrics droned on for more than three minutes. (Paris had spent several days on a Malibu beach shooting the video, which was directed by the same man with whom she had collaborated for the infamous and short-lived Carl's Jr. hamburger commercial.) The music video, like Paris's infamous X-rated see-all, was uploaded to the Internet and was part of the marketing for her inaugural eponymous album—a mix of reggae, pop, and hip-hop, which was being rolled out nationally by her label, Heiress Records, in conjunction with Warner Brothers. (She claimed she even composed some of the tunes, but most were written by lyricists who had worked for pop superstars like Gwen Stefani, Christina Aguilera, and Madonna.)

Always a star performer on the Internet, Paris's "Stars Are Blind" video was aired on MTV.Com's "Hot 5 on Overdrive," and was rated the all-time best performance on a single day. At the same time, the single became one of iTunes Top 20 downloaded songs overnight.

When New York disc jockeys began playing "Stars Are Blind," they expected to get hate e-mails and nasty text messages from outraged listeners who despaired of her singing. Instead, Paris was getting positive reviews.

One New York radio station program director, Scott Shannon, said he was "shocked" that "it actually isn't a bad record." However, two of his deejays expressed hope for Paris's sake that she isn't asked to sing live. As one pointed out, Paris "got significant [technical] help from [the record's] producers—though that's true for a lot of songs today."

Sharon Dastur, the program director for one of the Big Apple's major FM stations, observed, "Everyone realizes Paris Hilton is the epitome of pop culture, and we're a pop culture station. So we were going to let the listeners decide. Our jocks play it and ask what the listeners think."

Within the first week of the single's release, Paris's voice was being heard on more than fifty stations across the country, and in many such markets was the number one requested song. "We knew it was going to polarize our audience," observed Romeo, the music director and on-air personality of one of New York City's top stations, Z-100. "We were right . . . half of the calls said they hated the song, but it was still among the five top requested songs [and then became] our number one requested song. . . . Her timing is perfect, she has the sound of summer— pure pop with a reggae beat."

But media predictions that Paris's single would hit *Billboard*'s Top 10 in the first week failed to materialize. In fact, it didn't make the top 200 in the first week of release.

The *New York Post*'s music critic, Dan Aquilante, snarkily observed that "the socialite media whore demonstrates that, with enough time, loads of cash and electronic vocal manipulation, anyone can be a pop star. . . . The lyrics, which she reportedly had a hand in writing (sure), are mostly puppy-love growls that will appeal to young teens. Those older kids who knew Hilton's history will have a rough time finding the honesty in lines like, 'If you show me real love, I'll show you mine.' " He noted that her producers had " 'fattened up the skinny heiress' sound by layering her voice upon her voice—several times. The echo effect is almost imperceptible, but manages to erase any trace of thinness. It also erases any trace of identity." He speculated that Paris wouldn't sing live on stage because the "knob twisting production is so complicated" that "it would be nearly impossible to reproduce the sonics . . ."

The *New York Times* gave "Stars Are Blind" a glib mini-review, declaring, "The melody is a bit cramped, almost as if it were written to accompany a singer with moderate range (must be coincidence); the bridge is aimless, but it's over soon enough." The *Times* added, tongue-in-cheek, "A quick Internet search turned up very little information about the singer, name of Paris Hilton."

The nationally syndicated gossip columnist Liz Smith, usually known for her adulatory celebrity items, observed, "I do not think Madonna need worry."

The *Boston Herald*'s website declared, "Paris Hilton is once again a multimedia sensation—but this time there's no nudity involved." The site's critic, Heather V. Eng, described Paris as "an amateur porn star, reality TV simpleton, and the world's most famous person for doing absolutely nothing..."

Just before "Stars Are Blind" began receiving airplay, Paris told a magazine in Hong Kong that she had to overcome shyness—*shyness!*—to become a singer. (Interestingly, however, shyness was one of the problems her maternal grandmother, big Kathy, suffered from when she was Paris's age and was asked to get up and sing. "Kathleen always needed a few drinks in order to ease her nervousness," her friend Jane Hallaren recalls.)

Paris, on the other hand, admits to no need for such relaxants, her arrest in September 2006 for allegedly driving while under the influence notwithstanding.

"I have always had a voice and always known I could sing, but I was too shy to let it come out," she confidently revealed. "I think that is the hardest thing you can do, to sing in front of people. When I finally let go and did it, I realized it is what I am most talented at and what I love to do the most."

But when David Letterman asked her to sing for his vast television audience, she nervously declined, claiming she wasn't prepared. But she did reveal musical talents theretofore unknown. She boasted that she played both the violin *and* the piano.

Letterman moved on to other subjects, such as the latest season of her hit reality show, *The Simple Life 4: Till Death Do Us Part,* and the current state of her love life. Paris claimed that her much-publicized feud with costar Nicole Richie was strictly a publicity ploy to generate ratings, which is a complete contradiction from her earlier statements in which she claimed that Richie "cannot stand being around me because I get all the attention and people don't really care about her. . . . [W]hen I brought her on to my show, she got very jealous and turned on me for no reason. . . . She let fame go to her head. I never want to speak to her again—ever."

Some months earlier, appearing on CNN"s *Larry King Live* to plug her roman à clef about the Hollywood fast lane, Richie said one of the bitchy characters in her book had "things in common" with Paris. When asked about her relationship with Paris, she stated emphatically, "We're no longer friends" and that there was no chance they'd ever be friends again. "We do run into each other. We just don't talk." Admitting to having recovered from addictions to heroin, cocaine, and pills, Paris's friend since they were two years old confessed, "We just went in two separate directions. . . . I had to make some decisions in my life about what's right for me and what's not and so that's what I did."

Richie also acknowledged reports that she had been receiving "late-night prank calls." But she stopped short of accusing her former best friend. (Stories about the calls had been reported in the tabloids.) "I've been getting prank calls. I'm not going to say who they're from." (In season four of *The Simple Life,* in the wake of the feud that Paris maintained never existed, she and Richie were never seen on camera together.)

When asked by Letterman about her breakup with Paris Latsis, Paris Hilton contradicted assertions that his parents refused to have her in the Latsis family and had broken up the relationship. Said Paris, "We're just better as friends. . . . I just wasn't ready to get married. I just want to be single. I love it." She maintained she was thrilled not to have a man in her life and was savoring the freedom to pursue her money-making enterprises. "I'm single for the first time in my life," she continued. "I just want to be alone. I'm just going out with my sister and my girlfriends. It's cool not having to answer to anyone. I've never had time to get to know myself. I always put all of my energy into the man. I don't get to spend time on me. I'm just getting to know who I really am, until I can find someone else." (A year earlier, she was quoted in *Newsweek* magazine as saying she planned to start a family in 2007. But not long after her *Letterman* appearance, she announced to the world that she was going to remain celibate for a year. "I'm doing it just because I want to. One-night stands are not for me. I think it's gross when you just give it up. . . . You have to make guys work for it." Was a book on relationships next on Paris's to-do list?)

Anyone watching Paris's ladylike performance that night on the *Letterman* show would have thought her years of infamous partying were finally behind her, that she'd finally grown up. But later that night she showed up once again at Butter and, according to one report, confronted Lohan, yelling, "I can't believe you and Stavros! You are ridiculous!" Paris was said to have barraged the actress with insults and curses. Lohan took what was described as the "high road" and didn't return the fire.

After Lohan left the club, Paris, performing a one-eighty from her reserved appearance on Letterman's couch, did what was described as a "stripperish" dance on a banquette for a small group of professional basketball and football players.

That's hot.

With her album released, Paris hit No. 1 in *The Guinness Book of World Records,* not for her singing, but rather as "the most overrated celeb" based on polls in magazines in which readers chose their least favorite celebrity.

*That's* not *hot.*

**F**rom the start of my research, I felt that if one wanted to know how Paris Hilton became a singular phenomenon of the new millennium, one had to know where she came from. Since *House of Hilton* is the first contemporary independent biography of the hotel dynasty, I was faced with the daunting task of tracking down creditable, knowledgeable sources. This was especially true in attempting to paint an accurate as possible portrait of Ms. Hilton's never-before-scrutinized maternal roots.

While a historical and genealogical trail existed for the paternal side of her family because of the dynasty's decades-long, high-profile international business and social standing—Conrad Hilton's very readable 1957 autobiography, *Be My Guest,* was a start—I quickly discovered that, curiously, virtually nothing was publicly known about the maternal side of Ms. Hilton's genealogical tree. That part of her story had to be developed by tracking down dozens of private sources—few were known in the public domain—and interviewing them.

With all of that in mind, I would like to point out that all source quotes—persons interviewed by me or my researchers—are written in the present tense ("she says," "he asserts"). Quotes from all other sources, such as magazine articles, newspaper stories, and books, are written in the past tense ("he maintained," "she stated").

For example, all of the quotes attributed to the long-deceased Conrad Hilton came from *Be My Guest* or from numerous periodicals. Similarly, quotes attributed to Ms. Hilton's late maternal grandmother, for instance, came from interviews with family, friends, and acquaintances, or from sources otherwise stated in *House of Hilton.* Once again, the same is true of quotes attributed to Paris Hilton and her parents, among others.

The Hiltons over the decades have been boldface names in gossip columns, movie and scandal magazines—many, such as *Confidential,* are now defunct—contemporary daily and weekly tabloids, celebrity magazines, and a number of Internet sites, all of which were particularly valuable for my research.

I've attempted to cite these sources by name where applicable in the context of the book's chapters. Among them, in no particular order of importance, are: the *New York Post,* the *New York Daily News,* the *New York Times,* the *Los Angeles Times,* the *Washington Post, USA Today,* the *Wall Street Journal, US Weekly, People, Variety, Vanity Fair, Rolling Stone, Time, Newsweek, TV Guide, Life, Parade, Blender,* and *Radar* (and all of their related sites on the Internet).

Among the websites used for my research are:

Gawker.com
TMZ.com
PerezHilton.com
IMDB.com
Moono.com
SocialiteLife.com
NewYorkSocialDiary.com
RadarOnline.com
MetaCafe.com
CNN.com
GlamourGirlsOfTheSilverScreen.com
Eonline.com

# Selected Bibliography

Adams, Cindy. *Jolie Gabor.* New York: Mason/Charter, 1975.

Amburn, Ellis. *The Most Beautiful Woman in the World: The Obsessions, Passions, and Courage of Elizabeth Taylor.* New York: Cliff Street Books, 2000.

Bolton, Whitney. *The Silver Spade: The Conrad Hilton Story.* New York: Farrar, Straus and Young, 1954.

Collins, Joan. *Past Imperfect.* New York: Simon & Schuster, 1984.

Dabney, Thomas Ewing. *The Man Who Bought the Waldorf.* New York: Duell, Sloan and Pearce, 1950.

Finstad, Suzanne. *Natasha: The Biography of Natalie Wood.* New York: Harmony Books, 2001.

Frank, Gerold. *Zsa Zsa Gabor: My Story.* Cleveland: The World Publishing Co., 1960.

Heymann, C. David. *Liz: An Intimate Biography of Elizabeth Taylor.* New York: Birch Lane Press, 1995.

Hilton, Conrad. *Be My Guest.* Englewood Cliffs, New Jersey: Prentice Hall, 1957.

Hofler, Robert. *The Man Who Invented Rock Hudson.* New York: Avalon Publishing Group, 2005.

Johns, Howard. *Palm Springs Confidential.* Fort Lee, New Jersey: Barricade Books, Inc., 2004.

Kelley, Kitty. *Elizabeth Taylor: The Last Star.* New York: Dell Publishing Co., Inc., 1982.

Lambert, Gavin. *Natalie Wood: A Life.* New York: Alfred A. Knopf, 2004.

Leigh, Wendy. *One Lifetime Is Not Enough: Zsa Zsa Gabor.* New York: Delacorte Press, 1991.

Moore, Terry. *The Beauty and the Billionaire.* New York: Pocket Books, 1984.

Mungo, Ray. *Palm Springs Babylon.* New York: St. Martin's Press, 1993.

Parish, James Robert, with Gregory W. Mark and Don E. Stanke. *The Hollywood Beauties.* Carlstadt, New Jersey: Rainbow Books, 1979.

Reynolds, Debbie, and David Patrick Columbia. *Debbie: My Life.* New York: William Morrow and Company, Inc., 1988.

Wharton, Annabel Jane. *Building the Cold War: Hilton International Hotels and Modern Architecture.* Chicago: The University of Chicago Press, 2001.

Wood, Lana. *Natalie: A Memoir by Her Sister.* New York: G. P. Putnam's Sons, 1984.

# Acknowledgments

**I**'m indebted to so many people—more than one hundred sources—who helped make this book possible. I can't thank them enough for their generosity and kindness, their forthrightness and candor.

Along with the Hilton dynasty's enormous financial, philanthropic, and social success, scandal underscored the lives of a number of contemporary members of the family, and my probing into that colorful history opened some long-healed emotional wounds. In particular, I want to thank Trish Hilton, the widow of Nick Hilton, for agreeing to be interviewed for the first time about her often hellish life as his loving and supportive wife.

Over the years, especially as Paris Hilton came to fame, Trish and her two sons were contacted by journalists and TV talk show producers. Friends had suggested she write her own book. But she refused all entreaties to talk.

More than three decades after Nick's death, she still felt a strong sense of loyalty to her deceased husband and to the Hilton dynasty. With my book in progress, though, she finally concluded that the true story should be told, and she agreed to numerous interviews.

Beyond that, she opened many doors to sources who were in her and Nick's and the Hilton family's circle who otherwise would have been unknown to me, among them Carole Doheny, Bob Neal (who regretfully died as this book neared completion), and Noreen Nash Siegel. Their colorful remembrances of the Hiltons added greatly to this biography.

I also owe a special debt of gratitude to Pat Skipworth Hilton, the first wife of Conrad Hilton's third son, Eric. Pat's reminiscences about life in the Hilton family, and her thoughtful impressions and entertaining anecdotes about everyone from Conrad to Paris, were all-important.

When Paris Hilton's mother, Kathy, was quoted in the *New York Post* as telling people not to cooperate with me, it had exactly the opposite effect: it actually brought credible sources who had worked directly or indirectly in the Hilton organization to my attention. One of them was Neal Schwartz. Like others interviewed, he shared his memories and helped open previously locked doors.

Nothing of substance existed in the public domain when I began looking into Paris Hilton's important and colorful maternal roots, which became a key part of this book.

For helping me piece together the story of Kathleen Dugan Avanzino Richards Catain Fenton and her daughters, Kathy Hilton and Kim and Kyle Richards, I am forever grateful to Jane Hallaren, Mickey Catain and her brother Michael, Ken Avanzino and his sister Adele, Sylvia Richards, Diane Richards, Barbara Frank, Judy Goldstone, Kay Rozario, Lynda Bannister, Monty Brinson, John Jackson, and Pierce Jensen. I owe an extreme debt of gratitude to the many who helped fill in missing pieces. They include: Mary Ellen Akerson, Ellis Amburn, Tim Applegate, Jarred Barron, Martha Barone, Marcel Becker, John Blanchette, Josephine and Diane Campisi, Jeanne Carmen, Marlene Catain, George Christy, John Cohan, David Patrick Columbia, Bob Conkey, Pat Cox, Arthur Crowley, John Donaldson, Digby Diehl, Jean Dmytryk, Donna Dugan, Tom Fioretti, Rudy Florentine, Chet Frangipane, Joe Franklin, Mona Freeman, Melanie Gelb, Maynard Haddad, Nikki Haskell, Ken Heineman, C. David Heymann, Bibi Hilton, Francesca Hilton, Dave Johnson, Richard Johnson, Carol Kane, Bob Kelly, Keith Kelly, Bob and Janice Melvin Keller, Sally Kirkland, Gavin Lambert, Wendy Leigh, Rob Levin, Larry Linderer, Perry

Lopez, Skip E. Lowe, Joan Luther, Peter Mansfield, Jeanne Martin, John and Linda McCusker, Ailene Mehle, Barry Minkow, Elliott Mitchell, Hank Moonjean, Terry Moore, Brian O'Riordan, James Robert Parrish, Tom Parris, Bill Pawley, Grant Richards, Marjorie Roth, Milton Saxon, Phyllis Sherwood, Robert Siegel, Sam Staggs, Jackie Stallone, Barbara Sternig, Bob Suddarth, Les Sutorius, Gini Tangalakis, Donald Trump, Ralph Vanderpool, Frederick von Anhalt, Betsy von Furstenberg, Mamie Van Doren, Olga Viripaeff, Gerry Visco, Carol Wakeman, Christina Wolfe, Peggy Yakovlev. If I missed anyone, please know your help was deeply appreciated. There are those, not many, who asked for anonymity. You know who you are, and many thanks for your assistance.

A book like this cannot be written without the help of a strong team of inspired and experienced researchers who know where to look and how to interview—in this case, several of them published authors and journalists. My sincere thanks for due diligence and deep digging to Caroline Walton Howe, Judy Oppenheimer, Tom Lisanti, and Val Holley.

My agent, Elyse Cheney, did a masterful job by taking my idea to the perfect house. Steve Ross, vice president and publisher of Crown, got what I was trying to do from the moment he read my proposal. Luke Dempsey, my editor, is a rarity; his cuts and changes were inspired. His assistant, Lindsey Moore, helped smooth the process along. And for his eagle eye, many thanks to Random House attorney Matthew Martin.

# Index